Feminism as radical humanism

Feminism as radical humanism

Pauline Johnson

WESTVIEW
Boulder • San Francisco

96-246

FOR HARRIET

First published in 1994 by
Allen & Unwin Pty Ltd
9 Atchison Street, St Leonards, NSW 2065 Australia

Published in 1994 in the United States by
Westview Press
5500 Central Avenue
Boulder, Colorado 80301-2877

Library of Congress Cataloguing-in-publication Data available upon request

ISBN HC 0-8133-2357-6

ISBN PB 0-8133-2358-4

Set in 10\11 Plantin Light by DOCUPRO, Sydney
Printed by SRM Production Services Sdn Bhd, Malaysia

10 9 8 7 6 5 4 3 2 1

Contents

Acknowledgements

I would like to thank a number of people for their help, their patience and their concern about the book. Special thanks to my sister, Lesley, who read and offered very useful comments on the manuscript and was unfailing in her faith and encouragement. I am particularly grateful also to Maria Markus who took the time to read and offer some vitally important comments on the drafts. A big thank you to Patricia Bower who came to the rescue and did an excellent job unscrambling my typing. Finally, and above all, I thank John Grumley who has been hearing about, reading, criticising and offering invaluable suggestions on the book for years.

Early versions of three chapters have appeared in the following publications:
'Feminism and liberalism', *Australian Feminist Studies*, no. 14, summer, 1991
'Feminism and Enlightenment', *Radical Philosophy*, no. 63, spring, 1993
'The quest for the self: feminism's appropriation of romanticism', *Thesis Eleven*, no. 38, 1994

Introduction: the feminism that dare not speak its name

'Humanism', as Richard Bernstein has noted, has become something of a dirty word in recent times. It has come, in the new postmodern, post-structuralist theology, to stand for a 'kingdom of darkness' and is used by its critics to identify everything that they think is wrong with the modern world.[1] The crimes of humanism take on a particular complexion in contemporary feminist discussions. To admit to humanist allegiances is to show oneself insufficiently radical in one's feminism, having clearly not extricated oneself from an equality posture which is content to see the liberation of women into a sameness with men. A humanist feminist clearly reveals also her philosophical naivety, believing in the persistent 'truth' of a timeless, eternal human essence; she might even be supposed (worse) to be actively engaged in promoting those fictions of 'humanity's cause' which have underpinned the catastrophic, totalitarian formations of modern times.

The construction of the humanist enemy-in-our-midst is, perhaps, a psychologically intelligible manoeuvre for a social movement shaping its course and attempting to define its ambitions both against those ready attempts to accommodate feminism to the status quo and against the, now increasingly evident, efforts to turn back some of the material gains made by the women's movement. It is, however, unfortunate and rather ironic that the hegemony of anti-humanist sentiment within contemporary feminism is now such that it has become difficult to work up the courage to ask what humanism really means. As feminists can we really persuade ourselves that we have given up the value commitments of modern humanism? And what sort of feminism are we producing in the process? For all its renowned 'terrorism', the voice of humanism has become very timid and self-censoring in the main forums for the discussion of feminist ideas. And yet the contemporary women's movement is vital to us all; we all owe it a lot and should be prepared to join the discussion. I would, therefore, like to make a claim here for a serious consideration of the humanist character of modern feminism: a discussion which does not simply deride the concerns of an anti-humanist feminism but which is, rather, prompted by the perception that its critiques call for a strong response.

Many feminists today repudiate any suggestion that the goals and objectives of feminism could be absorbed into the wider project of 'humanity's cause'. They point to the tyrannical history of all attempts to extinguish human plurality and diversity under the banner of the 'unity of the species' and underline that images of a common humanity or of a human essence have been built on the back of a femininity construed as nature; as humanity's 'other'. The present book disputes none of this. It does argue, however, that an homogenising representation of modern humanism as simply a repressive, totalitarian construction of a common humanity suggests a one-sided interpretation of an ideology possessing a multitude of contemporary shapes. It needs to be underlined that modern humanism is not merely a doctrine which asserts the implicit unity of the species. Parallel with the aspiration to consider all humans within these universalising terms has been the equally strong desire to affirm particularity, to raise awareness and respect for the uniqueness of all forms of individuality: this desire has served as a basis from which to decry the totalitarian character of all images of a common humanity.

The idea of 'humanness' suggests a post-traditional consciousness in which particularistic integrations and traditional norms of conduct no longer serve as incontestable points of reference for virtuous behaviour.[2] Modern humanism played a vital role in 'disembedding' the modern individual from his or her identification with particularising integrations and local affiliations. No longer was identity to be 'received' as a taken for granted place in a community and social hierarchy. Modern humanism asserted that beyond this constellation of contingencies—locale, time, fortune—there exists a primary status as members of a generic 'humanity'. This capacity to identify oneself as a human being is based on two, seemingly antagonistic, but actually interconnected, value commitments. One of them is an allegiance to humankind as the only binding integration, the other is the commitment to the uniqueness of the human personality.[3] To modern humanism, then, we owe that dynamic concept of person—a concept which looks at individuals as unique, potentially autonomous beings, creating their own destiny, making themselves, struggling with the limitations externally imposed by existing institutions, norms and practices—which has come to be associated with a modern consciousness.

Modern humanism's dynamic concept of person has given rise to a wealth of diverse meanings, cultural and political causes and possibilities, among which can be discerned the distinctive, ever-changing interpretations of modern feminism. Contemporary feminism needs to be grasped as a particular, inchoate, permutation of the modern humanist allegiance to the idea of the uniqueness of the human personality. It stands both as a distinctive interpretation of the meaning of this commitment and as an index to its practical force. Historically, feminism has extended and added new meaning to the idea of the civil rights of all individuals and has qualitatively expanded our sense of the character of publicly significant human needs. At the same time, the politico-social phenomenon of contemporary feminism is itself dependent on the historical presence, albeit an embattled and fragile one, of those ideals of civil and human rights which are inscribed in modern social institutions.

While modern feminism is both a manifestation of and an interpretation of modern humanism, it is also, at the same time, a critic of all those constructions of an image of human subjectivity which presuppose the normativity of a particular socialised gender identity. The double-sided character of feminism's relations with modern humanism, as both its interpreter and its critic, does not, however, suggest any preferential discrimination between the above mentioned two faces of humanism's own value commitments. Contemporary feminism is as much a specific articulation of the universalising dimension of modern humanism as it is the inheritor and interpreter of the idea of self-determining individuality. Actually, these are not separable moments within modern humanism. In order, namely, to raise the value idea of the autonomous, self-constituted personality, it is necessary that individuals begin to establish their self-identity in terms other than the binding norms of those particularistic integrations and local affiliations which govern the contingency of their birth; in terms namely of their status as human beings.

As we shall see in following chapters, feminism has never established a fully satisfactory home for itself within any pre-existing formulations of humanist ideals: the efforts of the historical Enlightenment, of conventional liberalism and Marxism have all, in turn, been found wanting. Yet, against the self-representations of contemporary anti-humanist feminisms, I attempt to demonstrate that feminism's own efforts to interrogate and contest a host of formulations of the ideals of modern humanism do not establish feminism's own credentials as a rival to humanism. In its efforts to expose and contest old shibboleths and prejudices which encrust the main formulations of the ideals of modern humanism, contemporary feminism brings to bear its own hitherto silent and marginalised interpretations of the meaning and the potentials of these value ideas. Feminism's critique of previous attempts to interpret modern humanist values departs from an, at least implicit, commitment to the idea of a non-exclusionary humanity; a commitment which it has applied with potent critical force to protest all those images of a common humanity in which the particularising norms of a privileged, gendered experience are conferred with an alleged normative universality. Embracing, at the same time, humanism's own principled commitment to the idea of the uniqueness of each human personality, feminism discovers also that major interpretations of the ideals of modern humanism are actually pinned upon definitional images of the character of a normative subjectivity.

One of the prominent themes developed in the book is, then, that the self-representations of anti-humanist feminisms notwithstanding, feminism is a humanism. The first chapter attempts to set this argument in train by contesting the one-sidedness of the characterisation of modern humanism which typically underpins the perspective of anti-humanist feminisms. This argument does not entail, however, any call for a return to a homogeneous, centred, experience of the meaning of feminist aspirations. The contemporary women's movement has, hopefully, learnt too much from past mistakes not to resist, strenuously, any call to an imposed consensual understanding of the character of the good, the virtuously feminist, life. By asserting the humanist character of contemporary feminism, I seek fundamentally to redescribe the status of those ideals and principled commitments which, for anti-humanist feminisms, mark out feminism's character as an ideological rival to modern humanism.

The affirmation of feminism's character as a humanism means that modern feminism should not lose sight of its own fundamental allegiances to the value ideas of modern humanism despite the determination of its challenge to the prejudiced character of those images of humanity and personhood that infiltrate modernity and its culture at every level. This book is, in large part, concerned to gauge the reach of feminism's critique of the gendered, privileged character of those images of human subjectivity which support some of the major interpretations of the meaning of modern humanism. Feminism has, for example, discovered that the historical Enlightenment, nineteenth century Romanticism and classical liberalism all uphold images of the character of autonomous, self-determining subjectivity which confer normativity on a particular mode of social experience. And, again, not only in Marxism but also in Habermas' seeming sympathetic attempt to sustain the value commitments of modern humanism in terms which do not presuppose the normativity of any particular kind of human identity, feminism has espied the privileging of the characteristics of a certain gendered form of social subjectivity and its typical relations with others.

Upon the governing thesis that feminism *is* a contemporary participant in, and interpreter of, the ideals of modern humanism, this book builds a second, related theme. Feminism, I suggest, needs to *recognise* itself as a major interpreter of the cultural ideals of modern humanism. While there is no denying the contemporary popularity of an anti-humanist ideology (and I don't doubt that eternal scepticism has some value), an explicitly humanist feminism must, nonetheless, affirm the recurring vitality of emancipatory humanist ideals and its own lineages which are typically obscured in anti-humanist rhetoric. It does make a difference if feminism understands itself as an interpreter of, rather than an enemy to, modern humanism. Such a redescription has a powerful impact on the ways in which we might understand the character and role of feminist theory itself. Again, this point needs to be made in the context of a certain interpretation of the nature and status of modern humanism itself.

Against the background of a thoroughly discredited metaphysical construction of humanist ideals (a construction which seeks to underpin images of a common humanity in positive descriptions of irreducible human traits) we now encounter the emerging shape of an explicitly post-metaphysical conception of the meaning of humanism; a conception described here under the umbrella term 'radical humanism'. Briefly, 'radical humanism' understands humanism as an historical project born of conscious value choices and the vagaries of critical, social and political movements. An anti-humanist posture, which sees in the norms and ideals of modern humanism only the totalitarian ambitions of a particular, privileged subjectivity committed to the universalisation of its own will and interests, has certainly provided a much needed warning about the ever-present dangers which lurk within humanism's efforts to produce a universal category of humankind which breaks the bonds of traditional, particularising integrations. Yet, to radical humanism, this attempt at transcendent critique, which discovers in the point of view of modern humanism only the breeding ground for a totalitarian denial of the particularity of the marginal, overlooks the universalistic significance and emancipatory relevance such ideals have come to acquire for modern individuals. To radical humanism, the humanist ideas of freedom, equality and authentic self-realisation are not merely the rhetoric of a disciplinary regime; these values, which have taken shape in the course of historical development, must also be affirmed as modernity's crowning, if fragile, achievement.

One of the main things at issue, then, in feminism's capacity to recognise itself as an immanently critical interpreter of the ideals of modern humanism, is contemporary feminism's own sense of the achievements of modernity. If modern humanism is considered as the cultural reflection of a modernity immured in totalitarianism, then the stage is set for a feminism which considers itself engaged in a ceaseless struggle to extricate itself from the guilty norms and value commitments implanted within the institutional and cultural practices of modern social life. In this case, feminist theory ceases to affirm itself as a specific cultural reflection upon modernity and its prospects; it attempts, rather, to style itself as a radical alternative to a phallocentric logic seen to homogenise all discursive practices in the modern world.

If feminism fails to see itself as a specific manifestation and interpretation of progressive potentials in modernity, then it inevitably cuts itself adrift from a dialogic, reflective relationship with the practical, social and cultural experiences of women in modern society. Its construction of modern humanism as the cultural reflection of a totalitarian modernity means that an anti-humanist feminism can only underline its own alienation from those sociocultural arrangements and practices which organise the life experiences of women in modern society. Feminist theory thus, of necessity, severs itself from a reflective, interpretative relationship with the sense of frustrated potentials and dissatisfied cultural needs which has prodded the modern women's movement into existence. Concerned only to underline its own alienation from the organising norms and values of a phallocentric modernity, feminist theory comes to express the very limited and privileged life experience of a minority of feminist intellectuals.

The posture of radical alienation, which an extreme commitment to an anti-humanist feminism entails, can, in the end, only be given a rhetorical significance. Even the most radical feminists who feel themselves totally alienated from this culture and hold out no hope for its redemption would not want to give up the freedoms and opportunities produced by this society. At stake, then, in the recognition of feminism's own status as an immanently critical interpretation of the ideals of modern human-ism is the question of how the modern movement will direct and expand its critical energies and forces. Will it persevere with the vital task of reflecting upon present gender relations and of adding neglected depth to women's own self-reflections on the meaning and possibilities of their own struggles? Or will it dissipate itself in a hyper-radicalism which confuses sceptical rhetoric for reality and which loses touch with most of the urgent political and social struggles now preoccupying organised women's movements?

At issue also in the recognition of feminism's own status as interpreter of modern humanism is the construction of a positive, creative relationship with a range of other pre-existing attempts to interpret and implement the ideals of modern humanism. If feminism construes itself as the ideological opponent of modern humanism, then it can discover little more to interest it in the main formulations of modern humanism than an apparent repe-tition of that phallocentric logic thought to wind its way through the cultural reflections of modernity. In this case, the rich diversity of images of human subjectivity conceptualised in, for example, the historical Enlightenment, in nineteenth century Romanticism and in classical liberalism takes on a totalised significance. By affirming its own status as a reflection on the meaning of modern humanism, feminism does not, as already stressed, thereby resile from the radical critique of the gender prejudices which it discovers at the centre of a range of constructions of the character and vocation of human subjectivity. Rather, its critical engagement with these formulations takes on a new, creative and productive character. If, namely, feminism's interest in the various formulations of modern humanism ceases to turn simply on a determination to underline its own ideological break from the monotonous logic of phallocentric discourse, feminism is better able to enter into dialogue with past config-urations of humanism and to achieve a heightened self-under-standing of its own objectives from the perceived strengths and failures of a range of diverse interpretations of the ideals of modern humanism. For example, feminism's discovery of the prejudiced, privileged character of the conception of human subjectivity which informs the formulations of classical liberalism is, as I attempt to show, by no means the end of the story of the productive relations between feminism and liberalism. On the contrary, this critical engagement with the masculinist identity of the image of subjectivity in liberalism opens up the perceived necessity for new ways of conceptualising the meaning that autonomous subjectivity might have for modern women. In particular, the dilemma becomes: how to construct an image of autonomous subjectivity in terms which do not presuppose the bifurcation between the public and the private spheres which has become entrenched in liberalism's conception of the character of politically qualified subjectivity?

This study is, then, above all interested in the ways in which feminism helps to construct its own dynamic self-interpretation— its constantly unfolding understanding of the character of its own aspirations on the basis of its critical reflections on those images of human subjectivity and its historical vocation which it encounters in a range of modern cultural reflections. The book does not pretend to offer an intellectual history of the development of feminist ideas. Nor does it propose an intellectual history of competing formulations of the meaning of modern humanism. It is, rather, intended as a discussion of the hermeneutics of feminism's attempt to interpret itself, to understand its own aims and possibilities via its critical engagement with a variety of readings of the character of modern humanism. To this end I have selected what seem to me to be some of the more controversial but also some of the least finished areas of feminism's on-going discussions with a range of major sociocultural reflections on the character of, and prospects for, modernity.

This book reviews a spectrum of contemporary feminist theories and, while it has been my intention to avoid an overly polemical tone, I have not attempted to hide a lack of sympathy with some of the standpoints discussed. In the main, it is not the radicalism of their ambitions which today provides the major bone of contention between feminist perpectives. At least at the level of theoretically elaborated feminisms, the debate between the so-called feminisms of equality and of difference is, by and large, a superceded dispute. Rarely, today, does one come across a developed feminist theory which conceives the ambitions of feminism merely in terms of the opening up of already described rights and privileges of a hegemonic culture to embrace the equality of modern women. For the most part, feminist theories now conceive the ambitions of feminism in terms which encompass a demand for the recognition of the public significance of diverse human potentials and different ways of life. Yet, while the, variously interpreted, standpoint of a 'feminism of difference' appears virtually hegemonic, there is, nevertheless, substantial disagreement over the role of theory in the production of positive images of autonomous, self-determining femininity. My dispute with a range of contemporary feminisms principally turns, then, on a disagreement over the way in which the role and appropriate limits of feminist theory is conceived.

As I elaborate in chapter one, this dispute over the role of feminist theory in the production of positive images of feminine difference finally rests on a disagreement over the cultural potentials of modernity. An anti-humanist feminism cannot look upon itself and its own commitments as a specific manifestation and interpretation of progressive potentials in modernity. It is, accordingly, cut adrift from any practical role in clarifying and elaborating women's own self-reflections on the meanings and potentials of their own struggles. If it commits itself to a totalising description of the totalitarian phallocentrism of modern social life, feminist theory can only attempt to locate the well-springs of its own oppositional consciousness in an autonomous sphere of aestheticised images of non-subordinated femininity. An explicit opposition to this kind of construction of the role and the status of feminist theory is one of the main themes that holds the present study together.

1 Feminism and humanism

The last few decades have seen a momentous shift in feminism's attitude towards humanism. Writing in the late 1940s, Simone de Beauvoir had viewed feminism unambiguously as an expression of humanism in a quite straightforward sense. Indeed, the main feminist message of *The Second Sex* is the assertion that women must be considered first and foremost as human beings. For de Beauvoir, the oppression of women appears as the discriminatory denial of their right and task as human beings to freely choose their own identity and destiny. Feminism meant the demand that women should, along with men, enjoy the human task and responsibility of making themselves. What peculiarly signalises the situation of women is that she—a free and autonomous being like all human creatures—nevertheless finds herself in a world where men compel her to assume the status of the 'other'.[1] Latterly, however, the avant-garde of feminist theory has vigorously repudiated this early understanding of itself as a protest on behalf of the denied humanity of women in modern society.

Feminism today dismisses its former innocent reliance on the claims to universality and gender neutrality made on behalf of images of a common humanity. Indeed, contemporary feminism has played a crucial part in developing an unmasking critique of those images of universal human aspirations and priorities upon which its own disclosure of the oppressed humanity of modern women had formerly rested. Sandra Harding describes feminism's new, reflective and critical relationship to descriptions of a universal humanity in the following terms:

> . . . what we took to be humanly inclusive problematics, concepts, theories, objective methodologies, and transcendental truths are, in fact, less than that. Indeed, these products of thought bear the mark of their individual creators, and the creators in turn have been distinctively marked as to gender, class, race and culture.[2]

Kate Soper has also attempted to capture the significance of this change in feminism's attitude towards humanism:

> Today, there is a whole body of feminist writing which would shy away from an 'equality' which welcomed women (at last) as human subjects on a par with men. For this 'human subject', it is argued, must always bear the traces of the patriarchal ordering which has become more or less coextensive with 'human' condition as such.[3]

The appeal to a concept of a common humanity, once used to formulate feminism's own protest at discriminatory practices and prejudical ideologies encountered by modern women, is now often challenged as a repressive attempt to universalise specific kinds of culturally loaded experiences and aspirations. Today many feminists point to the underside of the allegedly triumphant march of humanist Enlightenment: the tyrannical history of a civilisation which has striven to extinguish human plurality and diversity under the banner of the 'unity of the species'. Specifically, they underline that images of a common humanity have frequently been built on the back of a femininity construed as nature; as humanity's 'other'. On this construction, feminism, seen as 'the quest for the registration and realisation of . . . feminine 'difference', 'appears as an ideological opponent of humanism, understood as a fraudulent and arrogant attempt to construct an image of a "common humanity" '.[4]

For many feminists today, 'humanist feminism' has come to signal a certain, very watered down, and ultimately self-defeating, feminist politics: a politics in which feminism is asked to content itself with the demand to be 'counted in' to privileged definitions of the character of a human identity. In this climate, my contention that feminism still needs to see itself as a particular interpretation of modern humanism is at least controversial and, for some, heresy. It might be immediately viewed as an attempt to turn back the clock on the major advances made in the self-understanding of contemporary feminism. It is, however, my aim to show that feminism's new-found concern to delineate a politics of feminine difference does not have to be viewed as a rupture from humanism. It is more appropriate to see this new phase of feminism as a further expression of the ideals of humanism, as a real enrichment of the values already inherent within these ideals.

Feminism's own powerful critique of the main formulations of the ideals of humanism has targeted the inevitably particularising standpoint which underpins all attempts to construe a universalising image of a common humanity. This critique has shown us that there can, indeed, be no going back to any presumed innocent description of a common humanity. Feminism has today, rightly, disabused itself of the fiction of a birds-eye view which seeks to suspend all particular, local, culture-bound affiliations in its description of a shared humanity. As we shall see in following chapters, feminism has successfully exposed the image of particular, gendered subjectivity hosted by various mainstream attempts to formulate a universalising conception of our common humanity. I have, then, no argument with contemporary feminism's efforts to search out and expose the prejudiced points of view which inform a range of attempts to formulate and to implement the ideals of modern humanism. I am, however, convinced that present feminist tendencies to inflate this critique of the universalising attitude of humanism into a thoroughgoing repudiation of the humanist credentials of contemporary feminism, to reconstruct humanism as an ideological rival, represents a dramatic overkill, a terribly one-sided interpretation of the character and the significance of modern humanism.

An anti-humanist feminism continually parades before us the sins of the universalising attitude of modern humanism. Citing the idea of our 'humanity' as the cultural product of a modernity whose history is scarred by a totalitarian denial of difference and human plurality, an anti-humanist feminism suggests only one way of viewing the implications of a humanist capacity to look at individuals in the abstract. On this construction, the 'disembedding' of the modern individual from those particularising integrations and local affiliations which appear as the contingent legacy of his or her birth appears only as a mechanism of a disciplinary society determined to impose upon all individuals a rigid, homogenising description of their identity.

Such critics tell a tale of the constant failure of the institutions and ideals constructed under the banner of modern humanism to reach beyond a repressive construction of the universality and normativity of certain culturally acquired aspirations. Yet, while scepticism in the face of all attempts to formulate, once and for all, a non-exclusionary image of a common humanity is certainly warranted, the emancipatory significance of the universalising

3

attitude of modern humanism ought not be so readily overlooked. Even in Enlightenment formulations, the humanist claim that all 'men' shared this status as members of a generic humanity allowed the modern individual to move and made possible claims to the rights of equality, autonomy and authentic self-realisation. 'Diversity' and 'plurality' can only be raised as value ideas by virtue of the space carved out by the universalising attitude expressed by modern humanism. It was this claim which first allowed modern individuality to attain a regulative status from which it could begin to assert its unique difference.

From the very beginning, these two value commitments were inevitably welded together. Humanism is a cultural ideal which seeks to construct an image of 'the unity of the species' as the only grounds from which claims to the rightfulness and significance of human uniqueness and diversity can achieve expression. This construction of the double-sided character of modern humanism does not seek, in any sense, to forestall the recent feminist challenge to the gender bias of major formulations of the ideals of modern humanism. Rather, the point to be made is that, when the feminist critics of humanism unmask the prejudiced, exclusionary character of a range of inherited images of a common humanity, they adopt an immanently critical posture. In establishing the inadequacy of such images in the face of human diversity and particularity, the feminist critics actually bring the various formulations of the ideals of humanism to account, not for their inadequacy with respect to a rival set of ideals and values, but for their failure to offer an adequate interpretation of the ideals of humanism itself.

The following chapter makes a case for looking upon modern feminism's own critique of the range of ways in which the commitments of modern humanism have been formulated as a contribution which 'pursues further' the emancipatory potentials of modern humanism. Modern humanism, I argue, is not to be reduced to a mere doctrinal assertion of the implicit unity of the species. The idea of our 'humanness' has to be raised, however, in any attempt to speak to those ideas of self-determination and autonomy which underpin the main principles of civil rights and modern democracy and which are, moreover, at the foundation of our personal attempts to express and realise our individual uniqueness. In seeking to construct itself in ideological opposition to modern humanism—seen as the cultural expression of a quasi-totalitarian modernity—a contemporary feminism not only endorses a one-sided and totalising vision of modern social life, it also blinds itself to the truly emancipatory dimension of modern humanism and neglects the degree to which contemporary feminism itself continues to be nurtured from this rich, on-going source of cultural values.

The dilemmas of modern humanism

The recent turn by some feminists against humanism needs to be understood as an aspect of a wider and on-going cultural critique of the ideals of Western humanism. The main impulse of this critique has its ancestory in the attitude expressed in Martin Heidegger's 'Letter on Humanism' which raised the problem of the imperialism believed immanent to the concept of humanism.[5] Taking its cue from Heidegger, the contemporary critique of humanism has supposed that there is no humanism which does not bring into play 'a metaphysics in which the human subject determines a role for itself which is necessarily central or exclusive'.[6] The efforts, namely, of modern humanism to abstract from all particular identities and affiliations to construe an image of a common humanity are seen as fundamentally misconceived. Each such attempt must evoke the universalising claims of a particular, culturally located subjectivity which seeks to stamp all other identities with its own distinctive mark.

To us, Heidegger's 'Letter' has bequeathed not simply a peculiarly potent formulation of the critique of the normative concept of 'man' which lurks in the depths of all attempts to evoke an image of a common humanity, it has also anchored a certain construction of what such a critique is supposed to entail. Heidegger's 'Letter' collapses the ideals of humanism into that one-sided construction of their meaning and potentials which has been adopted by the contemporary advocates of an anti-humanist standpoint.[7] With Heidegger, humanism comes to mean the self-assertion gone wild of a subjectivity determined to subject the world to the mastery of its own will. 'Humanism' refers to that modern mentality where:

> . . . primacy is assigned to a subject who represents an objective world and seeks to know and master it by experimentation and manipulation; setting upon and constraining nature to give answers to questions of reason's own determining.[8]

From Heidegger, the contemporary advocates of anti-humanism have inherited an all-encompassing critique of modern humanism. It is the fundamental commitments of humanism with its bent towards self-realisation, autonomy and the self-conscious life which are under attack here. The contemporary French Heideggerians have gone on to suggest that the modern humanist model of self-realising subjectivity must be construed as the 'origin' of the modern totalitarian implosion. It is this model of self-realising subjectivity determined to 'transcend all the determinations of the modern subject . . . [and to constitute] itself as *the* subject in absolute terms' which Lacoue-Labarthe discovers as the logic expressed by Nazism.[9]

The attack is, then, not on the particular formulations and interpretations of humanism but on the core value commitments of humanism itself. The objective of the Heideggerian legacy is the very ideas of authentic self-realisation, autonomy and self-determination which are flattened out to mean the will to mastery and subjection. Because it is the core of humanism, and not the failures of its interpretations, which is the objective of Heidegger's 'Letter on Humanism', it is not plausible to attempt to reconcile an acknowledgement of some of the achievements of humanism with the main sense of his anti-humanist posture. Hence, whereas for Barry Hindess, 'To think against humanism is not to deny everything that particular self-styled humanisms have stood for'; according to Heidegger, anti-humanism means precisely this kind of repudiation of the core of a humanist mentality and, thereby, its various manifestations.[10] Heidegger's anti-humanism is not an expression of despair at the constantly betrayed commitments of modern humanism to the idea of human plurality and to the principles of autonomy and self-realisation. His is a challenge to the 'damage' to human dignity which lies at the heart of the value ideas of modern humanism itself.

The centre of the debate around the contemporary significance of humanism is concerned not with a dispute over the formulation of humanist commitments to the idea of autonomous subjectivity and authentic self-realisation; up for discussion is, rather, the evaluation of the significance and the potentials of these core humanist value ideas. Against the Heideggerian legacy, contemporary advocates of humanism seek to establish that an anti-humanist attack on the humanist idea of self-realising subjectivity imperils the vital emancipatory potential contained within the heart of modern humanism. Luc Ferry and Alain Renaut point out that the dispute over the value ideas of modern humanism is finally a controversy over the evaluation of modernity and its achievements.[11] They use the term 'anti-humanism' to refer to the philosophical thematisation of a rejection of modernity which:

> . . . whether hostile or anguished, often unjust sometimes legitimate, was always done from a viewpoint of radical exteriority from which any compromise with modernity was always seen as a compromise with one's conscience.[12]

Among the most vigorous champions of contemporary humanism, Agnes Heller and Ferenc Feher have, nevertheless, no
illusions about the intolerant contempt for all particularity and
difference which has scarred the history of modern humanism.
As Feher sees it, a radical formulation of the cultural ideal of
humanism is burdened with the weight of its own oppressive
history. Humanism, he points out:

> . . . is in fact a European scenario. Man is seen as identical with
> the European man who embarked on the project of remaking the
> world in the image of the only progressive arrangement he was
> familiar with as well as prepared to recognize: nineteenth century
> Europe. This European scenario of humanism forcibly blended all
> differences. Within its own world, its own nation state and
> colonies, it tolerated neither particularity nor singularity. Difference
> (for example, the female difference, the difference of races, or that
> of sexual deviation) was persecuted or outright exterminated by an
> ethnocentric and oppressively universalistic humanism.[13]

If the contemporary defence of humanism mounted by Feher
and others concedes the devastating suppression of difference
which has attended the history of modern humanism, it needs
to be asked, on what fond hopes is the continuing allegiance to
this cultural ideal based? Grasping the nettle, Feher's own defence
of humanism does not disclaim the charge of an oppressive denial
of difference. Nor does he harbour any hopes that humanism
might somehow throw up a ready-made, non-exclusionary image
of a common humanity. Instead he conceives humanism itself as
a restless, incompletable project charged with ever-enriching its
core commitments understood as being the universalisation of the
ideas of freedom and self-determining autonomy. Allegiance to
these universal value ideas neither prevents the radical humanist
from questioning the particularistic shape of any of the historical
forms nor does it prevent their meaning being augmented as new
vistas are opened up by contemporary social struggles. Modernity
has, on this reading, meant the universalisation of the value
commitments of humanism with the obsolesence of provincial
standards and parochialisms. Yet, as these aspiring universal
standards are born on the wings of a real historical dynamic,
they can never entirely avoid the traces of their own historical
emergence, the limitations of their own embeddedness in particular, concrete conditions and societies. Contemporary humanism
still proudly endorses the values of freedom, rationality and
equality, yet it is not afraid to infuse these basic values with new
meanings which signify the enrichment and qualitative expansion
of the old.

Among the defenders of modern humanism, Agnes Heller, Ferenc Feher, Richard Bernstein, Jurgen Habermas and others concede the destruction wrought by the metaphysical conceptions which have swamped most former attempts to construct a non-exclusionary image of a common humanity.[14] Unlike the anti-humanists, however, the contemporary defenders of modern humanism see beyond this metaphysical husk an emancipatory core which lies at the heart of the humanist idea of self-realising subjectivity. There is a general accord among the contemporary advocates of humanism that the emancipatory potentials of humanist ideas ought to be pursued further, and there is even a consensus here on the need for a new 'post-metaphysical' construction of the meaning of these ideals. This new 'post-metaphysical' construction of the ideals of humanism rests on a determination to liberate the humanist 'subjectivity' from all connotations of arbitrary self-assertion and instrumentalising aspirations. As Habermas sees it, a 'post-metaphysical' humanism preserves the ideals of modern humanism long expressed in the ideas of a self-conscious life, of authentic self-realisation and autonomy, but disassociates all such commitments from the will and aspirations of any particular social subject. For post-metaphysical humanism these cultural ideals enjoin, rather, a commitment to the cause of radically democratic processes of communication and interaction between subjects.[15]

Much of what follows will employ the description 'radical humanist' as an umbrella term which designates a general orientation, but no homogeneous school of thought, among contemporary defenders of humanism. What finally separates contemporary radical humanism from the anti-humanism upheld by, among others, Michel Foucault, is its recognition of, and attempt to grapple with, the dilemma which lies at the centre of modern humanism. Anti-humanists find no tension at the centre of modern humanism between, on the one hand, the universalising attitude which seeks to raise claims on behalf of 'humanity as a whole' and, on the other, the always particularising character of any attempt to formulate an image of a common humanity. In this universalising attitude, anti-humanism espies only the determination of a specific subjectivity to mask its own will-to-power behind the ruse of a supposedly non-exclusionary conception of 'humanity as a whole'. Radical humanism, by contrast, insists on both the emancipatory achievements and potentials of that universalising value commitment and its being the pre-condition for the idea of the autonomous self-realisation of the unique personality which has taken shape in modernity. To the radical humanists, modern humanism is burdened by an irresolvable tension which invades its very core. This dilemma, between the universalising character of the claims and aspirations of modern humanism, which has a non-exclusionary interest in 'humanity as a whole', and the always particularistic terms in which these claims are framed, must not be made the occasion for a perilous attempt to dismantle this cultural ideal. On the contrary, the radical humanists grasp the nettle of the seemingly irreconcilable tension between the universalising aspirations of this cultural ideal and the particularising character of its formulations. Insight into the necessary limitations of all attempts to offer a universally applicable account of the meaning of these cultural ideals need not signify the end of what remains a dynamic and on-going quest.

Humanism: metaphysical or radical?

Agnes Heller has argued that to understand the peculiarity of modern humanism as a cultural ideal, it is necessary to look back to the revolutionary impact of the dynamic concept of man ushered in by the Renaissance.[16] Described as 'the belief in the unity of the human race and man's potential to perfect himself by his own efforts', humanism has a long and varied history stretching back to antiquity.[17] There is, however, no question of a direct, unbroken, legacy. The Greeks interpreted the ideal of human perfectability in terms of the static concept of man which prevailed in antiquity. Heller points out that the concept of person which infused Greek humanism meant that the individual's potentialities were seen to be circumscribed 'both in his social and individual life'; the ideal of human perfectability 'was one of objective limits, not the subjective projection of aims and desires'.[18] The unified totality of immediate social experience which characterised integrated, closed societies meant that:

> Man's . . . relationship to the community is identical with his relationship to 'defined existence'. To step outside the bounds of the given community is equivalent to destruction, and any kind of development is possible only within this circumscribed, untranscendable framework.[19]

In the dynamic conditions of accelerated socio-economic change which marked the Renaissance, people found themselves in a radically new situation which required a new way of behaving and a new way of understanding themselves. The dynamism of economic and social processes required 'a new concept of man . . . that of man as dynamic'. Henceforth, answering the question: 'How can I live and succeed amid the given movement of society?' gradually became an individual matter.[20]

The new dynamic concept of person gives a radically new content to the idea of a common humanity. In Heller's words, it holds that 'man is a relatively autonomous being, creating his own destiny, struggling with fate, making him self.[21] This new dynamic understanding of the concept of person which came to inform the various formulations of modern humanism spelt the end for any unitary human ideal. The dynamic concept of person was, for Heller, the other side of, and necessarily linked to, the same revolutionary transformation of social life which produced the disintegration of any unitary human ideal and the recognition of a plurality of images of the good life.

Heller makes the point that the dynamic concept of person which underpins contemporary humanism is the indispensable historical and conceptual underside of a recognition that for modern individuals there can be no unitary human ideal. This insight has a vital relevance to any contemporary attempt to evaluate and respond to the dilemmas which confront humanism today. The modern humanist, dynamic concept of person finds its way into those two, seemingly antagonistic, but actually interconnected value commitments of modern humanism which we noted earlier. On the one hand, the dynamic concept of person raises the claim that beyond the constellation of contingencies of one's birth there exists a primary status as members of a generic 'humanity'. Parallel with this aspiration to consider all humans in these universalising terms, a dynamic concept of person expresses a desire to affirm particularity, to raise awareness and respect for the uniqueness of all forms of individuality: this desire has served as a basis from which to decry the totalising character of all images of a common humanity.

A contemporary defence of humanism must conceive itself as an affirmation of the emancipatory value commitments of this cultural ideal. It adopts an immanently critical posture which strives to uncover the limitations and failures of the immense range of former attempts to implement and interpret the commitment of humanism to its key value ideas of freedom, life, equality, individuality and authentic self-realisation. Radical humanism rejects, however, the notion that the core value ideas of humanism inevitably rest upon any fixed metaphysical or anthropological formulation; that they must necessarily harbour the self-assertion of a particular subjectivity which strives to impose its own will and needs as normative and universal. Feher and Heller clearly recognise that the universalising dimension of modern humanism which seeks to abstract from all affiliations and particular integrations to construct an image of a common humanity can, and clearly has, functioned as an ideological legitimation for various forms of oppressive relations and institutional practices. Yet the humanist determination to raise individuals to the level of the universal does not, for them, simply express a totalitarian motivation. Indeed, on their account, the universalising perspective of modern humanism is, rather, tied to the liberal norm of the rights of humanity for, if all particularist determinations are to be suspended in our intercourse with humans qua humans, 'then every single individual being has to be protected against the force, pressure and interference of particularist integrations'.[22]

The radical humanist defends the value commitments of modern humanism as historical and, hence, contingent ideals which have, nevertheless, acquired an essentiality for us. The modern humanist ideals of self-determining autonomy and authentic self-realisation are values which have an historically acquired essentiality; these are the commitments of a cultural project through which we moderns seek to prosecute the desire for a good and rich life and to evaluate the character of specific forms of social relations and institutions. 'Radical humanism' is distinguished both by its determination to defend the ideals of modern humanism as contingent, historical values and by its efforts to grasp the consequences which this recognition of its historically contingent character might have for the 'cause' of modern humanism itself. To the radical humanism of, for example, Ferenc Feher and Agnes Heller, the value ideas of humanism are no gift of nature, eternal and inherent, but have come throughout the course of modern development to now claim a universal status.[23] Under this particular interpretation, the humanist commitment to the self-conscious life and its ideal of self-determining autonomy have been embraced almost universally in the modern world; they have become values relevant 'everywhere on our globe'.[24] Feher and Heller certainly do not suggest that the values of humanism are everywhere hegemonic and uncontested. Their point is only that it is increasingly difficult to find any corner of the modern world which remains completely untouched by the value ideas of contemporary humanism.

Radical humanism is, however, not merely distinguished by its historicising perspective on the universalising claims of modern humanist ideals. As already indicated, 'radical humanism' is here used to describe those various attempts to grapple with a dilemma seen to lie at the core of modern humanism. Feher describes the paradox of modern humanism in the following way: 'how to devise a universal category which is meaningful and all embracing without being oppressive and intolerant?.[25]Radical humanism recognises that modern humanism is pinned on a paradoxical relation between the universalistic character of its own aspirations and value commitments and the always particularistic, culture-bound terms in which these universalising claims are raised. There has been no single uniform response to this dilemma which is, for the radical humanist, integral to the very character of contemporary humanism itself. Major differences in the ways in which Habermas, on the one hand, and Feher and Heller, on the other, interpret and respond to the main dilemma of contemporary humanism will be examined in later chapters.[26] At this stage, I want to draw attention to the way in which the *recognition* of this dilemma distinguishes the standpoint of the radical humanist from the perspective of the contemporary anti-humanist. Radical humanism, to again make the point, conceives a tension between the universalising character of modern humanist ideals, which assert a non-exclusionary relevance for their claims, and the always particularistic terms in which these claims are made. The contemporary anti-humanist, by contrast, sees in the universalising claims of modern humanism only the cunning self-assertion of a particular subjectivity determined to seek legitimacy for its own will-to-power.

To highlight the main lines of this important dispute we can turn here to a brief discussion of its formulation in some of the main radical humanist challenges to the anti-humanism of the early Michel Foucault. Foucault's early formulations of an anti-humanist posture are mounted from at least two standpoints and a brief review of these distinct strands in his anti-humanism should allow us to delineate rather more precisely the terms in which radical humanism is prepared to defend the ideals of modern humanism.

Foucault has been vigorous and effective in his attack on the philosophical framework of humanism. According to him, a philosophical construction of humanism attempts to ground an image of a common humanity in a positive description of irreducible human traits. On this philosophical construction, the image of a common humanity ultimately refers to some sort of metaphysical postulate, like the Cartesian conception of the universal rational soul. In his attack on this kind of attempt to ground the image of a common humanity in an appeal to an a-historical Cartesian conception of subjectivity, Foucault joins with a host of contemporary critiques which challenge all attempts to supply philosophical foundations to an image of a common humanity. On this point, Foucault's is, then, just one voice among the general trend within mid-twentieth century philosophical

12

reflection towards a so-called anti-subjectivist stance. This anti-subjectivist turn rejects the alleged universality of some form of individual consciousness or set of common anthropological traits. It looks, rather, upon humanism as a specific cultural norm by means of which finite historical individuals seek to understand their own particular forms of existence and modes of intercourse.

With this line of argument the contemporary advocates of radical humanism have no difficulty. As we have seen, the standpoint of contemporary radical humanism fully disassociates itself from any metaphysical commitments. 'Humanism', on this construction, refers to a historio-cultural way of understanding persons which claims universality for itself and for its value commitments. The radical humanist posture seeks to elaborate its own commitment to humanist ideals which have 'taken shape' within modern society. The existence and practical necessity of these ideals can, however, be in no way supposed as 'guaranteed' by any metaphysical construction of the nature of subjectivity itself.

Radical humanism, has, then, no argument with Foucault's repudiation of all attempts to ground the ideas of modern humanism in a metaphysics of the subject. Foucault's early formulation of his critique of humanism goes, however, much further. He is opposed not merely to an attempt to provide philosophical justification of humanist ideals but calls into question the very notion that the cultural ideals of modern humanism could also serve as ideals with reference to which we criticise the traditions we inherit.[27] Fraser calls this second dimension of Foucault's anti-humanism—in which the ideals of humanism are seen as totally reducible to social practices of justification—the strategic aspect of his campaign against modern humanism.[28] The standpoint of a strategic anti-humanism points out that the values of modern humanism which stress 'autonomy', 'integrity' and 'human rights' are the ideological vessels through which the norms and expectations of a specific way of life have imposed themselves with a normative force on the existence of modern individuals. The ideals of humanism, which proclaim an emancipatory message, are in fact the repositories of certain normalising presumptions about an appropriate way of life and form of identity. Foucault seeks to have us recognise the dark underside of the ideals of modern humanism which finds the 'self-made individual' making him or herself over in terms of strait-jacket cultural descriptions of an appropriate subjectivity. Foucault refers to these modern forms of domination which stress the production of a disciplined and self-disciplined individual as the 'normalising discipline'. The values of modern humanism are seen as agents of the production of this kind of subjectivity; their spokespersons are the psychiatrist, the social worker, the therapist, the doctor and the bureaucrat who, supported by the newly developed social sciences, have vastly extended the scope of social control. On this construction, the anti-humanist rejects the rhetoric of humanism on strategic grounds because this rhetoric stands as an integral component of the new disciplinary regime.

There is, Thomas McCarthy points out, no major disagreement between, for example, Foucault and Habermas over the 'immanence' of the standards we use to draw distinctions between truth and falsity; right and wrong.[29] These standards are themselves embedded in concrete languages, cultures and practices. Yet, unlike Foucault, Habermas maintains that the fact that we always find humanist ideals embedded in particular contexts does not finally diminish the universalising significance and emancipatory relevance such ideals have come to acquire for us moderns. McCarthy makes the point better:

> The ideas of reason, truth, justice also serve as ideals with reference to which we can criticise the traditions we inherit; though never divorced from social practices of justification, they can never be reduced to any given set of such practices. The challenge, then, is to rethink the idea of reason in line with our essential finitude . . . that is, with the historical, social, embodied, practical, desirous, assertive nature of the knowing and acting subject—and to recast accordingly our received humanistic ideals.[30]

So far I have attempted to briefly chart two main options which face a contemporary evaluation of the legacy of modern humanism. A contemporary anti-humanism espies in the ideals of humanism the rhetoric of a disciplinary, totalitarian modernity. The standpoint of a contemporary anti-humanism objects not merely to all attempts to provide philosophical justification of the essentiality of the ideals of humanism, it also calls into question the kinds of claims made on behalf of humanism beneath which it discovers the rhetoric of a subject bent on mastery of self, others and the world of nature. A contemporary radical humanism has, on the one hand, no argument with the critique of a metaphysical humanism but is, nevertheless, determined to affirm the essentiality to modern individuals of the value ideas of humanism. The humanist ideas of freedom, autonomy, equality, life and authentic self-realisation are not, on this viewpoint, merely the rhetoric of a disciplinary regime; they are essential to those principles of civil rights and modern democracy and to that affirmation of the uniqueness of each personality which we have come to prize as the vital achievements of modernity. A contemporary defence of humanism does not, however, attempt to obscure the main dilemma which today besets the core of modern humanism. For its champions, the dilemma of the universalistic character of humanist ideals and the inevitably conditioned and therefore always limited, particularistic character of their formulation does not vitiate the essentiality of those ideals. A post-metaphysical humanism looks to the rich, historical accumulation of interpretations of these ideals which are constantly being augmented by the various shapes these ideals assume in the course of on-going social dynamism and ever-shifting terrains of social struggle. They insist that these basic ideals are never reducible to any one particular attempt to interpret and to implement them. These two principally opposed responses to the crisis of modern humanism describe also, as I now attempt to show, two main paths which have been explored in a contemporary feminist evaluation of its future with humanism.

Does humanist feminism have a future?

The main dispute between contemporary anti-humanism and the standpoint of the radical humanists does not, as we saw above, centre on any argument about the need to repudiate a metaphysical defence of humanism. Nor would even the defenders of humanism want to ignore the repressive episodes in the history of a civilisation claiming allegiance to these ideals. They also want to expose all those formulations of humanist ideals which rest on a dogmatic equation of the universalising attitude of modern humanism with the self-assertions of a particular mode of social subjectivity. The dispute centres, rather, on the evaluation of the significance of these ideals. Radical humanists continue to affirm the universalising significance and the emancipatory relevance which these ideals have acquired for us as modernity's greatest achievement.

The contemporary dispute over feminism's relations to humanism takes an essentially similar shape and direction. The main debate within contemporary feminism does not turn on any controversy over the need to repudiate all a-historical constructions of a timeless human essence. While generally recognising the lasting value we have derived from de Beauvoir's early investigations into the discriminatory logic of gender ideologies and practices in modern society, feminists today are sceptical about the a-historical image of human subjectivity which underpinned her early scrutiny of the oppressed condition of modern women. Many would now agree with Genevieve Lloyd's critique

15

of de Beauvoir's attempt to assume Sartre's construction of an inalienable human transcendence (consciousness of freedom) as the basis for her critique of the imposed immanence (attribution of stable qualities) of the condition of modern women.[31] By taking up Sartre's a-historical image of human subjectivity, de Beauvoir's early feminism has been shown to, implicitly, assume the universality and normativity of a particularising image of the character of our common humanity. Lloyd's critique discovers that, the Sartrean ideal of transcendence is, 'in a more fundamental way than de Beauvoir allows a male ideal . . . it feeds on the exclusion of the feminine'.[32] In its origins 'transcendence' is a:

> . . . transcendence of the feminine. In its Hegelian version, this is a matter of breaking away from the nether world of women. In its Sartrean version, it is associated with a repudiation of what is supposedly signified by the female body.[33]

The success of the feminist critique of the particularising, implicitly gendered, character of all attempts within modern philosophy to construct a timeless metaphysical image of human subjectivity has changed the terrain of the debate over the character of feminism's relations to humanism. The significant dispute now concerns itself with the question of feminism's relations to humanism viewed as a set of contingent historio-cultural ideals and commitments. The terms of this current dispute need to be clarified further. What is it that essentially divides the standpoint of anti-humanist feminism from that posture I will be calling radical humanist feminism? Radical humanist feminism does not resile from strong formulations of the critique of the repressive, particularising terms in which the ideals of humanism have been interpreted, implemented and institutionalised. The dispute centres, rather, on the question over whether this critique of the repressive formulations of the ideals of modern humanism can be seen to exhaust the significance of these ideals for contemporary feminism.

In a paper titled 'Feminism and Anti-Humanism', Elizabeth Grosz takes the view that the feminist critique of the masculinist terms in which the ideals of humanism have been interpreted forces feminism to assume the status of an ideological competitor to humanism. Feminists, she says, have begun to recognise that:

> . . . the universalistic or generic category, 'human', like 'he' or 'man', is in fact sex-specific, and thus not applicable to both sexes equally. The object of humanist inquiry—man—is the product or representation of one sex, the male, which takes upon itself to act as a universal or representative ideal for women as well.[34]

Humanism, Grosz continues, supposes a common humanity or essence, yet, at the same time, this 'commonness' is the result of highly specific, social, historical, class and sex-specific modes of categorisation.[35]

A contemporary anti-humanist feminism is, in the first instance, distinguished by its determination to part company from the universalising tendencies of modern humanist ideals. On this viewpoint, modern feminism's attempt to assert the singularity and particularity of an hitherto marginalised and unacknowledged female culture makes contemporary feminism an ideological competitor to humanism in which it sees evidence only of a totalising hostility to all difference and particularity. According to Grosz, an assertion of feminine difference is wholly incompatible with the universalising categories of modern humanism. 'For feminists, to claim women's difference from men is to reject existing definitions and categories, redefining oneself and the world according to women's own perspectives.'[36]

Diana Fuss similarly sees a decisive battle between the commitments of modern humanism and the efforts of contemporary feminism to achieve public recognition for the particularity of a socialised femininity.[37] She holds that the assertion of feminine difference can only be contemplated in the context of a break from the universalising claims of modern humanism. According to her, feminism can only hold out against the repressive formulations of modern humanism by opting for an essentialist construction of feminine difference. This strategic appeal to an essential or natural feminine difference supposedly provides us with an image which is not reducible to the universalising categories of modern humanism. As Fuss puts it: 'An essentialist definition of "woman" implies that there will always remain some part of "woman" which resists masculine imprinting and socialisation'. She goes on to suggest that the claim that:

'we are women from the start' has this advantage—a political advantage perhaps pre-eminently—that a woman will never be a woman solely in masculine terms, never be wholly and permanently annihilated in a masculine order.[38]

There have been numerous proposals for tackling this problem of how to conceptualise the supposed immunity of feminine difference from the imperialistic grasp of a male humanist culture. Some have sought to evoke feminine difference as the disruptive repressed of a humanist culture which recognises only the universal 'man'. Donna Haraway, for example, maintains that, in its efforts to constantly disrupt and puncture the pretended universality of humanist representations, feminism evokes the repressed otherness of the feminine. 'Feminist figures cannot . . . have a name; they cannot be native. Feminist humanity must, somehow, both resist representation, resist literal figuration, and still erupt in powerful new tropes, new figures of speech, new turns of historical possibility.'[39] Again, Cixous's metaphoric feminist utopia looks forward to the return of the feminine repressed. 'When the repressed of their culture and their society returns, it's an utterly destructive, staggering return, with a force never yet unleashed and equal to the most forbidding of suppressions.'[40] In this case, the repressed difference of the feminine is seen to be produced by humanist formulations which, in their efforts to construct an image of a common humanity, are perpetually caught evoking the 'other' of such an identity.

The title 'anti-humanist feminism' remains, then, an umbrella classification for all those feminisms emphatically in favour of severing all ties with the cultural ideals of modern humanism. Joan Scott summarises the main theme of this construction of an ideological opposition between a feminist sensitivity to difference and plurality and the universalising attitude of modern humanism.

> We need theory that will let us think in terms of pluralities and diversities rather than in terms of unities and universals. We need theory that will break the conceptual hold, at least, of those long traditions of (Western) philosophy that have systematically and repeatedly construed the world hierarchically in terms of masculine universals and feminine specificities.[41]

To Scott and others, feminism's ideological battle with the repressive universalism of modern humanism leads to a search for alternative modes of representing the particularity and diversity of concretely located individuals.[42] This viewpoint frequently looks to post-structuralist theory to support contemporary feminism in its search for ways of representing its own deep opposition to the normativism of humanist culture. Chris Weedon, for example, accepts fully Heidegger's supposition that any formulation of humanism as a cultural ideal is inevitably accompanied by a metaphysics of the subject to which she supposes post-structuralism provides a needed point of resistance. 'Unlike humanism, which implies a conscious, knowing, unified, rational subject, post-structuralism theorises subjectivity as a site of disunity and conflict, central to the process of political change and to preserving the status-quo.'[43]

For a significant trend within contemporary feminist theory the assertion of the difference, the particularity, of women within a highly differentiated, complex modern culture puts feminism in a relation of clear ideological opposition to the ideals of modern humanism. This attempt by a contemporary anti-humanist feminism to drive a wedge between the commitments of contemporary feminism and the values of modern humanism needs, I suggest, to be confronted on several distinct levels. The leading objective in the following discussion is to demonstrate that, by drawing on a one-sided interpretation of the character and significance of modern humanism, anti-humanism feminism construes the tension *within* the cultural ideals of modern humanism as a manifestation of feminism's own struggle *against* humanism.

Two related considerations are relevant to our attempt to underline the humanist character of feminism as both an established fact of the history of modern feminism and as a desirable self-understanding for its present and future. In the first instance, to the extent that feminism wants to offer itself as a principled advocate of any value ideas at all, it inevitably draws upon that humanist capacity to look upon individuals in terms which seek to 'disembed' them from the singularity of their lived context. Feminism itself participates, namely, in that universalising attitude which an anti-humanist feminism targets as its ideological foe. If the disembedding, universalising attitude evoked by feminism's efforts to raise ideological claims testifies to its own humanist character, so too, I argue, the nature of its principled commitments: its affirmation of the ideas of difference and uniqueness, further manifests feminism's status as a humanism.

In her recent work, *Feminism Without Illusions*, Elizabeth Fox-Genovese draws particular attention to the universalising character of the claims inevitably raised by modern feminism.[44] Feminism today does not understand itself as an attempt to raise claims aimed at improving the advantage of any particular grouping of women relative to the standing of others. 'The ideological claims of feminism are, on the one hand, universal. Therein lies their strength. The rights of women, like the rights of man, speak for all women independent of race or class.'[45]

Fox-Genovese makes the point that, to the extent that it embraces a commitment to social justice, feminism is itself a manifestation of the universalising attitude of modern humanism. This capacity to discuss women in the abstract is inevitably evoked by even those feminisms which proclaim their own anti-humanist character. We saw earlier that the anti-humanist posture within contemporary feminism typically maintains that its ideological battle with the precepts of modern humanism imposes the necessity for a 'redefinition of oneself and the world according to women's own perspectives'.[46] Yet what is involved here cannot be construed as a clash between the universalising pretensions of

19

modern humanism, on the one hand, and a contemporary feminist sensitivity to difference on the other. In the context of a highly diverse, pluralistic modern society, the notion of a 'feminine difference' is itself an homogenising construction which relies precisely on a humanist capacity to consider individuals in abstraction from their embeddedness within a constellation of specific historio-cultural contingencies.

This recognition that feminism is a manifestation of the humanist capacity to discuss individuals in the abstract does not imply that feminism is, thereby, committed to the imposition of an homogenising construction of the significance of the diverse sociocultural experiences and situations of women in modern society. Against the self-representations of an anti-humanist feminism, the claim made here is that, when feminism evokes the ideas of difference and particularity as values which ought to be defended, it speaks precisely in the language of modern humanism. In its appeals—either explicit or implicit—to the idea of a self-determining life freed from all imposed integrations, feminism offers further testimony to its own credentials as an interpretation of the ideals of modern humanism.

An anti-humanist feminism strikes out on an impossible course. On the one hand, it sees in all universalising constructions of the ideal of autonomous, self-determining subjectivity evidence of the normalising claims of a particular social subjectivity which seeks to subordinate all difference. We have seen that anti-humanist feminism resorts to various stratagems to evoke the difference of a marginalised femininity in terms which disrupt, rather than simply conform to, hegemonic descriptions of a human subjectivity. Yet, if anti-humanist feminism is called upon to account for its motivations; if it is called upon to offer any justification for its insistence on the need for creating space for the voice of a marginalised feminine subjectivity, it can only do so by recourse to a principled commitment to the cultural ideals of modern humanism. Its motivations can only be specified in terms, namely, of the ideals of self-determining autonomous subjectivity and authentic self-realisation: the ideals of modern humanism itself.

To the extent that contemporary feminism sees itself as a principled commitment to difference, plurality and to freedom from all imposed integrations, it appears not, as an anti-humanist feminism might suppose, as an ideological opponent to modern humanism, but as a manifestation and particular interpretation of these cultural ideals. Radical humanist feminism recognises that contemporary feminism is itself an articulation of an emancipatory social movement which presupposed a turn away from found 'natural' categories by way of abstractions. It looks, moreover, at humanism's commitment to the idea of the autonomy of the self-determining individual as not merely the ideological vessel of certain normalising presumptions about the character of appropriate subjectivity but, rather, as ideas essential to the ideals of modern civil rights, modern democracy and to that commitment to difference and to the uniqueness of each personality which we have come to affirm as modernity's great achievements. Feminism appears as advocate, beneficiary and specific interpreter of the meaning of these developments. And, as previously suggested, once called upon to give an account of its own motivations, anti-humanist feminism has no option but to speak in the language of those humanist ideals and perspectives it seeks to attack.

There is no 'school' of radical humanist feminists. I use the term, rather, to describe a certain identifiable attitude towards the relationship of feminism to the cultural ideals of modern humanism. Michele Barrett has captured an emerging trend within feminist theory concerned to retreat from the 'overkill' of an anti-humanist feminism. As she sees it:

> Recent discussion of humanism, and the closely related question of how to theorise 'the subject', has tended to oversimplify the issue and to leap from a critique of the transcendental subject to dogmatic anti-humanist conclusions that are neither justified nor, eventually, useful.[47]

What the very different feminisms of, for example, Kate Soper, Seyla Benhabib, Elizabeth Fox-Genovese and Michele Barrett, have in common is important.[48] Where anti-humanist feminism sees only a disjunction between feminism's commitment to difference and the universalising ideals of modern humanism, radical humanism looks upon feminism as itself a particular, inchoate, permutation of the cultural ideals of modern humanism. Benhabib, for instance, is clearly unpersuaded that the feminist and postmodernist critique of the universalist and moral theories of the present has emptied such theories of all emancipatory content and relevance.[49] On the contrary, to her, it seems, feminism needs to link itself to the task of reconstructing—not dismantling—a moral and political universalism:

> . . . committed to the now seemingly 'old fashioned' and suspect ideals of universal respect for each person in virtue of their humanity; the moral autonomy of the individual; economic and social justice and equality; democratic participation; the most extensive civil and political liberties compatible with principles of justice; and the formation of solidaristic human associations.[50]

It might seem that the 'old fashioned' and 'suspect' idea of universal respect for each person by virtue of their humanity continues as a major motivating ideological commitment of feminism itself.

The leading question which confronts contemporary feminism in its efforts to deal with the issue of its relations to the ideals of modern humanism is not, as I have been arguing: can feminism choose to adopt or to extricate itself from these cultural values? The question is, rather, what hangs on feminism's decision to affirm or to disavow the humanist character of the ideals it evokes? There is no denying that the history of main attempts to interpret and to implement the ideals of humanism has shown a systematic tendency to exclude and to marginalise the specific needs and aspirations of modern women. In this event, it might seem strategically astute to declare one's ideological opposition to modern humanism, seen as an accumulation of phallocentric stories of the attempted self-assertions of an imperialistic masculine subjectivity. As I now want to show, two considerations count against this move towards a strategic anti-humanist feminism. Firstly, feminism's critique of mainstream formulations of modern humanism is more, not less, telling if informed by a recognition of feminism's own engagement with these cultural ideals. Secondly, an anti-humanist feminism produces a certain political agenda which, I suggest, can only cut into the vitality and finally the broader relevance of modern feminist theory.

The opposition between a radical humanist and an anti-humanist feminism is not a dispute over the necessity for a principled recognition of difference and plurality. The disagreement is, rather, over two distinctive ways of formulating a commitment to difference. I have been describing a radical humanist posture as a constant attempt to grapple with that tension in modern humanism between the universalistic character of its ideals and the always particularistic viewpoint from which they are articulated. Applied to feminism, this attempt to grapple with the dilemma of modern humanism means a recognition of feminism's own status as a particular, permutation and interpretation of the universalising ideals of modern humanism which neither compromises its autonomy nor blunts its capacity to speak to the particular concerns of women.

'Difference', by this point of view, appears as a cultural ideal; as a value commitment inherited by us from our humanist traditions. As a cultural ideal or value which has taken shape in a pluralistic, highly differentiated modernity, 'difference' is open to a multiplicity of interpretations and formulations; there can be no single interpretation of the meaning of this universalising modern ideal. By contrast, an anti-humanist feminism does not see its commitment to 'difference' as a particular attempt to interpret and give shape to common cultural ideals. Anti-humanist feminism insists, rather, on its own status as the only true advocate of the idea of difference against the homogenising, universalising standpoint of modern humanism. Because it sees itself as the *bearer* of the idea of feminine difference, anti-humanist feminisms of various sorts attempt to parade one particular interpretation of the experience of feminine difference as the *essence* of women's experience of their particularity. According to Cixous, for example, feminine difference is marked as the 'utterly destructive, staggering return of the repressed'.[51] Others have attempted to capture the idea of feminine difference as the attitude of 'caprice' and the 'denial of all binding'.[52] The general point is that, despite its own vehement protest at the disciplinary consequences of all homogenising descriptions of human subjectivity, there is a definite homogenising, normative image of feminine difference advocated in a range of anti-humanist feminisms. In the following chapters I attempt to establish that an image of culturally and socially privileged femininity lurks within several anti-humanist attempts to advocate an image of feminine difference.[53]

The efforts of an anti-humanist feminism to drive a wedge between feminism's advocacy of the principle of feminine difference and a humanist insistence on a repressive, homogenising idea of our common humanity has tended to produce its own repressive, homogenising constructions of an image of feminine difference. Moreover, as stated earlier, this insistence that feminism is an ideological opponent of the ideals of modern humanism suggests a very one-sided interpretation of modernity and its achievements. From the perspective of anti-humanism, the ideals of modern humanism, which stress the moral autonomy of the individual and universal respect for each person in virtue of their humanity, are reducible to the normalising pretensions of a certain kind of social subjectivity. In this case it becomes impossible to speak either of the emancipatory gains, the fragile improvements and the frustrated hopes and expectations of a modern social experience. Yet, it is precisely this kind of experience of raised hopes and dissatisfactions which is, I suggest, the ground upon which the struggles of the contemporary women's movement continue to be enacted. As previously argued, if feminism fails to see itself as a specific manifestation and interpretation of progressive potentials in modernity, then it may marginalise itself and cut itself adrift from a dialogic, reflective relationship with the practical, social and cultural experiences of women in modern society. In its most extreme formulations, the construction of modern humanism as the cultural reflection of a totalitarian modernity means that anti-humanist feminism can only underline its own alienation from those sociocultural arrangements and practices which organise the life experiences of women in modern society.

A radical humanist feminism is distinguished by its efforts to constantly negotiate and grapple with the dilemma which its own humanist character has thrust upon modern feminism. For modern feminism, the attempt to grapple with this dilemma means the determination to uncover the multitude of ways in which the existing formulations of the universalising ideals of modern humanism are always encountered deeply encased in limitations and prejudices derived from particular gendered social experiences. It also means—in the context of a dynamic, open-ended social experience—the discovery of new, hitherto unsus-pected, meanings and scope for the ideals of modern humanism and it means a commitment to recognise the ways in which, in raising its own multiplicity of claims, feminism might catch itself out in the false, repressive presumption of the homogeneity of the needs, interests and aspirations of women in modern society.

In any discussion of contemporary feminism's relation to the value ideas of modern humanism, a consideration of the contro-versy over feminism's relation to the historical Enlightenment must take a central place. The chapter which follows attempts to establish modern feminism's own character as a particular reading of the meaning of contemporary Enlightenment. The function of this chapter is to further clear the ground for the standpoint taken up in the rest of the book. I suggest that much of the rationale for the adoption of an anti-humanist posture within contemporary feminism stems from a misreading of the character of the historical Enlightenment and the significance of the politico-cultural undertaking it has bequeathed to us.

2 The antinomies of the Age of Enlightenment

In recent years feminism has played a crucial part in a developing ideology–critique of the claims to universality made on behalf of a Western conception of human reason. Feminism has joined with other perspectives in modern cultural criticism to expose this concept of reason as a 'mere thing of this world' embodying the norms, values and priorities of particular historio-cultural practices. This distinctive participation of contemporary feminism in a broad-based critique of the claims of a sovereign reason appears symptomatic of the growing theoretical and ideological maturity of this vital social movement. There is, moreover, a considerable consensus within the recent femininst literature about the necessity and the general direction of this unmasking critique. An important dispute has arisen, however, over the question of the meaning, the consequences, of this critique for contemporary feminism itself. Certain feminists have supposed that the critique of the claims of transcendent reason establishes modern feminism on the path of counter-Enlightenment.[1] This position maintains that feminism requires a fundamental break from an Enlightenment commitment to the cause of reason and truth which is exposed as nothing more than a distorted and disguised will-to-power. There are, however, those for whom feminism's unmasking critique of Western constructions of a sovereign reason cannot be understood as an invitation to an anti-Enlightenment posture. Sandra Harding, for example, endorses feminism's debunking critique of the ways in which Western constructions of the power

25

96-246

of reason systematically embody the norms and priorities of a male-dominated culture. Yet, for her, this critique in no way heralds feminism's own break from the commitments of the Enlightenment.[2] Lovibond too has suggested that feminism now needs to take stock of its deep indebtedness to the 'emancipatory metanarratives' of Enlightenment.[3]

The following chapter investigates aspects of this disputed interpretation of the relationship between contemporary feminism and the so-called project of Enlightenment. The argument is that current attempts to sever feminism's ideological ties with the Enlightenment rest on a basic misinterpretation of the character and spirit of the Enlightenment. These feminisms have misconstrued the character of the Enlightenment on two counts. First, this critique is typically aimed at a caricature of the historical Enlightenment. This repudiation of the Enlightenment influence is based on a portrait of the legitimating temper of seventeenth century rationalism and fails to acknowledge the anti-dogmatic spirit which progressively emerged in eighteenth century intellectual life. The first part of the chapter argues that this fundamental misconstruction of the spirit of the historical Enlightenment has distorted feminism's understanding of its own Enlightenment legacy. The vital difference in the temper of these two periods is illustrated by a short comparison between the limitations of Astell's seventeenth century feminism and the radicalism of Wollstonecraft's late eighteenth century version.

The suggestion that contemporary feminism can be understood as an anti-Enlightenment posture, indicates, moreover, a failure to grasp the essential meaning of Enlightenment as an unfinished or unfinishable cultural 'project'. This interpretation of Enlightenment has mistakenly reduced the dynamic, on-going, self-critical process of Enlightenment thinking to a set of fixed principles and doctrines. Perhaps the most forceful expression of Enlightenment thinking as the aspiration which has infused the whole spirit of modernity is still to be found in Kant's famous essay 'What is Enlightenment?'. Enlightenment, Kant tells us, 'is the emergence of man from his self-imposed minority. His minority is his incapacity to make use of his own understanding without the guidance of another.'[4] Thus understood, Enlightenment means only a commitment to an on-going critique of prejudice and to the historical production of a self-legislating humanity. This commitment which has threaded its way through the intellectual trajectory of modernity exists as a living, dynamic aspiration which is fundamentally irreducible to any one single formulation. So it seems that the acknowledgement of feminism's own Enlightenment character by no means signifies its assimilation to any pre-existing goals and perspectives. On the contrary, feminism's current critique of Enlightenment formulations appears as another vital episode in the unfolding of the Enlightenment project itself. Feminism's discovery of the prejudices built into the various articulations of this project is nothing more than an extension and clarification of the meaning of the Enlightenment.

Enlightenment, I argue, needs to be viewed neither as a one-sided epistemology nor as the legitimating ideology of certain interests within seventeenth century society.[5] Enlightenment, said to have produced as its 'crowning achievement' a specifically modern culture of humanism, is not reducible to any one single interpretation of the character of its goals and perspectives. The final section of the chapter outlines modern feminism's own character as a specific, dynamic interpretation of the meaning of a contemporary, historicised interpretation of Enlightenment. It indicates some of the ways in which the meaning of contemporary Enlightenment and modern feminism come together. Both criticise existing social practices and attempt to reveal the radical social possibilities existing in the present. Feminism, I suggest, needs to understand itself as a vital part of this movement pushing back the frontiers of existing social possibilities.

Images of the Enlightenment in contemporary feminism

A certain interpretation of the postmodern 'turn' in contemporary feminism is up for review here. Basing itself on a totalising and abstract critique of Enlightenment rationalism, this brand of postmodern feminism construes modern reason as a guilty normalisation of a set of prejudices whose influence is uniformly felt throughout every aspect of contemporary culture. Alice Jardine's *Gynesis: Configurations of Women and Modernity* which seeks to jettison the entire legacy of the 'humanist and rationalist eighteenth century', is a typical example.[6] Susan Hekman also looks upon postmodern feminism as a fundmental break from a 'homocentric' Enlightenment tradition. She sees a fundamental unity of purpose between feminism and postmodernism. Both 'challenge the epistemological foundations of Western thought and argue that the epistemology which is definitive of Enlightenment humanism, if not of all Western philosophy, is fundamentally misconceived'. Both, she goes on, 'assert, consequently that this epistemology must be displaced, that a different way of describing human knowledge and acquisition must be found'.[7]

To Hekman and Jardine, Enlightenment embodies that colonising spirit of scientific rationalism which has, in the context of modern day epistemological disputes, reappeared in the form of positivism and empiricism. Hekman distinguishes her own feminist critique of Enlightenment from those postures which see in Enlightenment rationalism a privileging of the 'male' values of domination, rationality and abstraction against which they assert the claims of the supposed female values of nurturing, relatedness and community.[8] To Hekman, feminism is a vital participant in a contemporary challenge to the so-called epistemological attitude of Enlightenment. 'Enlightenment', on this account, means the oppressive, universalising assertion of certain, dogmatically assumed, truth claims. Feminism, by contrast, sides with a hermeneutic sensitivity to the conditioned, interpretative character of all knowledges. Against an Enlightenment 'epistemology' defined as the study of knowledge acquisition that was accomplished through the opposition of a (masculine) knowing subject and a known object, a modern feminist approach 'entails the attempt to formulate . . . an explanation of the discursive processes by which human beings gain understanding of their common world'.[9]

Jardine, Hekman and Flax share the conviction that feminism's critique of Enlightenment suggests an opposition in principle between two competing ideologies. Jane Flax, for example, sees in contemporary feminism and in the Enlightenment the clear and irreconcilable opposition of two ideological competitors. In her view, despite an understandable attraction to the (apparently) logical, orderly world of Enlightenment:

> . . . feminist theory more properly belongs in the terrain of postmodern philosophy. Feminist notions of the self, knowledge and truth are too contradictory to those of the Enlightenment to be contained in its categories. The way(s) to feminist future(s) cannot live in reviving or appropriating Enlightenment concepts of person or knowledge.[10]

In particular, Flax points out that contemporary feminism is deeply opposed to an Enlightenment construction of a sovereign reason which it exposes as resting on a 'gender rooted sense of self'.[11] On this account, the motto of the Enlightenment, *sapere aude*—'have courage to use your own reason'—confers an alleged normative universality on the supposed attributes of a modern masculine subjectivity. The attributes of passionate sensibility and intuitive understanding, associated with a socialised femininity, can only appear as impediments to be overcome in the development of the self-legislating Enlightenment personality.

According to this kind of interpretation of the significance of feminism's critique of Enlightenment, the latter appears only as a repressive epistemology whose grip must be broken in order to assert the excluded claims of the different and the marginal.[12] The prehistory of a feminist epistemology comes to appear as the repetitious logic of a totalitarian opposition between mind and body, reason and passion, reflection and intuition. What emerges is a portrait of a masculinised rational faculty which remorsely identifies itself and its power of universalising abstractions with human agency itself. The claims of the passions, of nature and of the uniquely individual appear as the mere objects of reason's limitless will to mastery. Because in the 'paradigm of Western reason' the human subject is identified with his or her own subjective reason, all difference is suppressed and an ascribed masculine psychology is conferred with an alleged normativity.

It is a particular interpretation of the significance of contemporary feminism's critique of Enlightenment which is up for review here. The disagreement is not with those feminist critiques which seek only to unmask the various ways in which Western constructions of the power of reason systematically embody the norms and priorities of a male-dominated culture. To the extent that a contemporary feminism understands itself as an immanent critique which seeks to rescue the emancipatory intent of Enlightenment from the various prejudices which cling to its 'master narratives' I have no argument. My disagreement is, rather, with those for whom this critique of the 'Western paradigm of reason' is seen to impose the necessity for separating contemporary feminism by radical surgery from the influence of Enlightenment thinking.

The dispute over the implications of feminism's own Enlightenment critique ultimately centres around significant differences in the ways in which Enlightenment itself is understood. To those, like Jardine, Hekman and Flax who understand contemporary feminism as the ideological competitor of Enlightenment, the Enlightenment appears as a repressive epistemology in which a masculinised rational faculty is seen to identify its own claims with human agency itself. An alternative viewpoint understands feminism as not merely a critic of, but also as a contemporary participant in, Enlightenment. Feminism, by this account, needs to be understood as a particular manifestation of that ideal of a self-legislating humanity which Enlightenment has injected into the spirit of modernity. As Harding points out, 'However a specifically feminist alternative to Enlightenment projects may develop, it is not clear how it could completely take leave of Enlightenment assumptions and still remain feminist'.[13]

To briefly remind, the Enlightenment interpretation proposed below suggests that the anti-Enlightenment turn in contemporary feminist thinking indicates two major misconceptions about Enlightenment. First, the feminist assault on the normalising claims of Enlightenment thinking frequently rests on a frozen image of seventeenth century rationalism and overlooks the progressive turn away from this interpretation of the meaning of Enlightenment which occured throughout the eighteenth century. Second, this particular misconstruction of Enlightenment is indicative of a more general misperception which confuses a *specific* meaning given to the ideal of a self-legislating humanity by the historical Enlightenment itself with the historicised, dynamic interpretation of this ideal which has become the meaning of contemporary Enlightenment.

The historical Enlightenment and its project

While Peter Gay has properly warned against any attempt to treat the Enlightenment as a compact body of doctrine, he discovers, nevertheless, a distinctive cultural climate in eighteenth century intellectual life. Despite the conflicting interpretations of the object of the newly discovered 'science of man', the historical Enlightenment agreed on the the ultimate self-responsibility of each individual. 'Whatever the philosophes thought of man—innately decent or innately power-hungry, easy or hard to educate to virtue—the point of the Enlightenment's anthropology was that man is an adult dependent on himself.'[14]

Ernst Cassirer finds, however, that d'Alembert's description of his own age as the 'century of reason' and the 'philosophic century' is too imprecise to capture the distinctive intellectual climate of eighteenth century intellectual life.[15] Cassirer and others point out that this self-description meant something quite specific to eighteenth century intellectuals. Namely, although they assume that there is unity, simplicity and continuity behind all phenomena, d'Alembert and his eighteenth century colleagues do not fall into the snares of the 'spirit of the systems' upheld by the seventeenth century rationalists.[16] In the great metaphysical systems of the seventeenth century, reason is in the realm of the 'eternal verities of those truths held in common by the human and the divine mind'. The eighteenth century takes reason in a different sense. 'It is no longer the sum total of "innate ideas" given prior to all experience, which reveal the absolute essence of things. Reason is now looked upon as rather an acquisition than as a heritage.'[17]

György Márkus has suggested that, for the eighteenth century, 'reason' appeared in what are, from a contemporary point of view, two rather incompatible guises.[18] In the first place, the eighteenth century intellectuals constructed a specifically critical construction of the power of reason understood as the critique of prejudice. Reason, on this account, assumed the negative character of critique. Reason concerned itself with the attempt to destroy the irrational 'superstitions' of the age, seen as the cause of all its ills.[19] On this construction, reason meant that new-born capacity to understand the world views of others not dogmatically, from the standpoint of the supposed 'eternal verities' discovered by reason, but as particular world interpretations expressive of a diversity of cultural experiences. The eighteenth century intellectuals, it has been said, discovered the concept of culture; they were the first to identify that now commonplace conception of the 'fashioning' of humans by their society.[20] The critique of prejudice contrived to establish an anti-dogmatic insight into the social–institutional supports behind a diversity of belief systems.

At the same time, however, the Enlightenment construction of reason as a 'heritage', also gave a particular, positive understanding of the character of the rational life. In this positive construction, rationality described an objective, albeit secular set of principles capable of guiding humanity's progress towards an enriched, fulfilled and harmonious social life. The eighteenth century's image of the rational character of the 'City of the Future' modelled on 'nature's plan' suggested that the high Enlightenment was unable to countenance the absolute relativisation of the cultural accomplishments of all historical periods and all societies. As Márkus notes, the concept of rationality also evoked a normative standard, a positive conception whereby the contributions of the diverse cultural products of other societies and epochs to the promotion of the rational, the harmonious and balanced life could be assessed.[21] So the destructive power of critique was to clear the way to a new rational social order ruled no longer by mere prejudice and superstition but by the 'highest' considerations of the well-rounded, harmonious development of human potentialities. Jacob and other major interpreters of the period particularly emphasise that high Enlightenment figures like Voltaire sought an order in society and government modelled after the new scientific conception of the orderly and balanced universe.[22]

Modern feminism's antipathy towards the anthropological underpinnings of an eighteenth century understanding of the rational life is clear and well-founded. The Enlighteners' supposition that the new rational society could be modelled after the principles of nature meant that traditional social arrangements continued to have powerful sanction. And yet, this understanding of the rational life meant also a new departure in the development of a modern image of the self; an understanding which, in fact, shares common ground with contemporary feminism's own critique of a one-sided rationalist conception of the self.

To the Enlighteners, the secular principle of human perfectability or self-improvement emerged as the clear successor to the rationalists' one-sided vision of reason's war on the unruly passions. Against the narrow asceticism of seventeenth century morality, the Enlighteners' understanding of the good, the rational life, encompasses the rehabilitation of the sensuous passions as a vital, creative force. Diderot, for example, insists that under the tutelage of reason's power of discrimination, a 'natural' sensuous love serves to unfold hitherto unrealised capacities for happiness and virtue in the personality of the lover.[23] And Emile's journey of self-development is radically incomplete without the love of his partner Sophie.[24]

Luhmann has emphasised that the rehabilitation of the passions evident in the Enlighteners' image of the rational, happy life is indicative of the inauguration of the modern concept of personality itself.[25] He points out that the psychology of the seventeenth century still worked with the old concepts of temperament and humour which allowed no room for personal development. This only changes in the course of the eighteenth century at which point people are now conceived as being changeable, capable of development and still unperfected. In the context of this new understanding of personality, marital love, a love based on 'tender confidence' and esteem, was given a vital place in the Enlighteners' image of the virtuous, happy and rational life. Fairchilds describes the new libertarian meaning of the Enlightenment's understanding of personality as follows:

> In the face of centuries of Christian asceticism, the Enlightenment propounded the possibility of individual happiness on earth: in the face of centuries of Christian disparagement, the Enlightenment rehabilitated the passions, including romantic love and sexual desire, as essential elements in such happiness.[26]

The discussion so far has been particularly concerned to differentiate some aspects of the notion of rationality typical of the high Enlightenment from the rationalism seen to characterise seventeenth century intellectual life. Jacob and other main interpreters of this period emphasise that the increased radicalism, the new critical character of an eighteenth century understanding of the notion of rationality was by no means a uniform or unambiguous development.[27] Nevertheless there are, I would argue, important differences here which need to be taken on board in the efforts of contemporary feminism to assess its own relation to Enlightenment. The anti-Enlightenment turn in contemporary feminism challenges what it has construed as the essential dogmatic spirit of Enlightenment thinking; it has focused particularly on its supposed one-sided rationalism and on its metaphysical pretensions. This image overlooks the important new critical spirit, the anti-dogmatic construction which came to infuse the conception of Enlightenment throughout the eighteenth century. This cultural commitment to the critique of prejudice laid down by the Enlighteners was constrained by their own positive conception of the character of the rational life.

Modern feminism can gain useful insights into both the radicalism and, from its own contemporary point of view, the fundamental limits of the Enlighteners' image of the rational life by considering the focus given to this image in Wollstonecraft's *A Vindication of the Rights of Women*. A brief comparison between Wollstonecraft's late eighteenth century feminism and the more conservative standpoint espoused in Astell's late seventeenth century feminism illustrates important discontinuities between the two constructions of the power of reason outlined so far. I suggest, moreover, that serious tensions which pervade the core of Wollstonecraft's feminism can be traced to limitations within the Enlighteners' own inaugural vision of the Enlightenment project.

Enlightenment feminism: Mary Astell and Mary Wollstonecraft

The Enlighteners' image of the rational life was quite plainly not intended to include women. Rousseau's Sophie 'made for man's delight', is esteemed only for her contribution to the self-development of her mate Emile. Contemporary feminist scholars have rightly drawn attention to the deep misogynistic currents which inform the perspectives of the main intellectual figures in the Enlightenment. Fox-Genovese, for example, points out that 'as heirs to the time-honoured notions of female inferiority, Enlightenment thinkers normally continued to view women as weak, troublesome, shrewish, false, vindictive, ill-suited for friendship, coquettish, vain, deceitful and in general lesser humans'.[28]

Yet, despite this failure to challenge an overtly patriarchal legacy, the Enlighteners' deliberations on the character of the rational life opened up hitherto unsuspected possibilities for the development of a far-reaching feminism. Wollstonecraft's feminism moved beyond a mere politics of anti-discrimination, which calls only for an end to the exclusion of women from existing social priorities to demand for women a vital place in setting the agenda for life in the 'City of the Future'. The Enlighteners' image of the rational life which emphasised the harmonious development of the individual's many sided possibilities opened up a new creative dimension in Wollstonecraft's late eighteenth century feminism.

To appreciate the novel radicalism of Wollstonecraft's feminism, it is useful to compare her Enlightenment standpoint with the limitations of a feminism which had already surfaced in the seventeenth century. Astell's *A Serious Proposal to the Ladies* made explicit seventeenth century feminism's identification with the rationalist's war on the degraded and unruly passions.[29] Aptly described as 'Reason's Disciples', Astell and her friend, Elizabeth Elstorb, placed great faith in the power of reason to expose the triviality, the moral unseriousness of the conventions governing the lives of the new bourgeois women. The seventeenth century feminist accepted her unpopular task as the upholder of the 'rules of reason' against an unrestrained life guided only by the pursuit of sensuous enjoyment. Astell explains the plight of the seventeenth century feminist as the defender of reason against the unruly, untutored passions thus: 'Custom has usurped such an unaccountable Authority, that she who would endeavour to put a stop to its arbitrary sway, and reduce it to Reason is in a fair way to render herself the butt for all the fops in Town to shoot their impertinent censures at'.[30]

In the first instance, Astell's feminism voiced the protest of middle-ranking and upper-class women at their effective loss of status and power in the new bourgeois society. Although the newly emerging bourgeois society certainly provided this class of women with substantial grievances, by its insistence on the rational legitimation of all social practices, it offered also the main ideological preconditions for the articulation of an early feminist standpoint. Writing on marriage in the year 1700, Mary Astell asked: 'If Absolute Sovereignty be not necessary in a State how comes it to be so in a Family? Or if in a Family why not in a State; since no reason can be alleg'd for one that will not hold more strongly for the other'.[31]

Luhmann and others have, however, pointed to the essentially conformist character of the seventeenth century construction of the power of reason.[32] To the seventeenth century European, it seemed that the rational life ultimately meant the observance of the rules and norms of the social environment against the tyranny of the unruly passions. And this seventeenth century image of the rational life which conditioned Astell's feminism placed serious limitations on the radicalism of her protest. Astell's feminism was simply not equipped to interrogate in any essential way the priorities of her society. *A Serious Proposal* could only demand an end to the systematic exclusion of women from the seeming fruits of an intellectual culture monopolised by men. Astell's feminism called for the end to the universality of women's exclusion from the elevated 'life of the mind' and their systematic relegation to the 'Trifles and Gaities' of the marriage estate.[33]

On first inspection, the standpoint of Wollstonecraft's *A Vindication* appears as merely the renewal of the perspective already established in *A Serious Proposal*. Mary Wollstonecraft clearly emerges as another of 'reason's disciples'. Wollstonecraft's demand that society recognise women as 'reasoning creatures' meant, however, something different and rather more radical than was implied in the feminism of her seventeenth century counterparts. To Wollstonecraft, the barbarousness of the lives of bourgeois women does not simply appear in the denial of any intellectual life to the women newly herded into the trivialities of the domestic sphere. The tragedy of the situation appears, more precisely, in the deplorable waste of women's potential to lead a life guided by the aspiration towards self-improvement and human perfectability. The Introduction to *A Vindication* announces Wollstonecraft's intention to 'consider women in the grand light of human creatures who, in common with men are placed on this earth to unfold their faculties'.[34] So it is the standpoint of 'improvable reason' which provides Wollstonecraft with the platform from which to challenge the unnaturalness and irrationality of the lives of women of her own class.

A late eighteenth century figure, Wollstonecraft has at her disposal a specifically critical construction of the meaning of the rational life: a construction which affirms as its reigning value the norm of the balanced development of all the individual's faculties into the self-directing adult personality. In the first instance, this image of the rational life appears as the platform for Wollstonecraft's scornful critique of the futility of the lives of bourgeois women in the newly de-politicised sphere of the household. To Wollstonecraft, bourgeois society had meant the creation of a whole class of women dehumanised and enslaved by their dependency. Wollstonecraft's feminism protests at the debilitating, one-sided development of women's human capacities in a bourgeois domestic life.

> Taught from their infancy that beauty is woman's sceptre, the mind shapes itself to the body, and roaming around its gilt cage, only seeks to adore its prison. Men have various employments and pursuits which engage their attention, and give character to the

opening mind; but women, confined to one and having their thoughts constantly directed to the most insignificant parts of themselves, seldom extend their views beyond the triumph of the hour.[35]

Denied the opportunity to develop a range of human potentials, the personalities of women could only become horribly distorted and impoverished.

Clearly, Wollstonecraft had no more stomach for the idleness and mere sentimentality which dominated early bourgeois domestic life than had her seventeenth century predecessors. What is, however, quite new is her conviction that our efforts to build an enriched and decent social life could be informed by an attempt to redeem those traces of a humanistic ethic presently locked within the distortions of bourgeois domesticity. Wollstonecraft despises the prison house of bourgeois domesticity with its futile and trifling preoccupations. And yet it is less the type of concerns nourished by the new bourgeois family that Wollstonecraft finds so repugnant than their one-sided and hence distorted form. In the bourgeois family the humanistic image of relations with others based on a 'tender confidence' only makes its distorted appearance as an irrational romantic love fanned by 'vain fears and fond jealousies'.[36]

What needs to be stressed here is that the standoint of 'improvable reason' does not simply articulate a judgement on the trivial irrationality of the lives of the new bourgeois women. It is also an invitation for a vital, creative participation in opening up new life possibilities for the enriched self-legislating personalities of the future. To Wollstonecraft, this creative dimension of the standpoint of 'improvable reason' suggests that a domestic ethic of affectionate care and duty towards particular others presently languishing in the artificial sentimentality of the private sphere is worthy of redemption as a public ethic. Wollstonecraft supposes that the bourgeois family both provokes and expresses a need to which it cannot adequately respond. The privatisation of the ethic of care and responsibility for particular others appears in the particular context of the bourgeois family in the unstable and distorted guise of transitory and possessive love. To Wollstonecraft, this need for relations of care and responsibility for others finds its most appropriate expression in the friendship which is to her 'the most holy band of society'.[37] Wollstonecraft's feminism preserves, then, the ideal of active citizenship. Far from conceiving the realm of private activities as a sphere which needs to be protected from political interference, Wollstonecraft encourages the politicisation of those perspectives and needs presently contained within a repressive private sphere. Ursula Vogel comments on this visionary aspect of *A Vindication*:

> . . . the role which we commonly identify as belonging in the
> private sphere, Mary Wollstonecraft perceives as a constitutive
> element of citizenship. Stripped of their familiar association with
> intimate affections, and merely personal interests, the task[s] of the
> mother attain the dignity of public virtues.[38]

Condorcet, too, argued for the 'admission of women to the rights of citizenship' on the basis of the civic importance of their 'gentle and domestic virtues' and on the basis of the distinctive character of their reasoning powers, seen by him as an expression of their specific interests and aspirations:

> Women are not governed, it is true by the reason of men. But
> they are governed by their own reason. Their interests not being
> the same as those of men through the fault of the laws, the same
> things not having the same importance for them as for us, they
> can (without lacking reason) govern themselves by different
> principles and seek a different goal.[39]

An evaluation of the utopian aspect of Wollstonecraft's programme is not particularly relevant here. What is of concern, however, is the peculiar radicalism of her feminism which supposes itself to have not merely grievances at systematic patterns of discrimination experienced by bourgeois women but also a vital positive contribution to make to discussions over the character of the rational life. Where Astell's feminism had demanded only an end to women's systematic exclusion from the life of 'reasoning creatures', Wollstonecraft appealed to the standpoint of 'improvable reason' to demand the participation of the distinctive voice of women in unfolding the meaning of the rational, happy life.

Timothy Reiss offers a very different interpretation of the radicalism of *A Vindication*. On his account, Wollstonecraft was prevented from arguing a truly revolutionary case:

> . . . because she argued within Enlightenment rhetoric, for the
> extension of equality without regard (at least) to gender.
> Wollstonecraft was asserting women's right to catch up with men,
> in the same way that Tom Paine (for example) argued that the
> enfranchisement of the dispossessed—whether colonials, the poor,
> or the aged must catch up with that of proprietors. It was always
> a matter of the right to participate in the system, not of the need
> to change it.[40]

Here, Reiss discovers only one aspect of the main trends in what is, from a modern point of view, Wollstonecraft's highly contractictory feminism. As previously argued, Wollstonecraft is not afraid of upholding those qualities with which education and circumstance supposedly endow women as vital ingredients in the fully humanised, improved personality.[41] In her view, bourgeois women have been constrained by a life dedicated to the cultivation of the sensibilities. And yet, as the following passage suggests, Wollstonecraft's feminism targets only the dehumanising, one-sided character of those 'feminine' qualities produced by bourgeois domesticity.

> 'The power of the woman', says some author, 'is her sensibility;' and men, not aware of the consequence, do all they can to make this power swallow up every other. Those who constantly employ their sensibility will have most: for example, poets, painters, and composers. Yet, when the sensibility is thus increased at the expense of reason, and even the imagination, why do philosophical men complain of their fickleness?[42]

Wollstonecraft's critique of modern gender relations had at its disposal an image of the improved, many-sided personality. Accordingly, her feminism recognises a positive contribution from a different feminine voice in setting the agenda for life in the 'City of the Future'. Wollstonecraft does not, however, manage to sustain this perspective. The appeal to an Enlightenment construction of the rational social life also makes way for a legitimating perspective on an existing gendered bifurcation of private and public roles construed as nature. In this case, we see that Wollstonecraft is not calling for a recognition of the distinctive voice of women as active citizens in establishing the character of new social forms. She seeks only a reappraisal of the public significance of the private duties presently performed by bourgeois women in the domestic sphere. 'Women', Wollstonecraft remarks 'may have different duties to fulfil; but they are human duties, and the principles that should regulate the discharge of them . . . must be the same'.[43] At such points, the radicalism of her challenge to the new bourgeois social arrangement which severed the lives of middle-class women from the new public sphere is seemingly overwhelmed by a naturalistic patriarchal ideology.

Despite its own overt radicalism, Wollstonecraft's feminism is haunted by an historically understandable, naturalistic construction of the gendered character of social tasks and duties. In this capacity her feminism does nothing to challenge the priorities and the practical arrangements of her society. It merely calls for the recognition of the vital importance of 'womanly' duties in the realisation of an harmonious, balanced social life.

In Wollstonecraft's feminism we see the aporetic manifestation of the two dimensions of an Enlightenment construction of the character of the rational life discussed earlier. On the one hand, Wollstonecraft employs the Enlightenment construction of the rationality of the balanced, harmonious life and personality as the vehicle for her positive feminist critique of both the one-sidedness of the lives of bourgeois women and the one-sidedness also of public discussions over the content of the good, the rational, social life. While women are denied the exercise of all their human faculties in the 'gilt cage' of bourgeois domesticity, so too there is insufficient public recognition of the humanising, ennobling, potentials of those virtues of 'tender confidence' and 'gentle forebearance' nurtured by the intimate sphere. On the other hand, Wollstonecraft's feminism does not attempt to challenge the seeming naturalness of a gendered division of labour.[44] In its positive construction, 'rationality' loses its critical power as an interrogation of existing social arrangements from the standpoint of the neglected claims of a diversity of human potentials. Seen, rather, as a vision of a balanced, orderly social life—a vision whose rationality is authorised by the supposed order of a harmonious universe—the Enlightenment appeal to reason has the effect of sanctioning an existing way of life. To the extent that it works uncritically within the aporia of this understanding of the character of the rationality, Wollstonecraft's feminism cannot itself entirely escape a naturalistic ideology which imposes an essential status on the culturally acquired roles and interests of modern women.

The naturalistic ideology which plagues *A Vindication* appears as a manifestation of the anthropolgical foundations of her typical Enlightenment vision of the rational social life. Despite the eighteenth century's stress on humanity's unique capacity for self-improvement, this enterprise is still seen to be circumscribed and shaped by anthropological givens. The Enlightenment had not yet fully achieved the historical consciousness which was to emerge in the nineteenth century. Human attributes continue to be seen largely as fixed anthropological traits. Far from suggesting the pursuit of historically posited goals and objectives, the ideal of the rational life appeared to the eighteenth century Enlightenment as the revelation of nature's own plan. Hazard points out that it was supposed that the light of reason would discover nature's plan and once this was fully illuminated all that remained was to conform the new society to it.[45] The capacity for the rational life was viewed in terms of eliminating the obstacles to the natural unfolding of 'human capacities', therefore it was viewed in the light of an anthropological discovery rather than as an affirmation of an historical project or task.[46]

This eighteenth century anthropology according to which reason appears as an inherent capacity in the individual and truth the revelation of nature's plan was unable to discover its own legitimating prejudices. These would only become apparent with the historicised perspective which was to emerge in the nineteenth century. From the point of view of an historicised consciousness, the Enlighteners' supposition that the new rational society could be modelled after the principles of nature ultimately suggested the failure of the historical Enlightenment's capacity to sustain a commitment to the cause of a self-legislating humanity. The philosophes were not yet able to formulate the Enlightenment project as a commitment to radical democracy which recognised concrete individuals as the arbiters of their own wills and needs. As Markus points out, the Enlightenment philosophers' search for the 'truth' of a rationally unified secular culture 'able to discover and to impose a unique direction towards human perfection upon all processes of change occurring in a dynamic society ultimately means the failure of the historical Enlightenment itself with respect to its own emancipatory vision'.[47]

Although it remained to later generations of Enlightenment thinkers to diagnose the root causes of the failure of the historical Enlightenment, the seeds of its own self-critique were already unwittingly implanted in the aporias of Wollstonecraft's feminism. The democratic impulses of Wollstonecraft's feminism, which saw her calling for a recognition of the distinctive voices of women in any discussion of the character of life in the 'City of the Future', was in conflict with her endorsement of an anthropology which construed an imposed gender division of labour as an expression of a natural order. Yet, as already noted, the anthropological underpinnings of her Enlightenment understanding of the rational life meant that traditional social arrangements continued to have a compelling sanction. In particular, as Jane Rendall points out, the Enlightenment's attack on the seventeenth century's concept of a divinely ordered patriarchal family was replaced by an equally repressive legitimating ideology of the family as a pre-political web of natural relationships.[48]

The contemporary meaning of Enlightenment

The twentieth century has, as Habermas stresses, shattered the optimism nursed by eighteenth century European philosophy. The extravagant expectations harboured by Condorcet and others that 'the arts and sciences would promote not only the control of natural forces but would also further understanding of the world and of the self, would promote moral progress, the justice of institutions, and even the happiness of human beings', have all but disappeared.[49] Yet, while the failure of the hopes nursed by eighteenth century philosophy is indisputable, the continuing relevance of their project is still evident to many amid the ruins of a catastrophic twentieth century society. As Bauman, for example, sees it, the failure of the historical Enlightenment to implement its own project does not mean that the project itself was abortive and doomed. 'The potential of modernity is still untapped and the promise of modernity needs to be redeemed.'[50]

The contemporary efforts of major twentieth century philosophers and sociologists like Jurgen Habermas, Zygmunt Bauman and Agnes Heller to affirm the continuing legacy of Enlightenment needs to be understood as the reassertion of fragile and tenuous hopes amid the disasters and catastrophes of twentieth century history. Their attitude is contested by those for whom the ambitions of the Enlightenment are held accountable for the totalitarian social forms which have scarred the history of the modern West. To Theodor Adorno and Max Horkheimer, the Enlightenment attempt to replace myth with Enlightenment and domination with liberation has only meant the reappearance of new, more subtle, forms of domination and the continuence of the innermost logic of myth.[51] The authors of the *Dialectic of Enlightenment* link the development of civilisatory rationality with the barbaric domination of the self, others and nature. The wild self-assertion of this civilisatory rationality, unchecked by any self-consciousness, betrays the persistence of myth deep within the ambitions nurtured by the Enlightenment.

Cautious in their reassertion of the continuing promise of Enlightenment, Habermas, Márkus and others refuse, nevertheless, to echo the philosophical despair embraced by Adorno and Horkheimer. Habermas does not dismiss the real obstacles to the effective realisation of democratic ideals in contemporary political life, yet he consciously retreats from the idea of a totalising instrumental reason. To Habermas, bourgeois public institutions were, and are, a positive force for progressive social change.[52] Discarding the view that they are merely part of the apparatus of domination in monopoly capitalist society creating the seductive appearance only of individual freedom, Habermas sees these bourgeois public institutions as the site and vehicle, albeit fragile and flawed, of contemporary social struggles and resistance to the logic of self-regulating bureacratic systems and processes.[53]

In his later writings, Foucault came to the view that the dispute over the significance of the Enlightenment legacy could be resolved by making a vital distinction between the tendency of the principles of Enlightenment, on the one hand, and those of modern humanism, on the other.[54] Enlightenment, Foucault argues, needs to be understood not as faithfulness to doctrinal elements, but as 'the permanent reactivation of an attitude'.[55] Its main principle of critique and 'permanent creation of ourselves in our autonomy' is seen to exist in a state of tension with the character of modern humanism which has always presented a positive conception of the character of human subjectivity, conferring, thereby, particular historio-culturally constituted identities with an alleged universal significance. Foucault's construction of Enlightenment attempts, then, to quarantine its legacy from all positive, universalising content conferring Enlightenment with the meaning only of an attitude of perpetual critique at those apparent necessities which rule our lives. This 'critical ontology of ourselves has to be considered . . . as an attitude, an ethos, a philosophical life in which the critique of what we are is at one and the same time the historical analysis of the limits that are imposed upon us and an experiment with the possibility of going beyond them'.[56] Yet it seems that positivity and the formulation of value judgements, repudiated by Foucault as the mark of modern humanism, are implicit in his own construction of Enlightenment as an aspiration towards a 'going beyond' and as an articulation of our 'impatience for liberty'. The legacy of Enlightenment to us always comes impregnated with particular positive constructions of the meaning of that bent towards 'the permanent creation of ourselves in our autonomy' which is, to Foucault, its on-going commitment. And yet, the meaning of this commitment is not identical with any of its particular formulations; Enlightenment is a regulative idea to be constantly recharged with contemporary historical content.

Kant's essay, 'What is Enlightenment?', still stands as a classical interpretation of the broad cultural meaning of the Enlightenment as the on-going, still radically incomplete project of modernity. Kant's essay underlines that Enlightenment exists only as a human task or goal. We live, he says, not in an Enlightened age but in an age of Enlightenment. The historical Enlightenment vision of a self-reliant humanity capable of legislating for itself must be embraced as the arduous task of every modern individual. The Enlighteners showed that Enlightenment required nothing but freedom, in particular 'the freedom of man to make public use of his reason at all points'.[57] On this account, Enlightenment means the freedom of self-legislation in those matters of public import which transcend the realm of the mere private duty of the citizen. In the end, Kant suggests that while Enlightenment remains a cultural and individual task it also and at the same time identifies the original vocation of human nature itself. Nature, he comments:

> . . . has evolved the seed for which she cares most tenderly, namely the propensity and the vocation for independent thinking: this gradually works back on the mentality of the people (whereby they become little by little more capable of the freedom to act) and also eventually even on the principles of government, which finds it advantageous to itself to treat people who are now more than machines in accordance with their dignity.[58]

Kant's view of Enlightenment is a call for a radical emancipation from the dogmas of the past and for practical autonomy. This is a call that has resounded down to our own time. The call was heard by Kant's contemporaries who applied Kant's critical method to his own philosophical presuppositions. Each succeeding generation of Enlightenment has submitted the certitudes of its own milieu to the same critical questioning in order to remarshal the energies and redefine the contemporary meaning of Enlightenment thus making another advance down the road that Kant had designated.

Hegel's philosophical critique of Kant represented the first bold acceptance of the Kantian challenge. He argues that the Kantian 'critique' had faltered at the very point where its critical impetus needed redoubling. Kant failed to question the self-thinking and self-legislating consciousness forming the very core of the transcendental philosophy. Hegel demonstrates the historicity of this consciousness and its demands and therefore immeasurably widens the emancipatory implications of the project of Enlightenment. Hegel rejects the naturalistic dressing of the Kantian imperative to freedom only to lay bare its sociopolitical preconditions. His philosophy underlines that freedom is born, nurtured and evolves not as a claim of anthropological human nature but in the particular historical soils favourable to its growth and metamorphoses. Yet, while Hegel exposes the historical dimensions of the preconditions and obstacles to Enlightenment, he was ultimately unable to carry this insight beyond philosophy and thereby infuse Enlightenment with an emphatic revolutionary sociopolitical message.

It was Marx who succeeded in putting Hegel's historicist understanding of the problem and project of Enlightenment on a radically new footing. For Marx, freedom is not a philosophical value compatible with the constraints, inequalities, horrors and pettinesses of the newly triumphant bourgeois order but a new social organisation immanent to the present class struggles of bourgeois society. Marx's own critique of ideology is, on the one hand, a definite continuation of the Enlightenment critique of prejudice conceived as socially induced deformations of reason. Yet, as Márkus notes, from the standpoint of Marx's theory of ideology 'a criticism of prejudices in the name of an impartial reason or an eternal and normatively conceived human nature is itself a deeply ideological heritage'.[59] Marx's critique of ideology preserves the Enlightenment's emancipatory vision in which human beings appear as creators of their own social world. Yet Marx's polemics against the prejudices and vested interests of the present are not conducted in the name of an ahistoric rationality. Marx's critique of ideology is 'conducted in the name of historically and socially defined, concrete and "limited" needs and sufferings which are produced and induced by the same social interests'.[60] With Marx, we see a real democratisation of the Enlightenment project in the sense that the call for emancipation and autonomy transcends the sphere of culture and science taking on a mass significance. (This remains true despite the no less apparent anti-democratic potentials which have informed the Marxian notion of class consciousness.) The fundamental cause of Enlightenment is now situated by Marx not simply as the task of an ahistoric rationality, not even as a matter of historically informed philosophy but as a matter of a concrete collective of individuals determining their own history on the basis of their own definite needs and aspirations. Other Enlightenment interpretations have followed Marx, discovering the crucial limitations of his own formulations of critique and revealing the tensions in his own understanding of social emancipation and autonomy. Each unveils a new dimension of the problem and a new terrain on which the battle for freedom and reason needs to be prosecuted in order to realise our historically accumulating sense of human dignity.

The assertion of modern feminism as an episode in Enlightenment thinking recognises feminism's own necessary participation in this, as yet, radically incomplete, open-ended project of cultural criticism. Feminism takes its vital and distinctive place in the project described by Kant as the future-directed optimism that people could emerge from their self-imposed minority to legislate for themselves. It remained for later generations of thinkers inspired by the historical Enlightenment to historicise and radically democratise the meaning of this task. Whereas the Enlighteners had appealed to the 'truth of nature' in order to impose a direction towards human perfection, the spirit of the Enlightenment since that time has sought to maintain the emancipatory temper which sees human beings as the creators of their own social world on the basis of the needs and the aspirations of concrete individuals themselves. This spirit was encapsulated in the broadening nineteenth century demand for constitutional reform, republicanism and finally social revolution and radical democracy.

Modern feminism is, I suggest, best understood as occupying a double relation to Enlightenment thinking. On the one hand, feminism's protest at imposed gender relations preserves and extends the Enlightenment's emancipatory vision in which human beings are affirmed as the determiners of their own social world. In particular, modern feminism needs to be understood as an interpretation of a contemporary historicised understanding of Enlightenment; it repudiates all Enlightenment formulations which turn on an appeal to an impartial reason and to an eternal and normatively conceived human nature. Modern feminism appears, then, as a vital moment in a contemporary interpretation of the cause of Enlightenment as a commitment to the cause of radical democracy. At the same time, the affirmation of feminism's own Enlightenment character does not suggest its assimilation to any fixed set of doctrines and principles. As its critic, modern feminism unmasks the failures of the various episodes in the Enlightenment tradition to fully interpret the meaning of the Enlightenment project. The narrow rationalism of seventeenth century metaphysics, the naturalising constructions of the Enligteners themselves, the so-called gender-blindness of Marxian categories, as well as liberalism's own construction of an abstract 'rights-bearing' subject, have all been appropriately targeted by this critical feminist perspective.

As a critic of the Enlightenment tradition, modern feminism is also and at the same time its manifestation and distinctive interpretation. Feminism constantly seeks to push back the legacy of our entrenched prejudices to reveal new social possibilities in the present. Ever since Wollstonecraft, feminists have affirmed their commitment to a qualitatively expanded interpretation of the meaning of Enlightenment. As we shall see in the chapters which follow, feminism has consistently attempted to expose the prejudices embedded within those definitional constructions of human subjectivity called upon in the various formulations of the meaning of Enlightenment.

Contemporary feminism has, moreover, attempted to open up our understanding of those activities and ways of doing things understood as the proper subject for public discussion and expression. The familiar feminist call for the politicisation of the personal sphere is one instance of feminism's vital and distinctive contribution to an on-going process of immanent critique in which generations of Enlightenment thinkers have opened up new terrains which need to be encompassed in a commitment to radical democracy. Modern feminism appears as a qualitative expansion of the contemporary Enlightenment project seen as an 'articulation of a broad-based program for critique and social change promoting the social recognition of diverse human potentials and ways of life'.[61]

The conception of the anti-Enlightenment character of contemporary feminism is a significant, by no means uncontested, theme in recent feminist discussions. The next chapter continues, from a different viewpoint, the challenge to this interpretation of the anti-Enlightenment commitments of contemporary feminism. It investigates the several ways in which modern feminism has attempted to appropriate main themes and perspectives developed by nineteenth century Romanticism. The chapter draws attention to the consequences of an attempt to construe the meaning of feminist aspirations along lines borrowed from the anti-Enlightenment impulses which cling to early Romanticism.

3 Quest for the self: feminism's appropriation of romanticism

If significant trends in contemporary feminism have turned their backs on the 'homocentrism' of the 'humanist and rationalist eighteenth century', they have not been long in discovering important new sympathies with the nineteenth century's own self-appointed rival to the main formulations of the historical Enlightenment. The increased interest shown by feminism today in the themes and precepts of nineteenth century Romanticism is hardly surprising. This first cultural revolution of modernity expressed the crisis of an old world and the emergence of the new. Its own rich ambiguities and polyvalences betray the first signs of cultural schizophrenia. A unique constellation of utopian expectations, shock and horror before the dynamic new were soon mixed with critique of the universal cultural illusions of Enlightenment and nostalgia for the eclipsed old. Amid a crisis of questioning their own former universalising normative ideas of humanity and equality, contemporary feminists are now eagerly exploring the rich veins of modernity's first attempt to question its own reigning values, to celebrate its own dynamic diversity and to recognise its own inchoate individualist subjectivity.

What do they really hope to find? Always Janus-faced (if not a hydra's head) nineteenth century Romanticism seems to promise two very different, and I think finally incompatible things. On the one hand, contemporary feminism has conceived an interest in the image of the concrete difference of the feminine evoked in the Romantic literature. Ursula Vogel, for example, discovers strong ties between the struggles of contemporary feminism against all imposed, merely one-sided, conceptions of the self and the efforts of the German Romantics to assert the diversity of human potentials which ought to be recognised in the cultivation of the harmonious and many-sided personality of the modern individual.[1] This first kind of interest, which investigates key images and motifs in the Romantic literature, is prompted by a perception of the potential support offered by a Romantic image of the self to a contemporary feminism concerned to discover terms for an unbiased reflection on the concrete differences between the sexes. A significant trend in contemporary feminism has, moreover, conceived of a second, quite distinctive sense in which it might exploit main themes and tendencies within nineteenth century Romanticism. This second kind of interest in Romanticism has, unwittingly, I suggest, contrived to appropriate the main sense of a Romantic world view as the basis for constructing a self-understanding of the meaning of modern feminism itself. The crucial difference here is that, whereas the former kind of interest is principally concerned to evaluate images of the feminine on behalf of the independently conceived goals and concerns of modern feminism, the latter kind of feminist appropriation of Romanticism understands the meaning of contemporary feminism itself in terms of a Romantic world view. Feminists as seemingly diverse as Judith Butler, Luce Irigaray and Alice Jardine have all, I argue, attempted to appropriate for feminism a very recognisably Romantic construction of the meaning of the emancipation of the self.

The following chapter discusses a seeming paradox which appears at the crossroads of the two different constructions of feminism's interest in Romanticism outlined above. The first part attempts to establish that the hopes that contemporary feminism might discover in Romanticism evidence for an unbiased reflection on the difference between the sexes have been disappointed. As its feminist critics have discovered, the weight of evidence suggests that Romanticism, no less than conventional liberalism, upholds an unmistakably naturalistic construction of the significance of feminine difference. In the second part of the chapter I attempt to show that a naturalising conception of feminine difference is a manifestation of assumptions embedded deep within the core of a Romantic world view. The final section sets out to establish that the very same dimension of a Romantic world view responsible for a naturalistic construction of feminine difference is precisely that aspect of Romanticism which has been appropriated by a Romantic feminism to supply the core of its own self-understanding. My argument is that a Romantic interpretation of modern feminism inevitably reproduces the very same problematic construction of the self and its relations with others which the feminist critics of Romanticism have uncovered in the Romantic literature.

Romanticism and the quest for a feminist definition of the self

Romanticism, it need hardly be said, is a highly complex phenomenon: one which admits a variety of not always consistent interpretations and emphases. The character of the Romantics' relationship to the historical Enlightenment is particularly subject to dispute. Seen by some as the precursor of a tradition of anti-Enlightenment, Romanticism is generally supposed to retain at least some of the goals of the Enlightenment. Ernst Cassirer emphasises the innovative character of Romanticism's relationship to the ideals formulated by the historical Enlightenment. In particular, he maintains that Romanticism helped forge that historicised consciousness which has come to shape the meaning of Enlightenment for modern individuals.[2] The Romantics progressively broke with that historical Enlightenment appeal to the 'truth of nature' thought to impose a direction towards human perfection. As Arthur Lovejoy explains, however, Romanticism did not, in the first instance, represent a turn from a conception of a morally significant universe.[3] It meant, rather, a shift in the way such a universe could be seen and the kind of role it could occupy. It meant, namely, a turn from a conception of the cosmos as a static mechanism 'radiant with order and value' to a conception of a dynamic, diverse cosmos in a constant state of becoming.

In his *The Triumph of Romanticism*, Peckham describes Romanticism as a revolution in the European way of thinking.[4] Elaborating on themes raised by Lovejoy, Peckham sees the main spirit of Romanticism as 'the revolution in the European mind against thinking in terms of static mechanism and the redirection of the mind into thinking in terms of dynamic organicism. Its values are change, imperfection, growth, diversity, the creative imagination, the unconscious.'[5] On this interpretation, Romanticism appeared in the wake of the collapse of the historical Enlightenment's efforts to model the social and the moral universe after the real structure of nature which was viewed as a static, well-ordered mechanism. This Enlightenment appeal to an orderly nature, put to the test in the French Revolution, gave way to the revolutionary thesis that 'the only conceivable source of value was the necessity for the individual self to create in order to maintain itself'.[6] For the Romantics, the truth of a diverse, dynamic, living world of nature can only be discovered through the projections of the unconscious and creative mind. The Romantics looked upon the Enlightener's belief in a natural order of interlocking purposes as a repressive dogma which could no longer capture the turbulent and fragmentary experience of modern individuals. And, according to many of their interpreters, the lasting significance of the Romantics lies in the early and still distinctive formulation they gave to that epochal question which has been the on-going legacy of the collapse of this Enlightenment anthropology: what, the Romantics asked, with ever-growing confidence, is the ground of value?[7]

George Herbert Mead has attempted to supply us with a sort of ideal type which captures some of the main aspects of the Romantic's efforts to grapple with the problem of values. On this account, the Romantics shifted from an early sense of the self as the casualty of a modern experience of isolation to an image of the heroic self who refuses to accept human limitation on the possibilities of his or her unique, creative self.[8] Mead's description of a characteristic Romantic attempt to drive a wedge between the unique self and the contingency of the social role is a formulation which has had a lasting influence on contemporary discussions over the meaning of Romanticism.[9]

It is, then, this overriding commitment of the Romantics to an ideal of the necessary independence of the unique self from the social role which informs Romanticism's distinctive attitude towards the world of nature. Whereas the Enlightenment had understood its historical task as the production of an orderly, balanced social world modelled after the image of the interlocking design of nature, the Romantic nature worship was designed to orient the individual away from all mere suffocating adaptation to the demands of an ascribed social role. Rousseau's proclamation in the *Confessions* has been taken as prototypical of this new sense of the unique self which was to mark the Romantic consciousness. Rousseau insists on the irreducible gap which separates the self from the homogenising constraints of the social role. Rousseau's self is like no other. I want, he says:

> . . . to show my fellows a man just as he is, true to nature; and that man is myself. Myself alone . . . I am not made like those I have come across. I venture to believe that I am not made like any other existing man. If I am not better at least I am different.[10]

In its general aspect, this insistence that a wedge could, and should, be driven between the self and its role has a definite emancipatory meaning. Indeed, such an understanding appears as the deep ideological precondition of that emancipatory interest which continues to motivate modern feminism. The Romantics gave, it is true, a quite particular formulation to this broad emancipatory interest. Yet even a first approximation of the specific character of Romanticism's understanding of the struggle of the self against the role seems to suggest no decisive barrier to its appropriation by contemporary feminism. We can, in fact, note in the Romantics' conception of the role as a violation of the diverse possibilities of the self an apparent sympathy with modern feminism's concern to break down and out of a restrictive, normative liberal conception of the self.

Conventional liberalism portrays individuals as legal persons bearing rights or as moral agents capable of rational choice, but these representations acknowledge only a formal individuality, what is general among people, not what makes them unique, various and original.[11] Liberalism clung to the ideal of the self-won independence of the strong, self-legislating personality and, as Nancy Rosenblum explains, to the Romantic consciousness which abhors all definitions, 'even this ideal of self-legislation and choice seemed cruelly limiting'.[12] Both Rosenblum and Vogel go on to underline a deep sympathy between the contemporary feminist critique of liberalism's definitional conception of the self and a Romantic resistance to the 'unlovely coldness' of liberalism's picture of political life. In contrast to the image of the self-governed personality evoked in conventional liberalism, the Romantic self is potentially full of feelings.

At first sight, the radical individualism of a Romantic world view might seem perfectly appropriate to the formulation of some of the main concerns of a contemporary feminist culture. The Romantic outlook contains at its centre an image of the unique self with potentialities and possibilities radically other and infinitely more open-ended than those suggested by the mere contingency of his or her sociocultural location. As Charles Taylor describes it, Romanticism is distinguished by its insistence that each individual is different and original and this originality determines how he or she ought to live.[13] And this commitment to the ideal that each one of us has an original path which we ought to tread would seem to be at least very consistent with an emancipatory recognition of the fact of human plurality and with the affirmation of the principle of the equality of life chances for all.

It is, in this light, rather striking that many modern feminist critiques have discovered that the Romantic literature does not characteristically affirm a plurality of diverse selves. Its feminist critics have, on the contrary, uncovered in the Romantic literature an image of a quite particular, masculine self. On the one hand, feminist critics like Alan Richardson, Marlon B. Ross and Mary Jacobus acknowledge the unmistakeable idealisation by the English Romantics of the supposed feminine qualities of emotion, compassion and sympathetic understanding.[14] The Romantic self typically recognises the humanising potential of a tender compliant femininity as salve to its own restless strivings. Thus, Wordsworth compares his own strange 'war against myself' to the recollected image of a maid who:

> Was wholly free, far less did critic rules
> Or barren intermeddling subtleties
> Perplex her mind; but, wise as Women are
> When genial circumstance hath favor'd them,
> She welcom'd what was given, and craved no more
> . . . For she was nature's inmate.[15]

The feminist critics stress that, for the Romantics, the image of a feminine difference assumes a fetishistic appearance whereby culturally acquired dispositions and potentialities take on the status of natural properties. For the English Romantics, the feminine becomes a channel through which the cultivated, unquiet Romantic self can appropriate the soothing simplicity of the world of nature. The Romantic self appears, namely, in the guise of the masculine ego determined to appropriate for itself the blessings of a feminised world of nature. Richardson points out that the image of the gifts of the mother's body, milk and tears gains significance throughout the period. Hence, for example, Wordsworth's Vaudracour seeks spiritual restoration at one of Julia's breasts while their infant sucks from the other:

> Oftener he was seen
> Propping and a pale and melancholy face
> Upon the mother's bosom, resting thus
> His head upon one breast, while from the other
> The babe was drawing his quiet food.[16]

The feminist critics of the English poets have discovered, then, that the Romantic self appears in the guise of a quite particular self. According to Ross, the Romantic self is an aggressively defined masculine ideal engaged in figurative battles of conquest and possession which is, at the same time, capable of incorporating into itself whatever attributes of the female it also desired to possess.[17] Richardson's essay on 'Romanticism and the Colonisation of the Feminine' develops its theme by attempting to unmask the conventional gender descriptions which continue to haunt the Romantics' ideal of the androgynous self. On this interpretation, while the Romantics' image of the completed personality is seen to involve the incorporation of so-called feminine qualities, these attributes continue to assume the appearance of merely natural imperatives. A feminine 'motherliness' and 'sympathy' takes on the restorative qualities of a tranquil nature whose blessings the masculine Romantic self is also happy to co-opt.

A review of the image of the self evoked in the works of the early German Romantics uncovers a similar story.[18] For Friedrich Schlegel, as for the English poets, in the feminine we encounter the world of nature in a human and, hence, appropriable form. In his passionate love for Lucinde, Schlegel's Julius believes himself to be 'looking deeply into the secrets of nature'.[19] And again, in Schlegel, the masculine confronts the feminine as an opposition between art and nature. 'In the end one must so recognise the nature in women as they the art in us.'[20] While a feminine capacity to 'harmonise experience and knowledge from an inner centre of intuitive understanding and reflective feeling' is embraced by the early German Romantics as vital to the unfolding of the enriched complete personality, these qualities are in no way construed as neglected cultural potential. As Firchow reads him, for Schlegel, the feminine represents an alternative to a restless masculinity which seeks to impose its consciousness on nature.[21] If he fails to recognise limit values supplied by the natural world (a world which takes on a human form in the shape of the feminine character) the cultivated masculine self can only appear as a hollow shell. To Schlegel, then, the value of feminine difference appears, precisely in its uncultivated character, in its opposition as the human form of nature amid the world of culture, the sphere of men.

In her interesting study entitled *Romanticism, Writing and Sexual Difference*, Mary Jacobus examines how diverse images of the feminine in the Romantic poets' work build a Romantic conception of the androgynous, whole personality.[22] Jacobus' deconstructive reading of the English Romantics attempts to go somewhat further than the unmasking, ideology–critique intention of Ross and Richardson. The main line of Jacobus' argument is that the identity of the 'feminised soul', regularly evoked and affirmed in Wordsworth, is hedged around by references to a competing, despised image of an embodied, natural feminine self. The image of a spiritual maternity, colonised by the Romantic ego, appears as a domesticated femininity whose unsubdued other surfaces in *The Prelude* in the figure of the prostitute. On this reading of Wordsworth's poem, 'the residual form taken by the mother is that of the prostitute. Cast out she becomes (by a neat symbolic reversal) an outcast.'[23] Wordsworth's Romantic ego contemplates this other image of the feminine with deep horror as a figure:

> . . . from humanity divorced
> The human form, splitting the race of man
> In twain, yet leaving the same outward shape.[24]

Jacobus' deconstructive reading of Wordsworth's *The Prelude* discovers that the Romantic self situates itself in relation to two rival images of a feminine difference. On the one hand, the Romantic self embraces the humanising potential of a tender, compliant femininity. On the other hand, the Romantic self contemplates with unconcealed horror the loathed image of an embodied femininity whose unkempt, passionate nature it is unable to assimilate. According to Jacobus, the purified and purifying image of woman which interposes itself healingly between man and his own unquiet, pre-existing, inner division, is hardly an image of sexual difference at all. 'Romantic women routinely appear in *The Prelude* at moments when Wordsworth wants to emphasise the continuity of his mature identity with an imaginary latency period, or undifferentiated sexuality, belonging to his Lake District Boyhood.'[25] An image of sexual difference only appears in *The Prelude* in the guise of the prostitute 'The Beauty of Buttermere'. Mary of Buttermere appears as the dark underside of a femininity no longer associated with nature but with a corrupt city life. She 'raises the spectre of a theatrical other, or dark temptress, whose urban fall shadows her Lake District purity'.[26]

Sexual difference appears, then, in *The Prelude* in the guise of the 'unmanageable sight' of the urban prostitute. Jacobus argues that casting out woman as prostitute serves to protect Wordsworth himself from consciousness of the failure of his search for the complete, unified personality. *The Prelude* projects as sexually differentiated, the experiential opposition between the necessity of the spiritualised poetic self and the corrosive signs of a materialistic modernity which threaten to engulf it. The projection of this experiential split, between the spiritualised self and an invasive urban environment as a sexually differentiated bifurcation between the Romantic self and its repudiated other (the loathed image of the fallen woman) restores the sense of natural harmony to the poetic identity.[27] This deconstructive feminist interpretation of the image of sexual difference in *The Prelude* offers itself, then, as a spoiling exposé of the purported natural unity of the self espoused by the Romantic poet.

Its modern feminist critics have, it seems, discovered a serious lapse in the efforts of the nineteenth century Romantics to evoke an image of the self as a creative project which tolerates no limitations on its own open-ended possibilities. The self which the feminist critics have uncovered in the Romantic literature appears, therefore, as a quite particular self: a self limited and shaped by a distinctive set of gendered social relations. This construction in the Romantic literature of an image of a very particular kind of self and its distinctive relations with others is not, I hope to show, any mere betrayal of the fundamental precepts of a Romantic outlook. A naturalising construction of the character of feminine difference and the constitution of the Romantic self as a colonising masculine ego appears, rather, as a manifestation of assumptions embedded deep within the core of a Romantic world view. Indeed, this construction of the self as a particular type of individuality with a particular set of relations with others is rooted in the distinctive understanding of the struggle between the self and its role which shapes the Romantic consciousness.

The following part of the discussion attempts to show that a Romantic construction of the struggle between the self and its role produces an image of a particular kind of self; an image which the feminist critics of Romantic literature have rediscovered in the guise of a colonising masculine ego. It is, I will argue, precisely this distinctive interpretation of the struggle between the self and its role which has been appropriated by certain trends in contemporary feminism to supply its own understanding of the meaning of the goals of feminism itself.

Feminism and Romanticism: the self in opposition to the role

As we have seen, nineteenth century Romanticism is usually marked out by its opposition to both an eighteenth century anthropology and to the restrictive image of the self upheld in classical liberalism. The Romantic outlook contains at its centre an image of the unique self; a self with potentialities infinitely more open-ended than those suggested by the mere contingency of his or her sociocultural location. For the Romantics, the disjunction between the self and its role typically appears as the heroic struggle of the self determined to unfold its own open-ended possibilities in opposition to the artificial, banal claims of a world of social convention. Yet the Romantics were, I suggest, unable to offer any discriminating account of the meaning of the social role. There is in their understanding no room for any substantive distinction between a conception of the role seen as the imposition of a repressive mask which estranges the individual from his or her unique potentialities and a conception of the role seen as the location of concrete individuals within the sense-giving norms of a specific sociocultural context.

These two conceptions of the character of the role yield distinctive images of the nature of the struggle between the self and the role. If the role appears only in the guise of a repressive mask, then the self enters into a life and death struggle against its own violation. A conception of the role seen as a recognition of the sociological fact that a highly diverse modern culture produces an immense range of sociocultural locations with their diverse governing norms produces, however, a very different image of the struggle between the self and the role. This latter conception yields an account of the self as a concrete, located and embodied individual; a self whose struggle with the role appears as a struggle over the interpretation of the role. The self, seen on this paradigm as a concrete located individual, seeks to challenge the meaning ascribed to his or her particular historio-cultural context. This struggle of the self over the interpretation of the role can encompass both a radical protestation against the ascribed limits of the role and an assertion of the public significance of the particular cultural needs it provokes.

The image of the Romantic ego is, then, forged out of a quite particular understanding of the heroic struggles of the self against the violation of its mask-like social role. The Romantic personality might experience this release from the world of mundane convention as an exhilarating triumph of the self. Equally this alienation of the self may be encountered in the harrowing mode of Coleridge's *Ancient Mariner* who, unable to join the wedding feast, feels himself a:

Heretic, rebel, a thing to flout.[28]

In the end, the radical character of this Romantic refusal to accept any definition on the limitless possibilities of the self finally suggests Romanticism's anti-Enlightenment formulation of Enlightenment goals.[29] The on-going Enlightenment commitment to the production, in Kant's classic formulation, of a self-legislating humanity appeared as an intolerable constraint on the rebellious, creative Romantic self. In Schlegel's view, for example, the determination to embrace the limitless possibilities of the self means overcoming 'the operation and laws of rationally thinking reason and [our transposition again] into the lovely confusion of fantasy, into the primordial chaos of human nature, for which [there is] no more beautiful symbol than the abundant throng of classical gods'.[30]

Peckham's interpretation of Romanticism stresses the typicality of this construction of the role as a repressive mask imposed on the 'primordial chaos' of the self. He emphasises that, for the Romantics, roles were seen not as modes of behaviour derived from the natural world, or dictated by a divine being or inherent in the individual's relation to his or her world, but as something that serves only to carry out a human intention, something, therefore with the character of a mask. And, Peckham continues, man cannot live without such masks, but, for the Romantic, the vital, the essential quality of experience came to be the realisation of what the mask concealed. And, 'since the hidden element was inaccessible it was necessary to create an anti-role, a role that was different from all other roles in that it could not be integrated into the social structure of interlocking roles'.[31]

Peckham's interpretation of the Romantic construction of the struggle between the self and the role underlines the positive meaning which this heroic struggle came to acquire. As he, Wilson and others point out, the notion of the heroic rebellion of the self against the role actually produces its own role, in the guise of an anti-role, the image of the Romantic subject or person: a specific type of human being and its characteristic mode of existence. The essence of this anti-role was that it was designed to symbolise the difference between the self and the role.[32]

According to Carl Schmitt's interpretation, the attitude of this characteristic Romantic self is defined by 'caprice, the denial of binding and predictable causality'.[33] Denying the claims of a normalising, conventional social existence on the supremacy of the creative self, the Romantic seeks to transform his or her own world into a work of art. The Romantic self:

> . . . conceives the moral regulation of life as a grim and
> spiritually numbing discipline, a predetermined pattern mapped out
> on a grid of ethical routines. Such a moral routinisation of
> existence would destroy the caprice, the irony and the imaginative
> play essential to the life of the aesthete and the eroticist who is
> committed to the task of living poetically.[34]

In the end, then, the image of the Romantic self as a constant project of the self beyond the constraints of the role is seen to yield a positive image of a particular type of human being and its typical relations with others. And it is this positive vision of the Romantic self, a vision at the core of the Romantic world interpretation, which has been targeted by the contemporary feminist critics of Romanticism. As we have seen, Ross and Richardson have unmasked this positive image of the Romantic self to disclose the figure of a colonising masculine ego. I suggest that this image of a colonising masculine self identified by the feminist critics of Romanticism needs to be understood as a specific outcome of the Romantics' own particular formulation of the struggle between the self and the role.

Schmitt points out that, in its efforts to free itself from the shackles of all conventional descriptions of the self, the Romantic ego 'plays off possible worlds against one another'.[35] And, in this sense, then, the Romantic self does display a vital interest in the concrete difference of diverse subjectivities. The Romantic self requires, namely, a recognition of a diversity of human potentialities in order to unfold a sense of his or her own open-ended possibilities. For Romanticism, it is, however, finally only the need of this colonising ego to feed its sense of its own ceaselessly expanding horizons which becomes the measure of significance of those diverse human potentials made possible by a modern culture. Because the Romantic can only recognise the social role as a mask which obscures the uniqueness of the self, the Romantic ego encounters the worlds inhabited by others as significant only as mere potentialities to be playfully, ironically appropriated by its own capricious self. The Romantic conception of the merely mask-like character of the social role means that Romanticism is unable to look upon the concrete difference of other selves in anything other than an ironic, colonising mode. As we have seen, for the Romantics, the role is seen only in the light of a violation of the unique self rather than as the site where concrete, located selves struggle to assert their own interpretation of the significance and possibilities of their specific sociocultural contexts. The Romantic's interest in the diversity of life descriptions is, thereby, guided not by any principled commitment to an equality of life chances for all but, rather, by the needs of the capricious Romantic ego itself. As their feminist critics have discovered, then, the Romantic's recognition of a feminine difference obtains its significance only in relation to the needs of the Romantic ego to realise an imaginitive extension of its own possibilities.

It appears that the feminist critique of the image of the colonising masculine self which underpins much Romantic literature strikes at the centre of the Romantic attitude. The feminist critique has effectively targeted the particular implications of a Romantic formulation of the self's struggle against the role. It is, then, a seeming paradox that this same vision of the heroic struggle of the self against the role has itself become a recognisable standpoint within contemporary feminism's interpretation of its own meaning. In the last part of the discussion I attempt to show that, in its efforts to evoke the defiant character of an assertion of feminine difference, a significant trend within modern feminism has adopted a pose virtually identical to the Romantic conception of the struggle between the self and its contingent role.

Romantic feminism: in search of the anti-role

As already stressed, some sort of conception of the struggle between the self and its ascribed social role is vital to the promotion of that emancipatory interest which has continued to motivate modern feminism. It is, then, merely a particular characterisation of the nature of this struggle which is up for review here. I am not interested in contesting those views which hold that feminism's challenge to all imposed constructions of a feminine identity should be mounted from the vantage point of some sort of natural, true feminine self-hood. It is not this search for an elementary, natural femininity which is supposed as the hallmark of what I want to characterise as a Romantic interpretation of modern feminism. Romantic feminism is distinguished, rather, by its search for an image of an anti-role supposedly able to symbolise the difference of the feminine self and its constraining cultural representations.

It is, I suggest, this search for a kind of feminist anti-role which informs the feminism of, for example, Judith Butler's *Gender Trouble: Feminism and the Subversion of Identity*.[36] Butler makes it quite plain that her feminism does not hold with any appeal to a disruptive image of an essential or true feminine self. Rejecting the repressive, homogenising dimension of those feminisms which seek to speak out against all imposed constructions of a feminine identity from the vantage point of a supposed authentic, natural feminine self, Butler seeks to establish the subversive character of a feminist anti-role. This image of an anti-role, designed precisely to symbolise the irreducible difference of the feminine self from all constraining cultural representations of the feminine, seeks to establish the merely playful, ironic attitude of the self to the plurality of cultural representations of the feminine which it encounters. Butler describes the subversive attitude promoted by this feminist anti-role in the following way:

> No longer believable as an interior 'truth' of dispositions and identity, sex will be shown to be a performatively enacted signification (and hence not 'to be'), one that, released from its naturalised inferiority and surface can occasion the parodic proliferation and subversive play of gendered meanings.[37]

In her efforts to repudiate all repressive, exclusionary constructions of a feminine identity, Butler produces an image of a heroic feminine self which challenges the limit character of all cultural descriptions of a feminine identity. To this rebellious femininity all ascribed constructions of the feminine appear as mere masks which provide occasion for 'parodic proliferation and subversive play of gendered meanings'.

Butler's feminism proposes a strategic appeal to the subversive attitude of a self in a mode of ironic play with the limit character of all ascribed gender representations. In a different context, Alice Jardine's concept of 'gynesis' suggests a further manifestation of this kind of attempt to evoke a feminist anti-role.[38] Jardine's neologism 'gynesis' identifies a certain reading of the representation of the feminine in philosophical and literary texts: a reading which seeks to subvert all claims to the representationalism of these descriptions. These images of femininity thus encountered appear as a mere plurality of 'effects' and the strategy of gynesis seeks to constantly underline the complex interrelations which produce these images in order to expose their lack of any fixed referent.[39] Again, as with Butler's proposal for a feminist 'subversion of identity', there is here no attempt to evoke a conception of a natural or essential feminine self. 'Gynesis' hopes to evoke a sense of ironic distantiation towards those representations of the feminine which, having no referent, can be playfully assumed, discarded or satirised. In Jardine's own formulation:

> . . . the 'woman-in-effect' can only be thought beginning with how the monological structures we have inherited are constantly reimposed and rearranged and (particularly) with how women both mime and reject those structures and even become their most adamant support systems.[40]

We saw earlier that, according to some of its major interpreters, Romantic literature typically evokes the image of a role which was supposed different from all other roles in that it could not be integrated into the social structure of interlocking roles. It is precisely this sort of search for an anti-role which has, I suggest, consistently guided Irigaray's feminism. As Butler sees it, Irigaray's feminism exemplifies that trend within modern feminism which supposes that 'feminine difference can never be understood on the model of a "subject" within the conventional systems of Western culture'.[41]

Elizabeth Grosz has pointed out that the concerns of the early Irigaray are mainly negative. Irigaray produces images of the feminine whose function is 'not referential but combative: [they are images] to contrast and counter dominant phallomorphic representations'.[42] Irigaray's entire oeuvre can be interpreted as a series of, variously formulated, attempts to capture the attitude of a rebellious, subversive femininity which resists, in the terminology of Diana Fuss, all 'enculturating definitions' of the feminine.[43] To Irigaray, it is useless to try to:

> . . . trap women into giving an exact definition of what they mean to make them repeat (themselves) so the meaning will be clear. They are already elsewhere than in this discursive machinery where you take them by surprise. They have turned back within themselves, which does not mean the same as 'within yourself'. They do not experience the same interiority that you do and which you mistakenly presume they share . . . If you ask them insistently what they are thinking about they can only reply: nothing. Everything.[44]

Helene Cixous also sees the project of contemporary feminism in terms of the search for a way of evoking the limitless possibilities of a non-compliant femininity:

> If woman has always functioned 'within' the discourse of man . . . it is time for her to dislocate this 'within', to explode it, turn it around, and seize it; to make it hers, containing it within her own mouth, biting that tongue with her very own teeth to invent for herself a language to get inside of.[45]

A Romantic interpretation of modern feminism is being distinguished here by the distinctiveness of its efforts to discover terms in which the non-referential character of all cultural representations of the feminine might be evoked without making any appeal to a constraining, homogenising image of a 'true' feminine self. The Romantic feminist attempts, namely, to forge a type of feminist anti-role which seeks to evoke only an attitude of non-compliance with all ascribed descriptions of the feminine. Romantic feminism is guided, then, by a clear and overriding concern to evade all constraining definitions which seek to ascribe an homogenising description of a feminine self and its possibilities. It would seem, however, that the strategic evocation of a type of feminist anti-role is not quite successful, for it inevitably carries with it a positive evocation of a particular type of feminine subjectivity; a subjectivity with the presumed capacity and will to maintain its ironic distance from all those cultural descriptions of the feminine which, mask-like, can never finally impose themselves upon her own capricious and ever-changing self.

The argument is, then, that the strategic evocation of a feminist anti-role inevitably hosts a positive description of a particular type of feminine subjectivity. This thesis finds support in Fuss's influential interpretation of the logic of Irigaray's feminism. On this reading, the production of a positive image of a feminine subjectivity is integral to Irigaray's strategic concerns. This evocation of a place-holder image of a supposed essential or given feminine identity is, however, guided only by Irigaray's overriding strategic concern to symbolise the violating character of all imposed constructions of a feminine identity. As Fuss sees it:

> The point, for Irigaray, of defining woman from an essentialist standpoint is not to imprison women within their bodies but to rescue them from enculturating definitions by men. An essentialist definition of 'woman' implies that there will always remain some part of 'woman' which resists masculine imprinting and socialisation.[46]

The strategic concern to symbolise the non-referential character of all cultural descriptions of the feminine which dominates Irigaray's entire oeuvre yields a positive image of a feminine subjectivity who refuses their invitation to exile her endlessly changing self to their smothering claims.

A Romantic feminism evokes the image of a particular kind of feminine subjectivity: a femininity which, in its heroic struggles with all ascribed definitions of the feminine, insists on our allegiance. And yet, Romantic feminism's own clear repudiation of the repressive character of all homogenising constructions of a feminine identity has itself supplied the substantial grounds for refusing its own implied claims on our allegiances. Romantic feminism's powerful critique of the repressive dogmatism of all totalising constructions of the feminine finally provides the foundation for the self-critique of its own implicit resurrection of a normative feminine identity.

Romantic feminism does, to be sure, explicitly disavow the 'truth' of its supposed merely strategic images. And yet, in the end, the suggestion that this feminism is not upholding an implctly normative image of feminine subjectivity is based on a confusion of genres. For all their evocative use of literary conventions, those feminisms I have been characterising as Romantic clearly remain within the genre of a politics and are, thereby, governed by its distinctive norms and conventions. The heroic rebellion of the non-compliant feminine self portrayed in such works cannot present itself as the expression of the poetic truth of one particular subjectivity which claims no normativity for itself. Guided by a strategic interest, Romantic feminism is clearly engaged in an ideological battle; it claims endorsement for the supposed correctness or adequacy of its understanding of the subversive character of a feminist attitude.

In an earlier part of the discussion we saw that the feminist critique of Romanticism has effectively unmasked the positive image of the self which suffuses much of the Romantic literature to disclose the figure of a colonising masculine ego. This feminist critique discovers, namely, that the Romantic ego houses a particular masculine subjectivity whose interest in a diversity of human potentials is guided only by its sense of its own inexhaustible needs to give reign to the imaginative extension of its own possibilities. It is, I suggest, precisely this kind of privileged self which makes its unacknowledged reappearance in a Romantic interpretation of modern feminism. After all, who else but the most socially advantaged could assume the persona of Irigaray's feminist who refuses to communicate anything about her needs? She, who thinks of 'everything' and of 'nothing'? And who else but the most culturally privileged could assume with Butler's feminist a merely playful, parodic attitude towards the limit character of those cultural descriptions of her identity she encounters?

The specifically negative character of the search for the anti-role, understood as the attempt to produce only a way of symbolising the non-identity of the self and its imposed cultural descriptions, actually produces a positive image of a feminine subject, an individual endowed with the capacity and the will to turn her back on 'the finite world of mundane existence'. So totalising is the dissatisfaction of this individual with the impositions of the world, it can be symbolised only in a public display of her refusal to seek public recognition for her own interpretations of her specific needs, experiences and aspirations. Clearly intelligible as a description of a psychological process in which the individual manoeuvres to protect his or her own self-interpretation from all violating miscomprehensions, this defensive psychological process cannot be adequately translated into terms appropriate to the practical concerns of a social movement. The Romantic search for the anti-role can only produce a highly homogenised construction of the diversity of material and cultural needs experienced by women in modern society. The totalising, merely abstract image of 'what women want' produced by this strategy is exemplified in the following passage from Irigaray's essay 'Women's Exile':

> When women want to escape from exploitation, they do not simply destroy a few 'prejudices'; they upset the whole set of dominant values—economic, social, moral, sexual. They challenge every theory, every thought, every existing language in that these are monopolised by men only. They question the very foundation

of our social and cultural order, the organisation of which has been prescribed by the patriarchal system.[47]

The Romantic search for the anti-role tends towards a totalising radicalism in its representation of the frustrated needs and aspirations of women in modern society. These aspirations are marked out by their inability to be communicated within the terms of present cultural descriptions and can, therefore, hardly be expressed as particular, concrete demands.

For the individual feminist, too, the image of the anti-role presents a totalising and static construction of her own distinctive needs and aspirations. It is, after all, only the struggle to communicate our own interpretation of our specific experiences and needs that can yield that practical self-understanding of our own particularity which is the goal of Romantic feminism itself. Enjoined to refuse all such struggles, the Romantic feminist becomes ensnared in the image of that particular type of feminine subjectivity hosted by the strategy of the anti-role.

We saw earlier that, according to the major feminist critics of Romanticism, the Romantic self appears as a colonising ego who measures the significance of the worlds inhabited by others in terms only of his or her own insatiable needs to imaginatively extend the scope of their own possibilities. So too the ironic attitude of the Romantic feminist for whom the multiplicity of representations of women offer the occasion for 'parodic prolif- eration and subversive play', homogenises the significance of these diverse representations around her own perceived needs. In her eyes, the plurality of ways of representing a feminine identity ceases to have significance as an index to the mutiplicity of materially and culturally unequal life conditions encountered by women in modern society. Concerned only to dramatise the non-representational character of all cultural descriptions of the feminine, the Romantic feminist can only overlook their particular significances as a range of, disputed, interpretations of the diverse and unequal situations encountered by women in modern society.

This particular objection gives a certain focus to the main line of my dispute with a Romantic interpretation of modern femi- nism. As I have attempted to show, a so-called Romantic feminism has imbibed a typically Romantic conception of the role which appears as a mask-like imposition on the seeming endless possibilities of the self. The Romantic formulation of the struggle between the self and the role finds its expression in the strategic evocation of a femininst anti-role: a strategy which is discovered to yield a positive description of a particular kind of feminine subjectivity and its characteristic relations with others.

The proposed connection, outlined here, between this type of intepretation of the meaning of modern feminism and the main tenets of a Romantic attitude allows us, I suggest, to diagnose the main sources of the problems with this feminist posture in the unintended consequences of the Romantic formulation of the struggle between the self and the role it has imbibed.

Contemporary feminism needs to firmly reject this Romantic formulation and to orientate its own self-understanding in terms of a radically different construction of the nature of the struggle between the self and the role. On this alternative formulation, the self does not appear as radically and irreducibly other than the social role in which it finds itself embedded. An active appropriator of the norms and meanings which govern the historio-cultural context in which he or she is located, the concrete individual both produces their own individuality and participates in transforming the potentials of the role itself by their efforts to practically interpret its significance. On this account, the struggle between the self and the role appears in the light of the practical efforts of the located individual to interpret and to reinterpret the governing norms and descriptions of the particular cultural context in which he or she finds him or herself. This practical struggle both allows the individual to unfold a sense of their own particular subjectivity and can open up possibilities for concrete transformations in the character of their social roles. Feminist theory has a vital task to perform in clarifying the meaning such struggles have for modern women: it points to the ways in which the role has provoked certain cultural needs which push radically beyond its own limits and helps to clarify the public significance and importance of the distinctive needs, aspirations and forms of conduct fostered by particular gendered social roles.

A balanced view of the legacy of nineteenth century Romanticism to contemporary feminism cannot fail to acknowledge some substantial gains. Romanticism, as we saw, played a vital role in forging that historicised consciousness which has come to shape the meaning of Enlightenment for modern individuals. The Romantics progressively broke from that historical Enlightenment appeal to the 'truth of nature' thought to impose a direction towards human perfection. To the Romantics we owe, also, the elaboration of a conception of individuality which stresses the diversity of unique personalities.

Georg Simmel has contrasted this Romantic conception of individuality with the historical Enlightenment idea of individualism.[48] The earlier construction had rested on a presumption of the essential similarity of all human beings endowed with universal rights or motivated by similar desires—this, Gerald Izenberg points out, was a conception abstracted from modern commercial society in which individuals were seen as pursuing uniform self-interest.[49] Simmel describes the explosive turn to a Romantic recognition of the qualitative uniqueness of each individual as follows:

> First there had been the thorough liberation of the individual from the rust chains of guild, birthright and church. Now the individual that had thus become independent also wished to distinguish himself *from other individuals*. The important point no longer was the fact that he was a free individual as such, but that he was this specific, irreplaceable given individual . . . The new individualism might be called qualitative, in contrast with the quantitative individualism of the eighteenth century. Or it might be labelled the individualism of uniqueness [*Einsigkeit*] as against that of singleness [*Einselheit*]. At any rate, Romanticism perhaps was the broadest channel through which it reached the consciousness of the nineteenth century.[50]

With Simmel, we need to acknowledge the vital role played by nineteenth century Romanticism in deepening our idea of and commitment to a conception of human diversity and difference. To the extent that Romanticism is heralded as a major source of a modern conception of the qualitative individuality and uniqueness of the human personality, feminism can only recognise its own profound indebtedness. Yet, as I have argued, an appropriation by certain contemporary feminists of a Romantic formulation of the meaning of individuality imbibes also a problematic construction of the character of the relations between individuals. Izenberg stresses that the Romantics' own definitions of individuality emphasised the idea of differences among unique individuals, 'of uniqueness understood as determined against others'.[51] This image of a self bent on an heroic struggle against all human limitations is, we have seen, finally shown to supply its own definitional construction of a privileged human subjectivity with a merely colonising, appropriative interest in the difference of the other.

Can a Romantic conception of the qualitative character of modern individuality be preserved without imbibing also a Romantic construction of the necessary antagonism between unique individuality and an impinging sociality encountered by the individual as his or her alienating limit? Habermas, for one, thinks this a very feasible project. In an interesting paper, 'Individuation through Socialisation: On George Herbert Mead's Theory of Subjectivity', Habermas has argued that Mead's social psychology seeks to dissolve a conception that the idea of a located, contextualised self is unable to give full reign to the idea of the qualitative uniqueness of each individual in their search for authentic self-expression.[52]

The aspect of Mead's analysis which appears especially relevant to the concerns of modern feminism lies in his insistence that modern individuality is produced via the individual's self-presentation of his or her 'critical appropriation of [his or her] life history'.[53] Individuality is seen as a modern form of identity formation in which the self is constituted not simply through the 'more or less perfect achievement of a given social type' but through an individual's own efforts to vouch 'for the more or less clearly established continuity of a more or less consciously appropriated life history' in the context of the pressure of social differentiation and the diversification of conflicting role expectations.[54] The advantages of this sort of perspective, which makes individuality a matter of the struggle to communicate a personal account of what one has made of the contingent circumstances of one's life history, is that, unlike the Romantic construction of an individuality forged in opposition to a contingent life history, it elaborates its conception of individuality in terms which give full weight to the diversity of social subjectivities. Romanticism, as we have seen, does not finally escape the evocation of the alleged normativity of a particular kind of subjectivity and its characteristic relations with others.

As we shall see in following chapters, this call for the elaboration of a conception of the self, understood as the efforts of each personality to critically appropriate the contingencies of an individual's circumstance, giving it the shape of a unique life-history, has been articulated by a range of major feminists today.[55] This call for a conception of the socialised self which fully accommodates our yearnings for individuality and diversity has gained particular urgency and focus in contemporary feminist attempts to rework the image of the self which underpins the principles of conventional liberalism.

4 Freedom and the encumbered self: feminism's changing relations with liberalism

Feminism and liberalism have travelled a long road together. This tortured relationship has a trajectory very different from the story of feminism's relations with Romanticism plotted in the previous chapter. In relatively recent times we have seen the appearance of a type of feminist theory which seeks to understand the aspirations of feminism within terms of categories and principles it has, unwittingly, borrowed from Romanticism. By contrast, this kind of appropriative relationship marks the earliest phase in feminism's history with liberalism. In this case, we see an early attempt to interpret feminism's own objectives in terms of principles and formulations directly borrowed from political liberalism giving way to a contemporary attempt to negotiate the troubling implications for feminism of its own searching critique of the gender prejudices built into main formulations of the principles of liberalism. We are now witnessing a redoubling of feminism's efforts to sort out this balance-sheet of deep obligations and equally profound objections to main categories and principles of conventional liberalism.

This chapter traces three main trends in the relations between liberalism and feminism; first, a feminist perspective whose protest at patterns of systematic discrimination encountered by modern women seeks to operate purely within the terms of liberalism's own categories and formulations. This episode in feminism's relations with liberalism utilises conventional liberalism's construction of the struggle of the autonomous indi-

vidual against the impositions of his or her found social context
to initiate feminism's own protest at institutionalised patterns of
discrimination encountered by modern women. The feminism of
John Stuart Mill and Harriet Taylor is paradigmatic here. I turn
next to a discussion of the main thesis of Carole Pateman's *The
Sexual Contract* as an example of a second major episode in the
relations between liberalism and feminism in which feminism
contests both the limited ambitions and the supposed patriarchal
assumptions of a liberal creed.[1] Contemporary feminist critics of
conventional liberalism have been concerned to unmask the image
of a particular gendered subjectivity which inhabits the conception
of the autonomous self upheld in a tradition of liberal thought
from J.S. Mill to John Rawls. The third part of the discussion
turns to a consideration of the various attempts to confront the
dilemma for feminism itself which is thrown up by this unmasking
critique. In what terms, namely, are the value commitments of
liberalism, which have underpinned feminism's own culture-critique, to be preserved in the light of the powerful feminist
challenge to the conception of politically qualified subjectivity
which has traditionally underpinned the critical values of liberalism?

The emergence of bourgeois society in the seventeenth century
precipitated a profound transformation in the concerns of political
philosophy. The political philosophy of modern liberalism was
predicated on the new ideal of a self-legislating individual subject.
Locke's vision of an idyllic prepolitical natural state presupposes
a collection of equal, autonomous, rational and sociable individuals. Locke no longer viewed the measurement of political life
in terms of a political ideal: the perfect functioning of a political
community. Like the other moderns, his measure is the empirical
nature of 'man as he is'. Only the self-determined well-being of
the abstract individual will henceforth be admitted as the measurement of goodness and rightness. Hence, whereas the ancients
had considered the relations between individual and state in terms
of conceptions of virtue and duty, modern liberalism construes
this relation in terms of obligations and rights based on contrac-
tual arrangements. This affirmation of individual freedom does
not mean the complete negation of an ideal of equality but there
is in Locke a general movement from the formal political equality
of all citizens before the law to differential political rights
depending on their actual social and economic situation. This is
especially clear in the case of women where natural equality is
quickly subordinated to natural differences which automatically
confers upon the husband authority over the wife because he is
'abler and stronger'.

The first point which needs to be emphasised about this new liberal interpretation of the social and political world is the disappearance of any conception of an objective standard of goodness and happiness. Chantal Mouffe points out that this constitutes the:

> . . . cardinal principle of Liberalism according to which there cannot be a sole conception of eudamonia, of happiness, which is capable of being imposed on all, but that each one must have the possibility of discovering his happiness as he understands it, to fix for himself his own proper objectives and to attempt to realise them in his own way.[2]

This is obviously still an emancipatory message today.

Liberalism posits the individual human subject as creator of their own values: as arbiter of their own will and needs. Yet, the peculiar abstraction of this understanding of the self-legislating, autonomous individual has long been emphasised. Modern critics of contract theory have long exposed its pretensions to abstract from the mere contingency of historical existence to derive the irreducible fundament of human nature. To its critics, contract theory inevitably only succeeds in conferring the status of the quintessential human on qualities and dispositions which are the mere reflection of peculiarly bourgeois relations. The main point to be emphasised at this stage is that liberalism understands the autonomous self only abstractly as merely a rational agent capable of entering into the self-assumed obligation of social contract. To liberalism, the rights-bearing individual appears as a disembodied self unencumbered by the mere accidentality of their particular history and context.

As we shall see, the shifting history of the relations between liberalism and feminism essentially turns on the latter's changing estimation of the coherence of the two dimensions of liberalism outlined so far. To liberal feminism, it is precisely its recognition of formal equality between abstractly conceived subjects which provides the basis for liberalism's critique of the institutionalised domination of women by men in modern society. For the feminist critics of liberalism, however, this conception of the unencumbered subject in fact harbours a normative ideal which seeks to universalise the life experience and aspirations of a modern masculine subjectivity. This chapter is, as already stated, concerned to discuss the difficulties which have arisen for feminism itself in the wake of its own unmasking critique of the implicitly gendered character of liberalism's image of the rights bearing, autonomous self.

Liberal feminism

The writings of John Stuart Mill and Harriet Taylor on the 'woman question' still represent the paradigmatic formulation of the main concerns of liberal feminism. As Susan Moller-Okin points out, Mill is the only major political philosopher to have set out explicitly to apply the principles of liberalism to feminism.[3] The arguments for women's emancipation formulated in 'The Enfranchisement of Women' and in 'The Subjection of Women' are characteristically guided not by any appeal to a conception of natural rights but, rather, by specifically utilitarian considerations. The libertarian right to active self-determination free from any material and ideological constraints is claimed for women as contributing not only to the happiness and self-advancement of women themselves but as enabling women to fully participate in the self-development of humanity as a whole. Mill and Taylor found in the principles of liberalism an array of critical values able to sustain a powerful protest at the practices of discrimination systematically encountered by women in modern society. Their protest appealed not only to the liberal ideal of a self-regulating individual subject but also to the notion of the formal equality of all subjects. Liberalism's abstract understanding of the individual which refuses to admit the relevance of traditional and cultural considerations, supplies the platform for liberal feminism's telling disclosure of formal and informal practices which undermine the rights of women to rational self-determination.

Mill and Taylor identify two main axes to the subjection of women. They suggest that arguments in support of the politico-juridical restraints on women are fundamentally circular. Women's supposed lack of aptitude for affairs of state is used to justify their continued exclusion from political life. Neither Mill nor Taylor are prepared at this stage to initiate a feminist interrogation of the forms of conduct and the kinds of priorities embedded within the norms of political life. Women, they agree, do not presently have an aptitude for political life but this is the effect only of their inadequate education.[4] Only by making all walks of life available to women can the question of their aptitude be properly decided. Mill and Taylor object also to the repressive tyranny of the ideology of femininity as an inhibition upon the liberty of women. The so-called nature of women is, they point out, directly produced by their relegation to domestic life which has both denied the unfolding of their potentialities and skills and has, at the same time, encouraged the distorted over-development of some of their propensities.[5]

In Mill's liberalism the idea of self-sovereignty does not appear as a natural right as Locke had insisted. Fearful that the newly politicised working class would seek to impose its own narrowly conceived class interests to the detriment of the 'common interests', Mill determined that the right of self-sovereignty should be reserved for those whose education had promoted a capacity for a sober appreciation of the good of all. Women's present lack of aptitude for political life is seen, thereby, not as a matter of any natural incapacity. Like the working class, bourgeois women are presently unable to get beyond their own partial and partisan viewpoint to achieve an enlightened, objective view of the interests of the whole. Lacking formal education, woman's propensity to 'build over-hasty generalisations upon her own observation' is a deficiency at once intelligible and surmountable.[6]

The right to self-sovereignty is acquired by the induction through formal schooling into an enlarged consciousness which overcomes or neutralises particular partisan affiliations and concerns. This conception of the sovereign individual upheld in conventional liberalism has been unmasked, by its socialist and now feminist critics, to disclose the self-assertion of a particular, privileged form of subjectivity. What needs, however, also to be recognised is that this conception of the autonomy of the sovereign self has functioned in the liberalism of Mill and Taylor to produce a powerful critique of those social conditions which, imposing on women a life of self-sacrificing duty to others, has prohibited the extension of their powers of judgement which are, in principle, equal to men's. The ideal of the sovereign self functions in the liberal feminism of Mill and Taylor to produce a hard-hitting critique of patterns of domination and violence in the nineteenth century family.

> If the family in its best forms is, as it is often said to be, a
> school of sympathy, tenderness and loving forgetfulness of self, it
> is still oftener, as respects its chief, a school of wilfulness,
> overbearingness, unbounded self-indulgence, and a double-dyed
> and idealised selfishness.[7]

There is no significant retreat here from the radicalism of Wollstonecraft's earlier assessment of the emerging patterns of bourgeois family life. Mill and Taylor cry out against the relations of domination and subordination in the family which produce and reproduce a tyrannical masculinity and a self-abnegating, unenlightened femininity.[8] What is lost in this nineteenth century feminist critique of the family is, however, the, already discussed, potential in Wollstonecraft's feminism to consider the domestic sphere as not just the object of critique but as the source also of positive values which ought to find expression in public life. Mill and Taylor are by no means tempted to try and find a formulation of the 'gentle and domestic virtues' adequate to life in the public domain. The standpoint of sovereignty of the autonomous self provided the basis for a critique of a marital structure 'contradictory to the first principles of social justice'. It could not, however, admit as public virtues any of those feminine capacities for 'gentle forebearance' which, if they sought to find a place outside their appropriate sphere, could only cloud the 'enlightened' judgement.

As Okin has noted, the indebtedness of contemporary feminism to the main principles of conventional liberalism is now widely acknowledged. Basic tenets of liberalism—'including the replacement of the belief in natural hierarchy by a belief in the fundamental equality of human beings, and the placing of individual freedoms before any unified construction of "the good"—have been basic tenets in the development of feminism too'.[9] These shared commitments have prompted Zillah Eisenstein to proclaim the liberal foundations of all feminism. All feminism, she claims, is 'liberal at its root' and the 'universal feminist claim that woman is an independent being (from man) is premised on the eighteenth century liberal conception of the independent and autonomous self'.[10]

Liberalism's feminist critics

Liberalism's feminist critics have by no means presented a united front. We can, nevertheless, distinguish a major concern threaded throughout the various feminist critiques. Feminisms of various political persuasions have objected to the limited ambitions of liberal feminism content to merely demand the end to discriminatory practices which thwart the access of women to the range of life choices already made available by contemporary sociopolitical institutions. The anarchist–feminist, Emma Goldman, heralded the liberal formulation of its goals as a 'tragedy' for the cause of women's emancipation.[11] Liberal feminism, she argued, has failed to call for the active participation by women in challenging the priorities of the market place. It has failed to recognise women's own potentially unique contributions to the elaboration of new life possibilities. Goldman despises the mere pursuit of an equality between the sexes which does nothing to achieve public recognition for the unique, hitherto marginalised, potentials and aspirations of modern women:

> Emancipation should make it possible for woman to be human in
> the truest sense. Everything within her that craves assertion and

activity should reach its fullest expression; all artificial barriers should be broken, and the road towards greater freedom cleared of every trace of centuries of submission and slavery.[12]

Insistent voices within the 'Second Wave' of modern feminism have also been raised against the implicitly gendered character of liberalism's image of the rational, autonomous self. Will we, June Jordan asks, liberate ourselves:

> . . . so that the caring for children, the teaching, the loving, healing, person-oriented values that have always distinguished us will be revered and honoured at least commensurate to the honors accorded bank managers, lieutenant colonels, and the executive corporate elite? Or will we liberate ourselves so that we can militantly abandon those attributes and functions, so that we can despise our own warmth and generosity even as men have done, for ages?[13]

The feminist critique of liberalism turns on the discovery of a covert anti-egalitarian dimension within liberalism as a political philosophy. The contention is that, despite liberalism's own evident commitment to the ideal of a self-legislating humanity in which each individual sets their own goals and definitions of the good life, liberalism itself inevitably imposes a strait-jacket definition of the appropriate ends of life. In recent years, we have seen the elaboration of a powerful feminist critique of the normative image of the self implicit in the ideal of autonomous self-determining individuality upheld by conventional liberalism. In essence, this line of argument holds that the abstract individualism of a liberal tradition, which refuses to admit the relevance of any concrete differences between embodied subjects, inevitably seeks to universalise the attributes of a single culturally constructed identity.

This feminist critique, exemplified by Carole Pateman, is a vital moment in a broad-based and on-going challenge to liberalism's appeal to a conception of an abstract, formal understanding of the individual subject unencumbered by the accidentality of mere history and cultural context. The self, liberalism's critics point out, is always encumbered: it is always a self which is located in history. Any appeal to an image of formal, abstract subjectivity can, therefore, only appear as a repressive universalisation of one particular, culturally constituted form of human subjectivity. This identity is conferred with an alleged normativity and becomes the standard by which diverse life priorities and experiences are measured.

Okin points out that the image of the self upheld in liberalism can only continue to appear as an abstraction from a peculiarly masculine set of life experiences as long as modern liberalism fails to resolve the problematic formulation of the separation of the public from the private which it has inherited.[14] The valuable legacy of liberalism's commitment to the idea of private persons deciding on their own preferred way of life continues, even in Rawls' formulation of the concerns of modern liberalism, to be bought at the cost of a legitimation of a gendered bifurcation between the public and the private spheres. The endemic failure of liberalism to dislodge its advocacy of the liberty of private persons to determine their own understanding of the good life from a conception of the supposed publicly uninteresting concerns of the personal, domestic sphere has rendered it deaf to the particularity of the perspectives and priorities voiced by modern women. As Okin puts it, 'if liberalism is to include all of us, women and men, it must address the challenge presented by the claim that "the personal is political" '.[15]

As we have seen, liberalism has understood social contract as the basis of a formal system of justice which displays an impartial disinterest in the merely contingent private concerns and needs of the specific individual. According to Pateman, however, the perception of civil society as a post-patriarchal social order in which contract between equal subjects replaces the power of mere status is based on an inherent ambiguity in the term 'civil society'.[16] In particular, Pateman discovers an ambiguous interpretation of the character of the private sphere which appears both as part of civil society and yet as separated from the 'civil sphere'. The private sphere is part of civil society to the extent that civil society is seen to be that form of association which replaces the state of nature. And yet, the *terms* in which the meaning of political life is described mean that the private sphere with its particularising concerns and needs again effectively assumes the status of a quasi-natural association. *The Sexual Contract* attempts to explain the origin of the ambiguous status of the private sphere in civil society by discovering the foundations of the story of social contract in an asymmetrical sexual contract. Pateman argues that although the archaic patriarchal order which gave authority to fathers and patriarchs became obsolete, it was replaced with an implied contract between male citizens which establishes the subordination of women to men. The 'sexual contract' which underpins modern society establishes what Pateman describes as 'fraternal patriarchy'. Modern 'fraternal patriarchy' ushers in a revised subordination of women which turns not on father-right but on the legitimation of exclusive sexual access. This sexual contract creates civil freedom as a masculine attribute dependent on patriarchal right and women's subjection in a domestic–intimate sphere.

> The private, womanly sphere (natural) and the public masculine sphere (civil) are opposed but gain their meaning from each other, and the meaning of the civil freedom of public life is thrown into relief when counterposed to the natural subjection that characterises the private realm . . . what it means to be an 'individual', a maker of contracts and civilly free, is revealed by the subjection of women within the private sphere.[17]

Pateman's efforts to unmask the patriarchal sexual contract which underpins the social contract hits at the heart of liberalism's self-understanding. *The Sexual Contract* challenges liberalism's pretended discovery of a non-discriminatory, impartial conception of human subjectivity freed from all particular cultural attributes. Pateman's rendition of the 'lost story' of sexual contract contrives to unseat the fundamental liberal assumption that the patriarchal separation of the private/natural sphere from the public/civil realm is irrelevant to political life. On this account, the meaning of the civil freedom of public life—seen as the universal bonds of contract between formally free and equal individuals—receives its definition from a counterposing private familial world constituted by seeming natural ties and by a seeming natural order of subordination.[18]

How is feminism to respond to such searching critiques of the main tenets of a liberal tradition? We saw earlier that there is widespread acknowledgement of the ideological debt which modern feminism owes to main principles of conventional liberalism. In the first instance, modern feminism has seen itself as a particular interpretation and elaboration of liberalism's recognition of the legitimacy of a plurality of descriptions of the good, the happy, life. And, as Eisenstein, for example, has shown, liberalism's assertion of the rights of the autonomous, self-determining individual has been a main ideological condition which has helped to prod into existence feminism's own protest at the patterns of discrimination woven into the life conditions of modern women. And yet, as the feminist critics of liberalism have shown, this discriminatory logic has, in turn, stamped itself on the very formulation of those liberal ideals and precepts which have, hitherto, been embraced as the vehicles of a feminist protest.

Feminism's own unmasking critique of the particular way of life and set of expectations housed by liberalism's image of rights-bearing, autonomous individuality has generated two different sorts of responses in the feminist literature. From one standpoint, the discovery of the implicitly gendered character of liberalism's image of self-determining individuality imposes the necessity for relinquishing this ideal as inappropriate to the formulation of the goals of modern feminism. According to Nell Noddings, for example, it would seem that contemporary feminism can only comfortably continue to recognise itself as a particular interpretation and manifestation of that aspect of the philosophy of liberalism which asserts the legitimacy of a plurality of descriptions of the good life.[19] In her *Caring: A Feminine Approach to Ethics and Moral Education*, Noddings attempts to derive a particular conception of the good, the moral, life from the so-called predispositions of modern women to the assumption of an attitude of care for particular others. Significantly, Noddings' call for a new public morality revitalised by a supposed feminine ethic of care for particular situated others sees itself as an assertion of a feminine description of the good life which seeks to present itself as a rival to, rather than a reinterpretation of, the universalising principle of justice for abstractly conceived selves.

Both Susan Moller Okin and Onora O'Niell have pointed to the serious limits of this kind of response to feminism's own critique of the image of justice for abstractly conceived individuals.[20] The feminisms of Nell Noddings and also of Carol McMillan in her *Women, Reason and Nature* insist on the necessity for a public recognition of significant difference of a marginalised 'feminine culture'.[21] Such attempts to interpret the meaning of modern feminism as a call for recognition of the public significance of a culture of feminine difference see themselves as opposed to, rather than concerned to re-educate, the voice of justice. 'They see attempts to incorporate women within the domain of justice as one more denial of women's difference.'[22] The incoherence of this attempt to protest on behalf of a marginalised 'culture of femininity' without due recognition of that formal liberal precept of 'justice for all' which is, at the same time, the ideological vehicle which carries this feminist protest is, I suggest, quite apparent. Noddings' assertion of the need for a public recognition of a supposed different feminine ethic makes its own claims within the terms of that very same liberal precept of universal justice which she nominates as the irreducible ideological rival of a feminine ethic of care.

Pateman clearly recognises the incoherence of any presumption that feminism can proceed as a meaningful cultural phenomenon without appealing to notions of universal justice and the rights of each individual. She points out that, even if existing formulations of civil freedom and equality have looked contemptuously upon the particular needs and concerns of women as irrelevant to its own 'impartial' concerns, the achievement of juridical freedom and equality is a necessary step towards women's autonomy. Pateman continues:

> The achievement will, with one important caveat, help in the task of creating the social conditions for the development of an autonomous femininity; the caveat is that women's equal standing must be accepted as an expression of the freedom of women as women and not treated as an indication that women can be treated just like men.[23]

Pateman thus announces the necessity for a whole new episode in feminism's dynamic relations with liberalism. From a powerful new voice in an on-going unmasking critique of liberalism's conception of the contracting self as disembodied subjectivity unencumbered by the accidentality of a particular history and context, feminism now affirms its interest in the reinterpretation of the main principles of liberalism in terms appropriate to the experience of 'women-as-women'. On this account, feminism's problems with liberalism essentially concern the restrictions which liberalism's definitional conception of the self impose on the recognition of the plurality and diversity of human needs and aspirations in general and specifically with regard to those of women.

This contemporary feminist interest in reworking the political ethics of liberalism to take account of the particular character of the needs and experiences of modern women can be seen as giving a special focus to a wider debate on the possibility of democratising the formulations of liberalism. Pluralist communitarian critics of liberalism, like Michael Walzer, are similarly concerned to attempt to determine the new ways in which liberal ideals of universal justice and equality might be interpreted in terms consistent with the broad-based critique of the disembodied image of the self which has supported the formulation of these principles in conventional liberalism.[24] Major feminist political theorists like Susan Moller Okin and Nancy Rosenblum have, however, serious misgivings about the capacity of communitarian pluralism to retain the vitality of the critique of domination which has been central to feminism's own efforts to appropriate the critical values of liberalism.[25]

Feminism and the pluralist communitarian reconstruction of liberalism[26]

Walzer clearly participates in the general thrust of the communitarian critique of political liberalism. Like Alistair MacIntyre, he rejects the efforts of political liberalism to establish universally applicable standards of morality and justice and turns towards a conception of justice which seeks to elucidate principles already present within a given society.[27] For the communitarian, notions of justice are said to exist already as part of a community's shared beliefs and traditions. As a *pluralist* communitarian, Walzer is, however, opposed to the viewpoint of the communitarian critics like MacIntyre who repudiate liberalism's efforts to drive a wedge between all notions of the 'common good' and a politics of individual rights. To MacIntyre, for example, liberalism appears as the mere legitimating political ideology of a culturally impoverished and fragmented modernity dominated by the experience of anomie.[28] Against these longings for a return to a type of *Gemeinshaft*, Walzer defends the image of a liberal pluralism with its rejection of any homogeneous ideal of the good life. Yet, Walzer's defence of pluralism is formulated in terms which challenge liberalism's own commitment to the notion of a simple formal equality between all individuals. According to him, the notion of mere formal equality precludes the relevance of any consideration of a diversity of needs and wills experienced by concrete individuals in determinate contexts and, hence, is totally inadequate to a pluralism of conceptions of the good.

Walzer's main theoretical innovation is, then, his attempt to replace a notion of simple formal equality with a theory of social justice whose goal is the realisation of a 'complex equality'. *Spheres of Justice* suggests that the notion of a simple formal equality is a repressive principle which reduces all difference to the terms of a single normative criterion. Only a principle of complex equality, which recognises a diversity of distributive criteria, is adequate to a highly differentiated modern society. This notion of complex equality suggests that different social goods be distributed not in any uniform manner but in terms of a diversity of criteria which reflect the plurality of those social goods and the meanings attached to them. According to Walzer, the regime of complex equality establishes:

> . . . a set of relationships such that domination is impossible. In formal terms, complex equality means that no citizen's standing in one sphere or with regard to one good can be undercut by his standing in some other sphere, with regard to some other good. Thus, citizen X may be chosen over citizen Y for political office

and then the two of them will be unequal in the sphere of politics. But they will not be unequal generally so long as X's office gives him no advantage over Y in any other sphere, superior medical care, access to better schools for his children, entrepreneurial opportunities, and so on.[29]

Chantal Mouffe suggests that 'the interest of the perspective adopted by Walzer is that it permits the critique of liberal individualism and its epistemological presuppositions while conserving and even enriching the contribution of pluralism'.[30] In other words, Walzer's theory of complex equality has, in Mouffe's estimation, managed to defend and radicalise liberalism's commitment to a pluralism of goods and values while replacing the 'impartial' principle of formal equality between undifferentiated individuals which has traditionally underpinned a liberal philosophy.

Nancy Rosenblum thinks quite differently.[31] According to her, Walzer's conception of complex equality forfeits the main democratic principles of liberalism on two counts. In the first place, Rosenblum is not convinced that the principle of complex equality has managed to preserve, let alone extend, the pluralist impulses of conventional liberalism. She suggests that only the perspective of simple equality which refuses to differentiate between social subjects on the basis of the mere contingency of cultural context and group affiliation is able to sustain the attitude of tolerance for the different vital to liberal pluralism. Liberalism, Rosenblum says:

. . . de-emphasises likeness and familiarity as sources of potential unity. It is designed to facilitate relations among citizens who may be strangers to one another and profoundly dissimilar: fairness assumes impartiality between friends and strangers. When membership replaces formal citizenship, the consequences of being a stranger can be harsh.[32]

A consideration of Rosenblum's objection highlights the vital role played by the notion of 'shared meanings' in Walzer's theory of complex equality. An appeal to criteria supplied by the shared meanings of a given community is, Walzer points out, indispensible to the elaboration of any conception of justice. On his interpretation, both the theory of 'complex equality' and the conventional liberal principle of a simple equality seek to articulate the shared meanings, the background assumptions, of that rhetoric of democratic pluralism which has gained an admittedly weak and embattled existence in main institutions of Western democracies. The theory of complex equality is opposed to the notion of formal equality to the extent that the latter is seen as an inadequate formulation of the ideals and presumptions which have taken shape in the political culture of Western democracies. Thus, when in accordance with the principle of complex equality we recognise the other concretely as a member of a specific sociocultural context, we embrace also a political ideal which recognises the legitimacy of difference and cultural diversity. For Walzer, then, both the theory of complex equality and the principle of formal equality offer themselves as formulations of the supposed common convictions, the background assumptions, upheld in the political tradition of Western democracies. Pluralist communitarianism historicises the liberal idea of universal human rights which is now shown to presuppose not the anthropological premise of isolated and unsituated subjects but the 'shared meanings' of the political tradition of Western democracies.

For Okin and Rosenblum, Walzer's appeal to a conception of the 'shared meanings' of our culture as a criterion for justice by no means puts an end to the difficulties which his theory throws up for a feminist appropriation. These feminist critics have deep reservations about Walzer's reliance on the notion of the shared meanings of our political culture. As Okin points out, the appeal to the idea of the supposed common convictions or shared meanings of a culture can act as a merely legitimating ideology for, she argues, 'when meanings appear to be shared, they are often the outcome of the domination of some groups over others, the latter being silenced or rendered "incoherent" by the more powerful'.[33] The reliance of the communitarian pluralist on the idea of shared meanings presupposes a cultural consensus which obscures vigorous and on-going disputes over the meaning of the notionally background assumptions of a democratic culture.

Further, and this is the second part of Rosenblum's critique of communitarian pluralism, the theory of complex equality is only able to sustain a limited political agenda which courts a pluralist tolerance for the different. This attempt to reformulate the main principles of liberalism in terms of a conception of the situatedness of particular embodied selves looses the utopian longing for the autonomy of the self-determining life which had been a main precept in conventional liberalism's conception of the struggle between the abstractly conceived self and the repressive constraints of an individual's social role. To feminists like Rosenblum and Okin, the failure of pluralist communitarianism to provide a way of conceptualising the aspiration of the situated self towards self-determination, towards a life freed from the coercive influence of imposed constructions of the identity of the self, makes it radically inappropriate to the conceptual needs of a contemporary feminism. In Rosenblum's view, Walzer's pluralist communitarianism, which searches for the experience of latent community embedded in our cultural history, finally appears as a conservative retreat from the priniciple of autonomous self-determination central to the liberal tradition.

Yet Walzer would insist that pluralist communitarianism has not, as its feminist critics suppose, forfeited liberalism's commitment to the idea of self-determining autonomy. To him, the idea of latent community does not retreat from, but offers a particular formulation of, the idea of self-determination. When Walzer appeals to the notion of latent community he refers not simply to mechanical, unthinking solidarity with a cultural identity whose authority is sanctioned by the mere weight of tradition. He is not, in other words, thinking of a traditionalistic relation to tradition but of a reflexive, peculiarly modern, relation to tradition.[34] As Walzer represents it, the idea of latent community suggests the experience of chosen solidarity with the value-directed social action of a particular community. *Spheres of Justice* suggests that forms of association like the club and the nation-state illustrate the goal-directed character of 'latent community'. Both are instances of associations whose policies and deliberations about practices of inclusion and exclusion offer a continuous commentary of the goal-directed character of the association itself. As Mouffe sees it, Walzer's particular interpretation of the notion of latent community offers a specific interpretation of the liberal ideal of an autonomous, self-determining humanity; an interpretation which affirms 'that the true human realisation is only possible when one acts as a citizen of a free and self-governing political community'.[35]

Yet this line of defence does not, finally, manage to establish that Walzer's communitarianism is able to sustain and to reformulate the utopian moment of conventional liberalism. Walzer's typology of a social life organised around the separation of spheres whose governing norms might not transgress their own bounds cannot finally offer any grounding for a politics which aims at the critique and trangression of imposed structures and definitions. *Spheres of Justice* sets its sights on the presumed achievable goal of a society capable of recognising the legitimacy of different goods. The resistance of the notion of separate spheres to a critical, transgressive politics is particularly illustrated by Walzer's attempts to distinguish the activities and norms supposedly appropriate to the private sphere. Okin draws attention here to Walzer's opposition to public child-care which he describes as the abandonment of children to 'bureaucratic rearing'.[36] For Walzer, the communal care of children suggests a damaging confusion between the norms and forms of conduct supposedly appropriate to the separate spheres. *Spheres of Justice* generally whisks over any consideration of the tyrannical results which might issue from making the family solely reponsible for the welfare of young children.

> Walzer's theory of complex equality prides itself on the non-utopian, achieveable, character of its goals. The aim of political egalitarianism is a society free from domination. This is the lively hope named by the word 'equality'; . . . no more high and mightiness; no more masters, no more slaves. It is not a hope for the elimination of differences; we do not all have to be the same or have the same amounts of the same things . . . equality as we have dreamed of it does not require the repression of persons. We have to understand and control social goods; we do not have to stretch or shrink human beings.[37]

Walzer's communitarian pluralist reconstruction of liberalism sacrifices that dimension of liberalism forfeited also by feminists like Noddings: a commitment, namely, to the idea of a self-determining subjectivity determined to 'stretch' itself beyond the impositions of its constraining social context.

The limits of political philosophy

As Axel Honneth sees it, the core of the debate around the communitarian reconstruction of liberalism hinges on the adequacy of its reformulation of the utopian impulses of liberalism: it turns on 'the question of how a political ethics must take account of the conditions of freedom of socialised subjects if it is to arrive at a convincing concept of a just society'.[38] As we have seen, for Pateman also the ideal of social justice is not exhausted by an ambition which seeks only the recognition of the equality of diverse goods. To her, feminism's critique of liberalism's formulation of the ideal of autonomous, self-determining individuality by no means extinguishes feminism's own commitment to the ideal itself. Yet, there is, as she puts it:

> . . . no set of clothes available for a citizen who is a woman, no vision available within modern political theory of the new democratic woman. Women have always been incorporated into the civil order as 'women', as subordinates or lesser men, and democratic theorists have not yet formulated any alternative. The dilemma remains. All that is clear is that if women are to be citizens as women as autonomous, equal, yet sexually different beings from men, democratic theory and practice has to undergo a radical transformation.[39]

Pateman has stated the problem with considerable force. Yet there is an important ambiguity in her construction of the *kind* of problem which might be at stake here. Having discovered the radical unsuitability of conventional liberalism's own description of the citizen, Pateman directs our attention to the failure of modern political theory to move beyond a negative, critical phase. Modern political philosophy is discovered to, as yet, lack any 'vision' in terms of which we might want to clothe a competing image of autonomous femininity. Pateman sees herself as simply opening up a question or posing a dilemma to which she does not pretend to have the answer. The inadequacy of feminist political theory to its task of undermining the 'life-supports' of the 'political fiction' it unmasks is lamented by her to the end.[40]

Perhaps one of the strongest notes struck in Pateman's feminism is the insistence that political philosophy be seen as itself established in, and limited to, reflection upon present social, gender relations. This historicising account of the status of political philosophy would seem to suggest that political philosophy can no longer be saddled with the task of proposing a transcendent vision of an alternative future. In this event, for effective clues about the possible shape of alternative conceptions of femininity, we would expect to look to the prospects opened up by the collective, concrete struggles of women in modern society. Yet, despite her own clearly historicising account of the status of political philosophy, Pateman contrives to throw the responsibility for the elaboration of the shape of an alternative description of citizenship back into the court of modern political philosophy itself. In *The Sexual Contract* and in the various essays collected under the title *The Disorder of Women*, Pateman implicitly evokes a return to a positive, norm-producing responsibility for political theory; political theory finds itself called upon to provide the shape of new, alternative descriptions of a citizen who is a woman.[41] In this construction of the norm-producing tasks of democratic theory Pateman herself implicitly burdens democratic theory with the, now thoroughly discredited, role of a metaphysics.

To move the discussion forward, we need to consider why Pateman seemingly finds it necessary to confer a norm-producing responsibility on radical democratic theory. I suggest that Pateman's totalising feminist critique of liberal democratic theory, together with the limitations of her perspective on the character of the lived experience of modern women, conspire to leave her nowhere else to turn but to metaphysics in her hopes for a vision of an alternative future for women.

According to Pateman, the feminist critique of the patriarchal content of its conception of politically qualified subjectivity penetrates to core assumptions of modern political philosophy.

> Feminism does not, as is often supposed, merely add something to existing theories and modes of argument. Rather, feminism challenges the patriarchal construction of modern political theory, and to engage with feminist criticisms political theorists have to be willing to think again about the fundamental premises of their arguments.[42]

There is no suggestion here of an immanently critical posture in which feminism reveals that liberal democratic theory proposes an inadequate, prejudicial formulation of its own ideals. The fundamental premises of modern political theory are seen to be so thoroughly contaminated that there can be no saving them. Feminism obliges modern political philosophy to 'rethink fundamental premises of their arguments' and feminist theory offers no guidance as to which core assumptions might be worth saving and rebuilding. If the main precepts of political philosophy are so totally shot through with the prejudices of a patriarchal culture, it does not seem that we can hope that any reconstruction of our political traditions and its ideals might yield that image of a feminine citizen which Pateman has called for.

Pateman's account of the story of the sexual contract which underpins the story of social contract also suggests a totalising and reductive perspective. Her notion of modern social relations as a 'fraternal patriarchy' rests upon a very one-sided sociology of the intimate sphere. From the standpoint of 'fraternal patriarchy', the intimate sphere and the particular place of women in it appears only as an arena of domination and subordination. The sexual contract, as we have seen, creates civil freedom as a masculine attribute dependent on patriarchal right and on women's subjection in a domestic–intimate sphere. There is, on this account, no sense in which the intimate sphere can be construed as the birthplace also of norms, modes of interaction and ways of doing things which might provide the starting point for a renegotiation of the prejudicial formulation of the ideal of civil freedom encountered in hegemonic images of politically qualified subjectivity. If we are to move forward with Pateman's call for a vision of citizenship not prejudicial to women qua women, we need to redress not only the one-sidedness of her attempt to reduce the meaning of the ideals of modern political philosophy to the status of mere emblems of fraternal patriarchy; the totalising character of Pateman's sociology of the intimate sphere must be overcome also.

Understood as an immanent critic of hegemonic descriptions of modern ideals of civil freedom, feminism targets those formulations of these ideals which it finds prejudicial to the recognition of distinctive aspects of the needs and aspirations of modern women. To Seyla Benhabib, Iris Young and others, the specific terms in which political liberalism has formulated its ideal of autonomous subjectivity has blinded it to the supposed publicly uninteresting concerns of the private sphere.[43] On this immanently critical approach, the substantive bifurcation which conventional liberalism makes between a public and a private sphere means that liberalism defaults on its own primary commitment to a pluralist discussion of possible modes of the good life. As Benhabib sees it, liberalism's vision of autonomy was, and continues to be, based on an 'implicit politics which defines the domestic, intimate sphere as ahistorical, unchanging and immutable thereby removing it from all reflection and discussion'.[44] A feminist reconstruction of the ideals of conventional liberalism requires, accordingly, an expanded notion of those activities and actions deemed the proper subject for public discussion and expression. On this account, the private should no longer appear coextensive with the particular needs and concerns of individuals located in the domestic, intimate sphere but as that aspect of an individual's life which he or she has the right to exclude from others. Young formulates this feminist call for a reconstitution of the public sphere as follows:

> The feminist slogan 'the personal is political' does not deny a
> distinction between public and private, but it does deny a social
> division between public and private spheres, with different kinds of
> institutions, activities and human attributes. Two principles follow
> from this slogan: (a) no social institutions or practices should be
> excluded a priori as being the proper subject for public discussion
> and expression; and (b) no persons, actions or aspects of a
> person's life should be forced into privacy.[45]

Young's immanent critique of liberalism endeavours to uncover the ways in which its naturalising construction of the status of the domestic, the intimate, sphere removes the concerns and needs provoked by this sphere from all public reflection and discussion. Importantly, however, she does not presume to install theory in the role of arbiter of those needs and values which ought to be given public recognition. Young seeks only to outline those formal structures and maxims which might allow women to speak for themselves.

At an earlier point in the discussion, we noted a certain tendency within contemporary feminism which seeks to restrict the role of feminist theory to that of mere advocate of an alternative feminine culture supposedly dominated by an ethic of 'caring' for particular others.[46] This trend was criticised for its failure to get beyond an endorsement of a mere pluralism of prevailing descriptions of the good to integrate a utopian commitment to the ideal of self-determining autonomy into its interpretation of the goals of modern feminism. This kind of feminism, typified by Nell Noddings, needs, however, to be clearly distinguished from an alternative construction of the ambitions of modern feminism which is, nevertheless, similarly persuaded of the need to assert the significance and value of those patterns of conduct and ways of seeing promoted by the positioning of women in the intimate sphere.[47] Clearly influenced by the stand taken by Carol Gilligan in her now contemporary classic *In A Different Voice: Pyschological Theory and Women's Development*, the feminism of, for example, Seyla Benhabib and Maria Markus has understood the call for an affirmation of the autonomy of women as women in the light of a practical need for the public recognition of the public significance of the distinctive aspirations and perspectives nursed by the particular life situations of women in modern society.[48]

Unlike Noddings, Markus does not interpret the role of feminist theory as that of mere advocate of presently constructed images of feminine diffference; nor does her feminism set itself the task of discovering an alternative image of the feminine uncontaminated by all normative, masculine constructions of the self. The attempt to answer the questions 'Who am I being a woman?' and 'What do I want to be?' is, Markus suggests, appropriately seen as a matter of the reflections by feminist theory on:

> . . . those neglected life-practices which, in addition to the
> institutionalised and semi-institutionalised forms of discrimination,
> continuously, throughout the whole life span of an individual,
> create or reinforce certain ways of seeing, thinking and acting. It
> has also become clear that some of the specific ways of
> experiencing the world, together with some associated personality
> traits, while functioning in the present as part of the mechanism
> of oppression, in virtue of being ascribed exclusively to women, in
> themselves may well contain certain cognitive abilities and
> emotional patterns that ought not to be lost, but be re-evaluated
> as possible components not only of women's liberation but also of
> the restructuration of the dominant culture.[49]

Theory, on this viewpoint, supplies a reflection upon the public significance of those supposed distinctive cognitive abilities and emotional patterns encouraged by the peculiar life experiences of women in modern society. In particular, feminist theory looks to the ways in which the recognition of the public significance of such potentials might require the restructuration and elaboration of new possibilities within the institutions and governing norms of Western democracies.

This interpretation of feminism's interest in the restructuration of the principles governing the character of modern public life underlines the distance of its emancipatory intent from the commitment of a pluralist communitarianism to the supposed 'shared meanings' of Western democracies. Yet, while contemporary feminism is seemingly increasingly conscious that common understandings of common ideals are not to be taken for granted, the projection of any goal aimed at the restructuration of the norms and institutions of an existing political culture presupposes a shared commitment to the betrayed and inadequately interpreted humanist ideals and principles of Western democracies.

A paradigm of social interpretation which at once confers an essentiality for us on those values of self-determining autonomy and social justice for all in which we recognise the contemporary legacy of Enlightenment, while permitting also an open-ended conversation about the significance and the scope of these values, would seem to hold out some promise to contemporary feminism in its efforts to interpret the character of feminism's own relation to the 'shared meanings' of a modern democratic culture. The next chapter moves on to consider claims that Habermas' communicative interaction theory can provide a paradigm of social interpretation which both upholds the universality of fundamental Enlightenment ideals without, at the same time, imposing a formulation of those ideals prejudicial to the plurality of needs and aspirations which issue from the diversity of ways of life and cultural identities which stamp a highly differentiated modernity.

5 Feminism and critique: from Marx to Habermas

Once the site of some of the most vigorous debates in modern feminist theory, the topic of feminism's relations to Marxism could hardly appear more exhausted than it does today. Contemporary feminism is, of course, not alone in its recent loss of faith and interest in the critical potentialities of Marxism. The reasons for this general crisis of confidence cannot be debated here. What can be discussed, however, is the more specific issue of the significance which contemporary feminism has given to its own turn away from Marxism. The following brief reconstruction of some main episodes in the rise and fall of feminism's interest in the capacities of Marxism as a critique of an alienated modernity is guided by a hermeneutical concern. What does the shifting character of feminism's interest in Marx's theory of alienation suggest about changes in feminism's understanding of its own role as cultural critique?

The early Marxist feminists had not, generally speaking, looked to Marx's theory of alienation to produce new insights into the lived conditions of women in capitalist society. It was, rather, the apparent capacity of this theory to anchor and to provide ultimate justification for the kinds of critical observations elaborated by feminists themselves that seemed the main attraction. Marx's theory of alienation had seemed to offer an account of our species' character from the vantage point of which the lived condition of modern women could be shown as a distortion and a travesty. It is not particularly useful at this juncture to again rehearse the motivations for feminism's collapse in confidence in Marx's theory of alienation. To my mind, the remaining relevant question is: what is the fate of the task which this kind of theory had once seemed to perform for feminism once the theory itself no longer seems qualified to perform it? Does contemporary feminism's turn from Marx's theory of alienation lead on to a search for new, less problematic, ways of justifying and establishing the rationality of feminism's own critical reflections on the lived conditions of modern women? Or is a more radical response called for, one which abandons altogether the demand for ultimate criteria capable of rationally justifying feminism's critical reflections?

This kind of hermeneutical interest is again the point of view which informs the subsequent, rather longer, discussion of contemporary feminism's relations to Habermas' radical endeavours to ground the normative commitments of social and cultural criticism. What does feminism reveal about its own sense of its options and future directions by the nature of its interest in, and the kinds of objections it raises about, Habermas' model of sociocultural interpretation and criticism?

Feminism and Marx's humanism

The question of Marx's credentials as a humanist has been debated endlessly and I do not propose to buy into a dispute over the existence of a 'rupture' in his thought which drew him away from early humanist commitments. My interest here is confined to a brief exploration of the efforts made by some early Second Wave feminists to appropriate an interpretation of Marx's humanism. I distinguish three main episodes in feminism's changing estimations of the significance of Marx's humanism. In the first we see the efforts of, for example, Sheila Rowbotham and Zillah Eisenstein to appropriate for feminism an anthropological reading of Marx's theory of alienation.[1] This first episode is quickly followed by the elaboration of a critical posture in which a so-called dual-systems theory discovered that Marx's anthropology is based on a gender prejudice that attributes significance to a very narrow range of human activities in modern society.[2] This second episode, in which feminism broaches a critique of the gender prejudices embedded in Marx's delineation of a presently alienated 'human essence', meant a major shift in the use feminism could make of Marx's theory of alienation. By endorsing the conception of a denied human essence which underpinned Marx's theory of alienation, the early feminism of

Eisenstein and Rowbotham had been able to look to the categories of Marxism to supply a perspective on the emancipatory potentialities dormant in the life conditions of modern women. The critique of the gender prejudices in the Marxist conception of human essence meant that Marx's theory of alienation was ruined for the dual-systems theorists as an instrument of cultural criticism. Henceforth, the Marxist theory of alienation appeared itself as an object of critique, and as a deficient description of the range of human activities in bourgeois society; a deficiency which dual-systems theory sought strenuously to redress.

It is, however, the third episode in this narrative which occupies the greatest contemporary interest. This last episode in the discussion suggests that feminism has a vital interest in the attempt to historicise the humanist commitments which underpin Marx's culture-critique intentions. It is said that this historicising interest requires a radical departure from fundamental aspects of Marx's own theory of alienation and points to the necessity for an alternative paradigm of social interpretation. To Seyla Benhabib and others, Habermas' theory of communicative action seems to offer a way of retaining the critical potential of the ideals of modern humanism without, at the same time, imposing a formulation of those ideals prejudicial to a recognition of the plurality of needs and aspirations of an increasingly pluralistic women's movement within a highly diverse modernity.[3]

The early efforts of Second Wave feminism to appropriate some main features of Marx's humanism emphasised two dimensions of the conception of labour in Marx's theory of alienation. Marx's theory of alienated labour refers, as both Eisenstein and Rowbotham pointed out, not only to the experience of the wage worker in capitalist society but presupposes also a philosophical concept of labour as objectification.[4] It is specifically the critical potentials of this philosophical concept of labour as objectification which early Marxist feminism sought to appropriate.

Marx's concept of labour as objectification refers to the historical creativity of individuals who, through their labour, not only reproduce and enrich the conditions of life but also augment human subjectivity with a wealth of new capacities, needs and potentialities. On this view, the dynamic of social reproduction meant the incessant expansion of human needs and abilities as producers constantly transformed their inherited world and, in so doing, enhanced their own capacities and aspirations. Marx's theory of alienation discovers an antagonism between these historically generated human possibilities both inscribed in the world of material objectifications and subjective needs and the reductionist logic of capitalism which views the individual who labours as a working animal, a mere instrument of production and creator of surplus value. This configuration of realised societal wealth and individual deprivation constitutes, for Marx, the fundamental contradiction of bourgeois society.

To Eisenstein, Marx's account of the antagonism between realised societal wealth and individual deprivation provides the basis for a critique of the full range of social relations entrenched in modern capitalist societies. There is, as she sees it, nothing about the theory of alienation which 'limits it to an understanding of class relations'.[5] From the point of view of this dynamic, creative concept of labour-as-objectification (which upholds the idea of the species' capacity for producing a supposed wealth of abilities and needs through the productive activity of humans), all merely instrumentalising forms of labour stand condemned. On this reading, an imposed gender division of labour means that the lives of modern women, and not just the proletariat, are characterised by an antagonism between their species' potential and the impoverished, one-sidedness of their existence in bourgeois society.

Eisenstein gives a sharply anthropologised reading of Marx's theory of alienation; the social and critical potentials of this theory are seen to rest on a bifurcation between human existence and its distortion in a capitalist–patriarchal social system. Marx's 'revolutionary ontology' of social and human existence posits:

> . . . within each individual a dialectic between essence and existence which is manifested as revolutionary consciousness in society. Both the criticism of class existence as alienating and exploitative and the revolutionary ontology of the theory make Marxist analysis critical to developing a feminist theory which incorporates but moves beyond a theory of class consciousness.[6]

The feminist critics of the type of humanist Marxist feminism which Rowbotham and Eisenstein had been developing throughout the latter part of the 1970s did not typically set their sights on the question of the adequacy of the Marx interpretation being offered. It should be said, however, that, to the extent that Rowbotham and Eisenstein's reading of the theory of alienation evokes an ahistorical construction of a thwarted species' potential for creative labour, this interpretation suggests a highly selective reading of Marx's own views.[7] As we have seen, Eisenstein's reading discovers in Marx's theory of alienation 'a revolutionary ontology of social and human existence which is manifested as revolutionary consciousness in society'.[8] When extended to women, this 'revolutionary ontology suggests that the possibility of freedom exists alongside exploitation and oppression since woman is potentially more than she is'.[9]

Eisenstein's anthropologised reading of Marx's theory of alienation, understood as the antagonism between human essence and social existence, evokes a clearly essentialising construction of human subjectivity. On this interpretation, 'autonomy' and 'creativity' appear as the presently distorted constituents of the subject rather than as historically developed human possibilities. They appear, that is, in the light of anthropological potentials rather than as a unique and contingent historical development. Thus interpreted, Marx's humanism appeared a rather easy target for the anti-essentialising consciousness which increasingly emerged with the development of Second Wave feminism. The philosophical anthropology discovered by Eisenstein and Rowbotham in the theory of alienation was found by its later feminist critics to rest on a repressive universalisation of a gendered social experience. This metaphysics of the subject was shown to necessarily involve the ascription of a normativity to selected aspects of a modern masculine subjectivity.

The critique of the feminist implications of an anthropologised interpretation of Marx's theory of alienation was spearheaded by the dual-systems literature which appeared in the early 1980s. On this view, Marx's theory offers an interpretation of social life based on an imposed, unitary model of human activity. The dual-systems model advocated by Mary O'Brien and others was, unlike the feminisms of Eisenstein and Rowbotham, not particularly concerned with the task of appropriating for feminism the critical potentials of Marx's account of the antagonism between human essence and social existence. The conception of labour as objectification which is so central to Marx's theory of alienation is almost entirely absent in the Marx interpretation offered by dual-systems theory. Marx had insisted on the antagonism between human essence—that species' potential for creative labour, in which humans are seen to accumulate through their own historical activity a wealth of many-sided abilities and capacities—and the distortion of this human essence in the merely instrumentalising forms of labour which characterise contemporary social existence. O'Brien and the dual-systems theorists can, however, see no evidence for a contrast between two antagonistic constructions of human labour. In the centrality of productive labour to Marx's theory of human essence, O'Brien, Hartmann *et al.* discover only a repressive attempt to universalise a gender specific mode of social existence.

Mary O'Brien's *The Politics of Reproduction* attempted to overcome the supposed inability of Marx's category of production to take account of many traditional female activities by introducing the complementary category of reproduction. At this time also, Heidi Hartmann's provocative essay on 'The Unhappy Marriage of Marxism and Feminism' targeted the 'gender blindness' of Marx's category of production. Hartmann attempted to supplement Marx's category of production, seen as the basis for an interpretation of specifically capitalist relations of production, with an interpretation of patriarchy, understood as a relatively independent set of social practices of domination and coercion. Marx's analysis of capitalist relations of production appeared inadequate to an investigation of patriarchy understood as 'a set of social relations between men, which have a material base, and which, though hierarchical, establish or create interdependence and solidarity among men that enable them to dominate women'.[10]

The humanist Marxist feminism of, for example, Rowbotham and Eisenstein, had attempted to appropriate Marx's account of labour as objectification as the basis from which to ground a critical perspective on the one-sided, merely instrumentalising character of those social relations, forms of conduct and modes of activity in modern society which, they insisted, dominated not only the lives of the proletariat but women as well. On this reading, Marx's conception of labour as objectification describes a species' potential for the self-production of a limitless range of human capacities, abilities, skills and needs via the historical activity of humans themselves. The dual-systems literature suggests, however, that this account of labour as objectification is not, as it pretends, an abstraction from the historical activities of the species as a whole. For O'Brien and others, the concept of labour as objectification appears as simply an illegitimate essentialisation of an, otherwise descriptively useful, account of the productive activities of the wage worker in bourgeois society. Marx's paradigm of production is, accordingly, seen as a deficient description of the range of human activities and forms of life in bourgeois society. Writing in the early 1980s, Iris Young, for example, finds that Marx remains blind to the fact that:

> Such traditional women's tasks as bearing children, caring for the sick, cleaning, cooking etc., fall under the category of labour as much as the making of objects in the factory. Using the category of production or labour to designate only the making of concrete material objects in a modern factory has been one of the unnecessary tragedies of Marxian theory.[11]

According to O'Brien and others, the main task confronting a dual-systems Marxist feminism is to propose 'a modification of

Marx's sociohistorical model, which must now account for two opposing substructures, that of production and that of reproduction. That, in fact, improves the model.'[12]

The third episode in this on-going feminist discussion over Marx's paradigm of production marks a new level of theoretical complexity and opens up a radically new alternative paradigm of social interpretation and critique. On the one hand, the feminism of, for example, Seyla Benhabib and the later Iris Young, vigorously endorses the critique of the gender prejudices built into Marx's concept of human essence developed by the dual-systems theorists.[13] As Benhabib sees it, contemporary feminism confronts the paradigm of production with questions which probe at its core assumptions. Namely, is the concept of production which is based on the model of:

> . . . an active subject, transforming, making and shaping an object given to it, at all adequate for comprehending activities like child-bearing and rearing, care of the sick and the elderly? Can nurture, care and socialisation of children be understood in the light of a subject–object model when they are activities which are so thoroughly *intersubjective*?[14]

Unlike dual-systems theory, however, Benhabib is not concerned only with the question of how to redress the descriptive deficiency of Marx's monological model of the character of human activity. Her concern is, rather, with the wounding impact that this critique of the monological character of the model of human activity upheld by the paradigm of production has had on Marxism's status as a critique of the alienation of modern social life. To Benhabib, the criticisms directed by contemporary feminism towards Marx's paradigm of production suggests, not simply the need for an additional model for interpreting human activity. What is required is a radical alternative to Marx's own deeply reductive paradigm of human activity.

The next part of the discussion reviews some of the arguments raised by, in particular, Benhabib in support of the supposed necessity for a paradigm shift within feminism towards Habermas' communicative interaction model as a means of social interpretation.[15] The feminist arguments developed by Benhabib against the presuppositions of Marx's paradigm of production see themselves as partner to, and as an elaboration of, Habermas' hard-hitting critique of the monological character of the Marxist paradigm.[16] Her feminist critique endorses and extends Habermas' main charge against the paradigm of production which finds that Marx reduces the broad range of human communicative interactions to the model of instrumental activity alone.

In a number of important early essays Habermas laid down the outlines of a critical response to Marx which was to fundamentally shape the direction of his own monumental reconstruction of critical theory. Central to this reconstruction was the critical dissection of Marx's paradigm of production. Habermas' potent critique discovers that Marx's attempt to construe an image of a human essence on the basis of an extrapolation from the supposed creative, self-productive character of human labour rests on a repressive essentialisation of one particular form of human activity and the mode of social existence which supports it. Marx, Habermas maintains, had conceived human self-development in terms of an all encompassing processual exchange with nature through labour.[17] As we have seen, on Marx's paradigm, the formative processes of social labour are seen to constantly revolutionise the productive forces of society building an irresistable reservoir of new capacities, needs and aspirations. According to Habermas, however, this model of the emancipatory dynamics within bourgeois society falsely equates the development of productive forces (the continuous expansion of a freely expressed wealth of human skills, capacities, technologies) with the cause of social emancipation as such. Marx, on this view, had equated two dialectics which, having different tempos, trajectories and possibilities, ought to have been separated. Rationalisation of the productive forces at the level of the subsystems of purposive–rational action (technology, economy) while facilitating the growing mastery of nature from the standpoint of instrumental control, should not be confused with the rationalisation at the level of the institutional frameworks of communicative interaction that removes restrictions on free communication and self-reflection and encourages sociopolitical emancipation.[18]

Benhabib emphasises that this equation in Marx between the development of productive forces and the cause of social emancipation points to his lingering commitment to a philosophy of the subject.[19] Marx's theory of the objectifying character of human labour is seen as a particular formulation of a philosophy of the subject described as an understanding of human self-formation based on the idea of an interaction between subject and object. Whereas the rationalist tradition from Descartes to Hegel had accorded a privileged status to knowledge in the new understanding of human self-formation based on the idea of an interaction between subject and object, Marx had shifted the emphasis to those activities which not only create something and transform the object but also throw the subject into ever new constellations and thereby develop its potentialities.[20]

As already noted, to Benhabib, the subject–object model of human activity which supports Marx's paradigm of production makes it inadequate for an understanding of the typically inter-subjective character of human activities in bourgeois society and particularly inappropriate in interpreting the activities of women.[21] In particular, she suggests that, to the extent that the philosophy of the subject upheld by the Marxist paradigm gives a universal, normative status to an instrumentalising subject–object relation, it proves unable, in principle, to offer any substantive critique of the patriarchal social relations whose instrumentalising logic it expresses. Moreover, the monological model of human activity fixed by Marx's philosophy of the subject means that the paradigm of production can only offer an homogenising conception of the meaning of human emancipation. On this account, Marx's paradigm of production is unable to recognise a plurality of needs, aspirations and goals provoked by the diversity of social life in bourgeois society and is, consequently, unable to provide adequate normative foundations for contemporary social theory.[22] Benhabib insists that contemporary feminism would find an ideal of emancipation modelled not on the ideal of a free, untrammelled expression of human subjectivity but after the idea of 'uncoerced will formation in a communication community' more suited to its own insistence on the necessity that an emancipatory politics give due recognition to a pluralism of social subjectivities.[23]

The turn to the paradigm of communicative interaction

From the time of his Habilitationsschrift published in English as *The Structural Transformation of the Public Sphere*, Habermas has consistently turned away from any conception of the meaning of social emancipation understood on the model of the self-realisation of the subject.[24] In place of all such constructions of social emancipation steeped in a philosophy of the subject, Habermas developed an account of intersubjective communicative processes and their emancipatory potential. It is Habermas' ambition to preserve the main values of Enlightenment without, however, seeking to construe any particular form of human subjectivity as the appropriate bearer of Enlightenment hopes. In place of an interpretation of the meaning of Enlightenment based on a philosophy of the subject, Habermas had proposed an interpretation of human emancipation understood as the revitalisation of a form of democratic public discourse in which social integration is based on rational–critical debate between differently placed social actors; on processes of communication rather than on domination. Habermas looks to the immanent possibility in the present for a human emancipation modelled not on the idea of a free, unconstrained expression of human subjectivity but after the idea of 'uncoerced will formation in a communication community'. The emergence of an autonomous sphere of political reasoning and discussion is also central to the project of the moderns.[25]

In Habermas' early work this theme of the necessity and possibility of establishing democratic public discourse as the dominant mode of co-ordination of social life is given a rich historical and sociological focus. *The Structural Transformation of the Public Sphere* charts the triumph of the bourgeois public sphere in the vibrant institutions of a free press, clubs, philosophical societies and the cultural life of early liberal society and through the revolutionary establishment of parliamentary and democratic regimes and its decline under the pressures of a late capitalist economy and state.[26] In particular, Habermas sets out to plot the paradoxical history of the bourgeois public sphere whose expanding scope has been achieved at the cost of the dimunition of its function. He points out that the early bourgeois public spheres—conceived 'as the sphere of private people come together as a public'—were composed of limited segments of the European population, mainly educated propertied men who 'conducted a discourse not only exclusive of others but prejudicial to the interests of those excluded'.[27] The transformations in the public sphere which Habermas describes turn on both its continual expansion to include more and more participants and the development of large-scale social institutions as mediators of individual participation. In the conditions of the large, democratic social welfare state the communicative interconnectedness of a public could only be 'brought to life within intraorganisational public spheres' in a process whereby opinion formation and expression is wrested by the organisation's members from the bureacratic, formal channels of a publicity staged simply for the purpose of manipulation or show.[28]

Yet, as Craig Calhoun points out, *The Structural Transformation* was not able to find convincing sociological grounds for the hopes Habermas had invested in the possibility of a regenerated public sphere. The early Habermas 'ultimately cannot find a way to ground his hopes for [the] realisation [of democratic public discourse] very effectively in his account of the social institutions of advanced or organised capitalism'.[29] Habermas' growing pessimism about the democratising potentials of the social institutions of advanced capitalism does not provoke him, however, to a despairing revocation of Enlightenment hopes. As Calhoun explains, Habermas endeavours to find alternative empirical grounding for the promises of contemporary Enlightenment. Habermas' subsequent turn to the theory of communicative action moves away from the early hopes invested in the critical potentials carried by main civic institutions of bourgeois society. He now looks to the character of expectations raised by participants in the transhistorical human activity of communicative interaction, to establish that the ideals of democratic interaction between free and autonomous social actors is still invested by us with an unambiguous normativity.

It seems, however, that Calhoun's interpretation of Habermas' turn to the communicative interaction theory overstates its case. Habermas' diagnosis of modern societies consistently refuses to give way to total pessimism regarding the democratising potentials of the main civic institutions of late capitalism. In this light, the turn to the communicative interaction theory appears not so much as an attempt to find an alternative location for the flagging hopes invested by the early theory in the civic institutions of bourgeois society. At issue, rather, is Habermas' long-standing concern to overcome the normative deficiency he had recognised in orthodox Marxism. As we have seen, Habermas' critique of the paradigm of production finds that orthodox Marxism lacks any clear normative foundations. Because the Marxist paradigm is shown to itself presuppose a monological, subject–object model of human activity, it is unable to provide any normative foundations for its own condemnation of the typicality of instrumentalising forms of human intercourse in bourgeois society. It is this 'normative deficit' in Marx's paradigm which the turn to the communicative interaction theory hopes to rectify.

The theory of communicative interaction argues that modern social theory has lost sight of the changes and diversification of forms of rationality which have occurred in modernity. In particular, Habermas sets out to identify the neglected rational potential of modern culture described as communicative reason. In clear dispute with the bleakly pessimistic analyses of the *Dialectic of Enlightenment*, Habermas maintains that instrumental and functional reason do not reign completely uncontested in bourgeois society. In our efforts to arrive at understanding, to interact communicatively with others, we use quite independent norms to judge the rationality of the performance. These norms of communicative rationality, which govern our efforts to reach understanding with others, attest to the survival of the normativity of a democratic public ethos, which continues to be presupposed by us in the face of the technocratic instrumentalism which has ursurped the role of the steering mechanism of modern social life.[30]

Habermas' renowned conception of the 'ideal speech situation' represents an attempt to designate those conditions (such as reciprocity and symmetry) which would have to obtain between participants in a discourse if the demands for 'discourse free from domination' and 'unconstrained dialogue' were to be realised. The ideal speech situation describes those rules and conditions which would have to be observed and met by participants in a dialogue 'if we were to say of the agreement they reach that it was rationally motivated, dependent on the force of the better argument alone'.[31] The *Theory of Communicative Action* centrally maintains that the norms embedded in the 'ideal speech situation' are counterfactually presupposed in all communicative acts as a condition of their possibility and validity. In our efforts to arrive at understanding with differently placed social actors we implicitly make a prior commitment to the symmetry condition which stipulates the equal right of all to be considered rational and free beings.[32] The values and normative commitments necessary to a democratic public ethos are, then, conferred by us with an unconditional essentiality in all our efforts to enter into communicative interactions with others. The norms of symmetry and reciprocity counterfactually presupposed in all communicative acts as the condition of their possibility and validity serve to facilitate the critique of institutionally distorted communication engendered by the relations of domination reigning in bourgeois society and as criteria for defining the ideal of undistorted communication in a radical democracy.[33] Habermas' communicative action theory suggests, then, that the standards for a critique of the coercive, undemocratic character of social relations are implicit in the norms of rational speech which aim at reaching understanding between differently placed social actors. Immanent critique is a matter of reconstructing what is 'intuitively known by every competent speaker'.[34]

The advantages to contemporary feminism of Habermas' project of cultural criticism seem significant. Habermas appears to offer a promising starting point in feminism's search for a non-discriminatory foundation from which to elaborate its critique of the irrationality of the gender-relations inscribed in the institutions of bourgeois society.[35] Habermas gives to the values of modern humanism the meaning of a radical democracy which aims at a negotiated consensus of the competing claims made by differently placed social actors. The ideals of modern humanism are not, for him, identified with the claims to self-realisation of any particular kind of social subjectivity and his or her characteristic mode of existence. Rather, the ideals of modern humanism circumscribe, for Habermas, a particular mode of social inter-course between social actors in a complex, variegated modernity. The norm of freedom counterfactually presupposed in all com-municative acts, insists not on the rights to the subject's unham-pered self-assertion of his or her will and needs; it means, rather, the suspension of all internal and external constraints of action and the right to follow the 'force' of the better argument only.

In its ambitions, at least, Habermas' theory of communicative action seems to hold out the promise of a progressive overcoming of the dilemma of modern humanism outlined in an earlier chapter. It seeks to raise as universal the principles and ideals of modern humanism without identifying the realisation of these ideals with the claims and mode of existence of any particular kind of social subject. Habermas' paradigm promises to establish a standard for a critique of anti-democratic social institutions and unequal social relations which avoids that threat of a smothering of the other which haunts other attempts at universalistic moral and political philosophy. Benhabib stresses that at the core of the communicative action theory is the image of open conversa-tion, that is, conversation where one is obliged to listen to other voices.[36]

Habermas' efforts to interpret the ideals of humanism as an aspiration towards a radical democracy in which social integration is achieved not through domination or by coercion but through a negotiated consensus between differently placed social actors suggests an understanding of social justice in which claims raised by the different voices of women might be heard. The universality of the ideals of modern humanism are defended by Habermas but these ideals are understood in the theory of communicative action as formal presumptions made by us about the ideal character of intersubjective relations; relations in which social integration is achieved through rational consensus rather than coercively through the agency of money and power. On this reading, Habermas' paradigm of social interpretation holds out to feminism the very attractive promise of sustaining a critique of present social relations and institutions from the standpoint of a future-directed ideal of a radical democracy in which the plurality of goals and needs of a highly differentiated social life, including those specific goals, needs and aspirations of women, gain full recognition.

Habermas, to be sure, says virtually nothing about gender in *The Theory of Communicative Action* and Nancy Fraser has marshalled a strong critique of the failure of Habermas' sociology to thematise the 'gender subtext' of the social institutions and processes it analyses.[37] Her two main papers on the sociopolitical dimensions of Habermas' work—one from the Craig Calhoun collection titled 'Rethinking the Public Sphere: A Contribution to the Critique of Actually Existing Democracy', which concentrates on the early Habermas, and her article of the politics of the communicative action theory titled 'What's Critical about Critical Theory? The Case of Habermas and Gender'—constitute some of the most serious feminist critiques of Habermas' work.[38] For my purposes, the former, rather less well-known paper is most relevant. The following brief discussion of the feminist critique of Habermas' reconstruction of critical theory attempts to demonstrate some important parallels between Fraser's main objections to the early Habermas and the feminist critique of the communicative action theory developed by, in particular, Seyla Benhabib.

Fraser's essay on *The Structural Transformation of the Public Sphere* sees itself as an attempt to reformulate and defend the main task undertaken in Habermas' early work. The notion of the revitalisation of the public sphere is, on the one hand, envisaged by Fraser as the appropriate direction for an emancipatory politics today. Habermas' commitment to the revitalisation of the public sphere affirms an historicised reading of the Enlightenment project; a reading which looks to the institutionalisation of the idea of democratic relations between a plurality of social subjects rather than to hopes for the realisation of the appointed historical mission of a unified humanity. To Fraser, however, Habermas' formulation of the meaning of a revitalisation of the public sphere is, at the same time, a deeply problematic one. By focusing on the chances for rejuvenation of the 'liberal model of the bourgeois public sphere' in the fundamentally altered situation of late twentieth century society, Habermas' analysis buys into a particular construction of the meaning and limits of the idea of the public sphere which prejudices the idea of democracy from the start.

According to Fraser, in taking over the normativity of the liberal model of the bourgeois public sphere, *The Structural Transformation of the Public Sphere* perpetuates classical liberalism's construction of dichotomous relations between the private sphere, seen as the locus of particularising interests and needs, and the public arena, in which participants are required to 'bracket' their particularity attending only to the persuasion of the 'force of the better argument'. Fraser argues that Habermas simply takes over the model of rational, democratic intercourse developed by conventional bourgeois constructions of the public sphere. This model requires the bracketing of all particularity and, hence, all considerations of social inequality and different needs in the pursuit of a consensual agreement over common interests. This bourgeois conception taken over by Habermas 'assumes that a public sphere is or can be a space of zero degree culture, so utterly bereft of any specific ethos as to accommodate with perfect neutrality and equal ease interventions expressive of any and every cultural ethos. But this assumption is counterfactual'.[39]

Joan Landes also finds that Habermas takes over an inherently limited construction of the meaning of the public sphere; a construction which is particularly prejudicial to the attainment of due recognition for the public significance of the 'different voice' of modern women. As Landes sees it, because in the model taken up by Habermas the public sphere and the conditions for publicity presupposed a distinction between public and private matters, 'it was ill equipped to consider in public fashion the political dimension of relations in the intimate sphere'.[40] The early Habermas is shown to have failed to fully challenge the idea of the public actor as a particular type of subjectivity; whose qualification for publicness rests on a capacity for abstraction from private identity and particularising concerns. On Fraser's argument, Habermas' proposal for a revitalised public sphere and for a newly constructed intimate sphere, made responsible for the construction of primary identity, perpetuates a gendered construction of those needs and aspirations which might gain recognition in the 'open conversation' of democratic public discourse. Habermas' construction of the meaning of radical democracy is too limited for Nancy Fraser. She suggests that 'public deliberation need not be understood as simply *about* an already established common good; it may be even more basically an occasion for the clarification . . . of interests'.[41]

The ambitions of Habermas' early model of a rejuvenated public sphere, which implicitly assumes a harmony of interests, appear insufficiently radical for his feminist critics. Does the later theory of communicative rationality fare any better? Again, this paradigm of social interpretation seems to promise much to a feminist theory engaged in the search for a non-discriminatory foundations from which to elaborate its critique of the irrationality of modern gender-social relations.

As we saw earlier, the theory of communicative interaction rejects the standpoint of a totalising condemnation of modernity which sees evidence for only one mode of human intercourse in modern societies. Habermas' theory holds that modern societies have produced a number of qualitatively distinct modes of association and forms of intercourse. To him, critical theory now has the task of helping to promote the immanent possibilities for the flourishing and institutional protection of that particular mode of intersubjectivity which presupposes the rationality of democratic, non-coercive relations between differently placed social actors. Habermas' theory finds that processes of communicative interaction presuppose—in clear opposition to the instrumentalising relations which characterise interactions in the capitalist economy and the modern administrative state—as a condition of their possibility and validity, counterfactually posited norms of 'symmetry' and 'reciprocity' between social subjectivities.

It is vital to the critical intentions of Habermas' model of modern social life that he is able to sustain his claim that the differentiated domains of social life carry with them certain unambiguous norms of the mode of social interaction presupposed as necessary and appropriate to their proper conduct. In entering into communicative relations with others, competent participants undertake to have their performance assessed in terms of its observance of the rules of reciprocity and symmetry and in terms of their preparedness to listen only to the force of the better argument. For Benhabib, however, Habermas' model of the norms presupposed in communicative interaction suggests an ambiguous and, ultimately narrowly gender-blind, image of the character of democratic relations between social subjects. This model, which suggests that our interest in communicative interaction with others is governed by a norm of formal reciprocity, requires us to abstract from the individuality and concrete identity of the other. On this account, the norms of our interaction are primarily public and institutional ones.

Like Fraser, Benhabib pursues a feminist critique of Habermas' model of communicative interaction in the spirit of immanent critique: she finds Habermas' own formulation inadequate to the ideal of 'open conversation' between differently placed social subjects. On this account, Habermas' model of communicative action cannot be viewed as a description of formal procedures counterfactually presupposed by anonymous selves who, mushroom like, emerge from nowhere.[42] The participants in the model of communicative action described by Habermas are particular, located selves. The idea that rational discussion requires an attitude of disinterested impartiality which refuses to allow the force of the better argument to be blurred by any consideration of the impact of circumstance and particularising context is, Benhabib points out, the projection of an ideal of moral autonomy which only reflects 'the experience of the male head of household'.[43] For Benhabib, Habermas' model of communicative interaction remains complicit with the gender-biases of liberalism's bifurcation of the public and private spheres which his feminist critics also discovered in Habermas' early work.

Benhabib makes the point that Habermas does not abstract the norms governing communicative action from that site where our processes of communicative interaction normally occur. The norms governing processes of interaction in the private sphere yield, she suggests, a conception of communicative rationality quite different from the Habermasian model. These are the norms of:

> . . . friendship, love and care. These norms require in various ways that I exhibit more than the simple assertion of my rights and duties in the face of your needs. In treating you in accordance with the norms of friendship, love and care, I confirm not only your humanity but your human individuality.[44]

This critique of Habermas' model of communicative rationality does not argue with the universalistic moral and political ambitions of his theory. Benhabib holds, however, that Habermas' own formulation of these universalistic ideals contains 'unjustified assumptions' about the character of politically qualified subjectivity. Habermas' communicative interaction theory overlooks the public significance of that mode of communicative interaction in which participants seek democratic relations in which the significance of concrete difference is not simply bracketed as immaterial to the pursuit of reciprocity but in which the self-actualisation of difference, the capacity to unfold one's individuality in its uniqueness, is counterfactually presupposed by the terms of the relationship. Benhabib follows Carol Gilligan in describing this rival image of communicative interaction as the standpoint of the 'concrete other'.[45]

> The standpoint of the 'concrete other' . . . requires us to view each and every rational being as an individual with a concrete history, identity and affective-emotional constitution . . . Our relation to the other is governed by the norm of *complementary reciprocity*: each is entitled to expect and to assume from the other forms of behaviour through which the other feels recognised and confirmed as a concrete individual being with specific needs, talents and capacities.[46]

Habermas tries to show that it is competent social actors themselves who, in the on-going linguistic interaction or 'communicative action' presuppose reciprocity and symmetry as the norms in terms of which participation is to be judged. The feminist critique developed by Benhabib and by Fraser suggests that the 'competent speaker' evoked here is actually the masculine citizen of liberal political philosophy.

In raising the claim to the public significance of the norms of rational communicative interaction presupposed by 'the standpoint of the concrete other', Benhabib is not simply seeking to highlight the norms of a mode of interaction whose distinctiveness has been missed in Habermas' typology. She claims also that the 'standpoint of the concrete other' reinvests the model of communicative interaction with an interpretation of a core commitment of Enlightenment which appears to be lost in Habermas' model of the norms raised in communicative relations between 'generalised others'.

We saw earlier, that Habermas seeks to respond to the powerful assault on Enlightenment hopes unleashed by the theorists of the dialectic of Enlightenment. Habermas' theory of communicative interaction attempts to establish that an instrumentalising subjectivity is not the only contemporary reminder of the Enlightenment's emancipatory hopes for the development of the self-legislating human personality. His theory both preserves and seeks to transfigure the content of such Enlightenment hopes. In Habermas, the value commitments to the ideals of 'self-legislating autonomy' and the 'fully conscious life' are preserved as the emancipatory values of modernity. The status of such commitments are, however, at the same time changed from their original meaning as a commitment to the birth of a certain kind of subjectivity to a description of the norms of a particular, radically democratic mode of human intersubjectivity.

In supporting the project of transfiguration of Enlightenment values, Benhabib points, nevertheless, to a significant loss provoked by the particular terms in which Habermas' model of communicative interaction seeks to articulate the meaning of contemporary Enlightenment. Specifically, Benhabib describes the reconstitution of Enlightenment values carried by the communicative interaction theory as a loss of that utopianism which had inspired the image of emancipation upheld by the historical Enlightenment. Habermas' transfiguration of the emancipatory values of Enlightenment makes, however, gains as well as losses:

> Habermas has attempted to re-establish the link between Enlightenment and emancipation, and to bring the project of emancipation into the light of the public by going back to the Enlightenment legacy of practical reason. His project requires the fulfillment of the universalistic promise of bourgeois consent theories which, since the seventeenth century, have always limited such universalism on the basis of sex, class, race and status considerations. But even when we concede that the realisation of bourgeois universalism is a necessary condition it hardly seems sufficient.[47]

Habermas, we have seen, seeks to make the values of Enlight-enment no longer simply the expression of the will and aspirations of a particular subjectivity. Yet, to Benhabib, this universalising commitment needs to be wedded to an ideal of democratic intersubjectivity which insists not *merely* on the absence of coercion and on a tolerant admission of difference. In her view, only an ideal of intersubjectivity modelled on the standpoint of the recognition of the 'concrete other' gives due weight to the idea of the self-development of each personality which had been central to the utopian message of the Enlightenment. As we saw earlier, in opposition to the standpoint of the 'generalised other', the point of view of concrete otherness undertakes a mode of intersubjectivity which is committed not merely to absence of coercion but to the elaboration of those circumstances which might foster the individual's capacity to develop potentials in interaction with and beyond the contingencies of his or her 'found' context.

This reworked model of communicative interaction is not based on any conception of an, in principle, opposition between the point of view of justice, which adopts the standpoint of the generalised other, and the point of view of specific needs, which takes up the standpoint of the concrete other. In the struggle to communicate the specificity of our needs, we also raise claims about their justice, we offer reasons for why these claims should be met. This process of communication (understood as a form of interaction between social actors committed to the standpoint of the concrete other) suggests a model of intersubjectivity in which, through an individual's struggle to communicate who they are, the person comes to a heightened self-understanding of the character of his or her own individuality.[48] It is, however, also a process in which the struggle to communicate claims about the rationality and the justice of needs and aspirations imposes a recognition that while 'one has to admit that every need and desire reveals the traces of a unique life history [it also reveals] traces of shared values of the culture into which we are born and the socialising institutions which have shaped us'.[49]

Benhabib has attempted, then, to suggest a model of commu-nicative interaction which redresses some of the limits which feminist (among other) critics have discovered in Habermas' model. Her account of communicative interaction seeks to over-come the particularity of the image of politically qualified sub-jectivity which Habermas' feminist critics discover clings to his particular ideal of communicative discourse. Benhabib's ideal of communicative action attempts, moreover, to reinvest an image of emancipatory social relations with a utopian commitment to the ideal of the self-development of each human personality.

Scratching where it does not itch?[50]

In a certain broad sense, Benhabib seeks in a reworked interpretation of the communicative interaction theory the same sort of practico-theoretical potentials which an earlier generation tried to discover in Marx's humanism. In both cases what is pursued is a paradigm for interpreting modernity and its potentials which might serve as the basis from which to elaborate a critique of the irrationality of gender relations inscribed into the fabric of bourgeois society. From the standpoint of Marx's humanism, it was specifically the critical potentials of his philosophical concept of labour as objectification which earlier Marxist feminism sought to appropriate. The appeal of Habermas' communication theory has rested, rather, with his attempt to transfigure the meaning of Enlightenment values, now understood not as a construction of the will and aspirations of a particular subjectivity but rather, as ideals to be protected and maintained by the institutionalisation of democratic intersubjectivity. It is, however, not merely the adequacy of these paradigms to the feminist hopes invested in them which is today subjected to serious interrogation. For some feminists, it is now necessary to ask: from what point of view does it *matter* that the feminist hopes invested in these major paradigms of social interpretation have been disappointed? Is, namely, contemporary feminism 'scratching where it does not itch' in trying to establish grounds for asserting the irrationality and illegitimacy of those coercive gender relations which it condemns?

On this point, Iris Young adopts a rather equivocal position.[51] As we have seen, Benhabib thinks that feminism needs to link itself to the task of restructuring—not dismantling—moral and political universalism. By contrast, Young seems to suggest that what comes out of the feminist critique of Habermas' theory of communicative action is the collapse of all pretension that we can confer our particular values and cultural commitments with any universalising scope. An emancipatory politics ought not envision a renewal of public life as a recovery of universalising Enlightenment ideals. Emancipatory politics means the reconstruction of a heterogeneous public sphere which fully recognises human plurality and the limitless diversity of ways of life in a differentiated, pluralistic modernity. For Young, emancipatory politics today can have no truck with the tame 'Enlightenment ideal of the civil public where citizens meet in terms of equality and mutual respect'. Refusing to consider individuals in abstraction from 'their particular situations and needs', progressive politics is committed to a conception of a public which:

> . . . in principle excludes no persons, aspects of persons' lives, or topics of discussion and which encourages aesthetic as well as discursive expression. In such a public, consensus and sharing may not always be the goal, but the recognition and appreciation of differences, in the context of confrontation with power.[52]

Yet Young's formulation here of the ideal of a heterogeneous public sphere appears as an interpretation of the universalising Enlightenment ideals whose restrictive normativity she has condemned. Rather than achieving a break from the Enlightenment ideal of a civic public 'where citizens meet in terms of equality and mutual respect', Young offers an elaboration and a particular interpretation of the potentialities of the meaning of contemporary Enlightenment.

The general point is, then, that feminism itself is always engaged in raising universalistic principles or value ideas which claim the rightfulness and rationality of certain social arrangements and forms of conduct. Feminism constantly evokes universalising ideals which claim legitimacy for all independently of any consideration of 'the particular situations and needs' of specific individuals. And because feminism itself is inevitably committed to making critical judgements about the rationality of certain gender relations and norms, it needs, I suggest, to attempt to reflect upon the character of its own universalising value ideas. It must be stressed that this kind of critical self-reflection is not guided by any purely epistemological interest in the discovery of supposed 'secure' foundations which might guarantee our knowledge claims. We constantly make universalising claims about the rightfulness and rationality of certain social relationships and ways of doing things and yet we know that these claims can have no guarantor and no ultimate justification. To György Márkus, this cultural condition, in which we cling to ideas and beliefs that are known to lack legitimacy, 'seems to be the classical case of "bad faith" '.[53] We are still inheritors of Enlightenment but we now recognise, against the historical Enlightenment itself, that these ideals have no anchorage in any anthropological truths. We need the universalising ideals of Enlightenment but know that they cannot be ultimately justified; in this sense Enlightenment appears as the 'bad faith of our culture'.[54]

If universalising Enlightenment ideals which continue to underpin our critical reflections and our positive orientations cannot be finally justified, we can, however, seek to adopt a relatively anti-dogmatic relationship to these ideals. Our capacity to adopt such an orientation to the inherited 'prejudices' of our culture requires, first and foremost, an insight into the presence of universalising value commitments within the judgements we constantly make about the character of our lives. We might not be able to provide legitimacy for the universalising ideals of Enlightenment, but, recognising ourselves as personalities which have taken shape under the tutelage of these ideals, we also begin to grasp our place as their active interpreters. As Charles Taylor has observed, at issue here is the conviction that 'it is more honest, courageous, self-clairvoyent and hence a higher mode of life, to choose in lucidity than it is to hide one's choices behind the supposed structure of things'.[55]

6　Feminist alternatives and postmodernism

Should feminism travel the path of postmodernism? To some the formulation of this question might seem to have already prejudiced the issue. In what sense, it could be asked, can the history of recent attempts to grapple with the meaning of modern feminism be disassociated from the 'main game' of those cultural reflections lumped under the title 'postmodernism'?[1] Moreover, is it possible to distill, from among the contemporary avalanche of literature on the issue, any coherent understanding of the postmodern attitude and perspective? Perhaps it is more realistic to ask: which out of the several rival interpretations of postmodernism should feminism choose in its efforts to deliberate on its own present configurations and its future possibilities? In making its choice between competing constructions of postmodernism, contemporary feminism chooses itself; it comes face to face with the need to determine how it will direct and expand its own critical energies. How will it look upon and weigh up the significance of the various images of modern social life which seemingly underpin several leading interpretations of postmodernism? And in what way will feminism today view its relationship to the kinds of ambitions and hopes which have, in the past, motivated the modern women's movement?

The term 'postmodern' is generally assumed to signal an attitude which loudly proclaims the end of all innocence with respect to the universalising perspectives and value commitments which have taken shape in modernity. 'Postmodernism' describes a definite experience of inhabiting a world in which it has become apparent that those Enlightenment commitments to the universalising ideals of 'freedom', 'authentic self-realisation' and the 'self-conscious life' are rooted in the sand of contingent historio-cultural circumstance. Those dwelling in postmodernity are marked by a radically historicising consciousness: a consciousness which has lost all faith in the efforts of modern philosophy to grasp the role of arbiter among all competing constructions of the 'good' characterising a heterogeneous modernity.

There is, perhaps, nothing particularly new here; no radical break from the portrait of a rationalised modernity, with its 'struggle of the gods', painted by Weber many decades earlier. Perhaps it is, then, only the heightened awareness of the contingency of all values and cultural commitments which marks the postmodern attitude: this, together with a new willingness to suggest that an historicising consciousness must be prepared to put the fate of the universalising value ideas, which the moderns regarded as their greatest achievements, also on the line. The divisions within the postmodern literature over this question of the contemporary fate of modernity's universalising value commitments are extreme. Within recent feminist discussions, for example, the differences are very marked. For some, feminism cannot align itself with those interpretations of the meaning of postmodernism which see in all universalising value commitments only a failure of nerve in the face of modernity's historicising consciousness.

This is the view adopted by Nancy Fraser and Linda Nicholson in their essay entitled 'Social Criticism without Philosophy: An Encounter between Feminism and Postmodernism'.[2] To Fraser and Nicholson, feminism appears, on the one hand, as a project whose critical impulses are directed at all attempts to ground modern universalising value commitments in a speculative conception of the nature of human subjectivity. At the same time, however, the critical impulses of modern feminism, its affirmation of the ideas of social justice and self-determining individuality, also speak to feminism's own universalising value commitments. In particular, Fraser and Nicholson look to the connections between the concerns of contemporary feminism and the challenges to the role played by modern philosophy in contriving to obscure the historio-cultural character of the value stances which have come to assume an essentiality for modern individuals. Fraser and Nicholson suggest that writers like Richard Rorty and Jean-Francois Lyotard begin by arguing that:

Philosophy with a capital P is no longer a viable or credible enterprise. They go on to claim that philosophy and, by extension, theory in general, can no longer function to ground politics and social criticism. With the demise of foundationalism comes the demise of the view that casts philosophy in the role of founding discourse vis-a-vis social criticism. That 'modern' conception must give way to a new 'postmodern' one in which criticism floats free of any universalist theoretical ground.[3]

Fraser and Nicholson consider that the challenge by, for example, Rorty and Lyotard, to the norm-producing role of philosophical reflection has not dissolved but only reconceptualised the problem of the legitimacy of normative judgements. Postmodern feminism does not, on this account, cease to evoke claims about the character of just and rational social arrangements; it can, however, no longer fail to recognise that its own critique of the present is inspired by the affirmation of historio-cultural value choices which 'float free of any universalist theoretical ground'.

To Jane Flax and Judith Butler, by contrast, for feminism the demise of foundationalism means the emancipation from all attempts to raise and justify claims about the rationality and legitimacy of given social arrangements. According to them, postmodernism's challenge to the arbitrating pretensions of all constructions of transcendent reason establishes that any reflection on the rationality of particular cultural forms and modes of intercourse is an unwarranted attempt to again cloak social authority behind the mysteries of metaphysical speculations.[4] Flax, in particular, interprets any suggestion that it might be necessary and possible to develop an alternative understanding of normativity as a failure to come to terms with the full emancipatory consequences of the postmodern challenge to the arbitrating role of the philosopher. She adopts the view that any attempt to construct an alternative understanding of normativity is itself ultimately committed to the resurrection of the illegitimate authority of a self-proclaimed sovereign reason.[5] There are, for Flax, only two alternatives. If traditional foundationalism is obsolete, claims about the justice and legitimacy of given social arrangements appear as hollow, unwarranted appeals to a collapsed authority. According to Flax, any attempt to pursue an alternative understanding of normativity appears as simply another proposal for reviving the old dream of the arbitrating role of transcendent reason. Feminism, on this view, still has to learn the full, emancipatory implications of the postmodern challenge to the norm-producing pretensions of philosophical reflection.[6]

By contrast, Fraser and Nicholson remind us that the advent of postmodernism should be seen as the demise of one particular mode of seeking to justify our claims concerning the rationality and legitimacy of certain social practices and arrangements. On this point of view, to suppose that the undermining of the role of the philosopher-arbiter has been accompanied also by the collapse of the need and the possibility of seeking rational assent for normative claims is to concede far too much to the self-aggrandising representations of modern philosophy itself.

The main disputation over contemporary feminism's ties with postmodernism has its roots, then, in a fundamental disagreement over the normative requirements of social criticism in the wake of the collapse of the idea of the hegemony of a sovereign reason. I want to explore two main responses to this issue outlined above. First, the stronger claim that postmodernism's challenge to the norm-producing pretensions of philosophical reflection does not mean that social criticism has to discover a new way of justifying its own normative underpinnings. This first part of the discussion considers the idea that postmodernism dissolves normativity as a problem for feminism. I am, in particular, interested at this point in looking at the way in which one strand within modern feminism has responded to the postmodern challenge to all normativity by contriving to renegotiate the status of feminism itself. Feminism, on this account, is no longer to be understood as social criticism in which claims about the rationality of certain social arrangements and forms of conduct can be debated and contested. In what form, then, does this kind of feminism—a feminism concerned to divest itself of the task of a social critic of an irrational and unjust society—seek to appear? And, what might be the impact and the limits of this contemporary attempt to renegotiate the status of modern feminism? To put the question slightly differently, we need to ask: what are the implications for feminism of adopting that radical critique of reason which has been elaborated by a range of postmodern thinkers? How must feminists persuaded by the suggestion that feminism could offer no rationally justified grounds for its critique of modern gender relations seek to construe the nature of feminism itself?

The postmodern challenge to the modern episteme

The work of the early Michel Foucault can be counted among those for whom 'postmodernism' does not mean an attempt to put the Enlightenment presupposition of universal rationality and normativity on a new, historicised footing. The project of Enlightenment, appears on this perspective, as a perilous and essentially misguided undertaking. In the work of Foucault and in the writings of Jean-Francois Lyotard, we find, I suggest, examples of a certain construction of the meaning of postmodernism whose influence has been widely felt in contemporary feminist discussions over feminism's own current meaning and options.

In *The Postmodern Condition*, Lyotard argues, that 'postmodernism' designates a general condition of our time in which the 'grand narratives of legitimation' have lost all plausibility.[7] The main theme of this early work is that we can no longer hope to discover in the historical narratives of the Enlightenment, Hegelianism and Marxism a key capable of unlocking the hidden truth of Western civilization. These narratives are now radically out of step with the heterogeneity and fragmentation of a contemporary lived experience. In the postmodern era these so-called metanarratives come to appear as simply a polytheism of competing stories each of which supplies only local and context-specific criteria of validity. All modern attempts to unbind norms and values from their location within the governing rules of a particular discursive practice seem both implausible and totalitarian to those imbued with a relentlessly historicising postmodern consciousness. The modern episteme, as an allegedly universal framework, is viewed as an episteme of domination.

Lyotard does not limit himself, then, to a challenge to the norm-producing pretensions of philosophical reflection. His critique decries all suggestions that the legitimacy of discourses might be questioned in terms which transcend the constitutive norms of the discursive practice at issue. In this wider aspect of Lyotard's postmodern challenge to the modern episteme, Judith Butler, for example, finds a common cause with the concerns of a contemporary feminism similarly persuaded that legitimation in the postmodern era must quit the realm of the universalising metanarrative.[8] This sympathy with postmodernism seen as a critique of the universalising attitude of a modern consciousness is evident in the following passage from Butler's essay 'Contingent Foundations: Feminism and the Question of "postmodernism"':

> . . . the point articulated forcefully by some recent critics of normative political philosophy is that the recourse to a position—hypothetical, counterfactual or imaginary—that places itself beyond the play of power, and which seeks to establish the metapolitical basis for a negotiation of power relations, is perhaps the most insidious ruse of power. That this position beyond power lays claim to its legitimacy through recourse to a prior and implicitly universal agreement does not in any way circumvent the charge, for what rationalist project will designate in advance, what counts as agreement? What form of insidious cultural imperialism here legislates itself under the sign of the universal?[9]

To Butler, a modern insistence on the rational legitimation of all social practices now appears reducible to a mere manifestation of the 'will to power' of a particular mode of social subjectivity.

Susan Hekman is similarly persuaded that a postmodern feminism is committed to an unmasking critique of the gender prejudices which inform all attempts to raise claims on behalf of the supposed rationality of particular social forms and modes of intercourse.[10] Hekman finds Foucault's particular formulation of the critique of the relations of domination inherent in the modern episteme especially relevant to the concerns of modern feminism. Her interest here is primarily with that formulation of the radical critique of reason and the rational subject which Foucault developed in the 1970s in the context of his power/knowledge studies. From the early 1980s Foucault's attitude towards the contemporary legacy of Enlightenment undergoes a significant change; a change which substantially alters his understanding of the character of his critical project. We shall see in a later part of the discussion, that this 'turn' in Foucault's attitude to the 'philosophical ethos' of Enlightenment has also had significant reverberations in the efforts of contemporary feminists to interpret the character of their own critical project.

For Hekman, as for Irene Diamond and Lee Quinby, the attraction of the standpoint of the earlier Foucault rests precisely with the radicalism of his challenge to the modern idea of subjectivity.[11] This analysis finds that the very idea of human subjectivity is fully complicit with the efforts of certain kinds of historio-socially constituted identities to impose as universal and normative their own acquired characteristics and perspectives. Diamond and Quinby identify Foucault's exposure of the disciplinary credentials of modern subjectivity as a major site at which feminist and Foucauldian analyses converge.

Foucault is not to be understood here as simply emphasising the historio-social constitution of subjectivity. This much had already been done by Herder, Hegel, Marx and others. Yet, whereas the heirs of Enlightenment had retained the idea of an historically formed subjectivity as a critical standard against which to judge social conditions that oppress its self-affirmation and unfolding, Foucault, at this juncture at least, insists on the wholesale repudiation of the idea of subjectivity. To him, not only is the idea of subjectivity a specific historical product, both the universality and unity of which is illusory, but the idea of human subjectivity is also a product of social repression and subjugation. Foucault's earlier work represents, then, a constant attack on the very idea of subjectivity itself. For him, subjectification has always been a historical mode of subjugation. The modern subject is a 'fictive atom of an ideological representation of society', product of overlapping discourses and disciplinary practices.[12]

> The individual is not to be conceived as a sort of elementary nucleus, a primitive atom, a multiple and inert material on which power comes to fasten . . . In fact, it is already one of the prime effects of power that certain bodies, certain gestures, certain discourses, certain desires come to be identified and constituted as individuals. The individual is not the vis-a-vis of power; it is, I believe one of its prime effects. The individual is an effect of power.[13]

Feminists like Biddy Martin and Jana Sawicki have found that Foucault's challenge to the idea of human subjectivity has a double-edged significance for contemporary feminism.[14] On the one hand, as Martin sees it, the critique of the idea of human subjectivity has extended the reach of feminism's own understanding of the extent of, and mechanisms at work in, the marginalisation of women within Western culture. Feminist criticism must, she maintains, be engaged in elaborating:

> . . . the extent to which the phallocentric meanings and truths of our culture have necessarily repressed multiplicity and the possibility of actual difference by appropriating difference, naming it in opposition, and subsuming it under the 'Identity of Man'. Feminism shares with poststructuralist criticism a critique of the hegemony of the identical and the desire for other forms of discourse.[15]

Martin's feminism clearly embraces the radicalism of Foucault's early challenge to the idea of human subjectivity which seeks to expose 'the workings of power in the will to truth and identity'.[16] The novelty of Foucault's posture lies in its determination to go beyond a mere disclosure of the historio-cultural constitution of all images of human subjectivity to challenge also the repressive universalisation of the characteristics and aspirations of a particular, located identity carried by all appeals to the idea of self-determining, autonomous subjectivity:

> I don't believe the problem [of the constitution of objects] can be solved by historicising the subject . . . One has to dispense with the constituent subject, to get rid of the subject itself, that is to arrive at an analysis which can account for the constituent subject within an historical framework.[17]

To Martin and others, this early Foucauldian inspiration to 'get rid of the subject' alerts contemporary feminism to the necessity of a radical extension of its critique of the ideological mechanisms used to delegitimise and to conceal the public significance of the distinctive kinds of identities which have been forged by the peculiar historio-cultural experiences of modern women.

Sawacki points out that Foucault's critique of the idea of human subjectivity has helped also to expose the repressive universalisation of culturally acquired characteristics which informs all those attempts to speak on behalf of the denied 'truth' of feminine subjectivity. She finds that an appropriation of Foucault's challenge to the idea of human subjectivity underlines the necessity for a sensitivity to difference in the formulation of feminism's own goals and perspectives.

> Foucault's analyses of power and sexuality put into question the viability of using essentialist notions of sexual identity as a basis for building a feminist theory and politics. However, they have highlighted the importance of keeping open the question 'which desires are liberating.'[18]

This formulation suggests, however, a tension in Sawacki's efforts to reconcile her own feminism with the early Foucault's Nietzschean idea of the subject as a mere 'fiction' which unknowingly serves the 'will to power'. Feminism, as Sawaki understands it, recognises the need to uphold a distinction between coercive and non-coercive identity construction: it calls for guidance on the question of 'which desires are liberating'. Feminism raises claims about the justification and rationality of certain forms of social intercourse and conduct. The difficulty, however, is that such claims are disallowed by Foucault's own radical anti-subjectivism. For him, as already pointed out, subjectification has always been an historical mode of subjugation. So while feminists like Martin and Sawacki continue to struggle with the question of how to formulate the ideal of self-determining autonomous subjectivity in terms which do not simply legitimate and conceal the public significance of a culturally acquired feminine identity, the early Foucault still thinks to dissolve the problem by repudiating any commitment to the modern ideal of self-legislating subjectivity as simply a repressive fiction. On this account, the modern idea of the subject, a product of particular discourses and disciplinary practices, simply inhibits public recognition of the discourses of the marginal, the different. Foucault refuses to recognise that this ideal of self-legislating subjectivity might also supply the grounds for an immanently critical perspective on all those social arrangements and ideological representations which thwart its realisation and limit its interpretation.

Those feminists like Hartsock, Martin and Sawacki, who wish to retain the idea that feminism represents a politics committed to a protest at the irrationality and injustice of certain modes of social intercourse and forms of life, discover a stumbling block to a wholesale feminist appropriation of Foucault's anti-humanism in the radicalism of his early critique of the idea of the subject. To others, however, the challenge led by, for example, Foucault and Lyotard to all attempts to propose grounds for the rationality and legitimation of discursive practices opens up an opportunity for radically rethinking the status of the discourse of feminism itself. Feminism, on this construction, must now disassociate itself from all attempts to raise universalising claims about the rationality and legitimacy of certain modes of intercourse. Feminism now offers itself as a discursive practice which claims our assent as an 'aesthetics of existence'.

An anti-humanist ethics

Martin Jay has pointed out that its disavowal of the necessity and the possibility for the rational legitimation of discursive practices has led some of its critics to mistakenly suppose post-structuralism as being disinterested in all ethical considerations.[19] As Jay points out, this retreat from normative reflections on the character of the good life does not automatically suggest a retreat also from all interest in the reflections of the modern individual on the possibility of a personal ethics. The retreat from normativity suggests, rather, a resignation from all attempts to construct intersubjectively recognised criteria from which the justice and virtue of certain life forms can be assessed. Lyotard suggests, accordingly, that our inevitable judgements on the quality and appropriateness of certain life choices are based on mere practical and aesthetic considerations; they can claim no intersubjectively recognised validity. 'We judge without criteria. We are in the position of Aristotle's prudent individual, who makes judgements about the just and the unjust without the least criterion'.[20]

There is, then, in the various writings of Lyotard, Foucault, Levinas and Irigaray a serious attempt to redescribe the object of ethics in the context of a heterogeneous modernity repulsed by any quest for an idea of justice linked to the supposition of consensus.[21] As Jay points out:

> If one had to single out the most common aspect of this dispersed body of thought, the likeliest candidate would be its shared resistance to defining the ethical in terms of a system of norms, rules, laws or values, which can be codified in a rigorous way.[22]

For Lyotard, a commitment to the principles of justice does not necessarily impose any consensus over the meaning of the good life. The idea of justice which he has in mind anticipates a social condition in which all forms of life enjoy the same right to autonomy and the unimpeded development of their creative play. The collapse of the plausibility of all emancipatory philosophies of history means the release of the creative potentials of a pluralism of forms of life, or social language games, from the shackles of modern rationalism. To Lyotard, the postmodern condition means that 'the grand narrative has lost its credibility' and therewith the supposed need for, and possibility of, an arbitration between the competing claims of divergent social language games. The collapse of the modern fiction of the metanarrative dissolves the struggle over the competing claims to legitimacy and rationality of all those social language games which are now seen to supply their own local and context-specific criteria of validity.

This call for the liberation of all social language games from the impositions of discredited philosophies of history has also reverberated throughout contemporary feminist circles. We hear its echo in, for example, the recent efforts of Luce Irigaray to forge an ethics of sexual difference. Drawing on the work of Emmanuel Levinas, Irigaray has attempted to propose a sexual ethics of difference in which men and women create themselves according to radically different principles.[23] Irigaray's proposal for an ethics of alterity is not concerned to provide any substantive vision of the orientation and character of a self-making femininity. Her ethics attempts, rather, to supply an insight into the ways in which the feminine self needs to construct the difference of the other in the struggle to affirm her own autonomy. In clear opposition to the universalistic basis of Kantian ethics, the struggle to maintain the irreducible difference of the feminine self becomes the substantive content of Irigaray's ethics of sexual difference. An ethics of sexual difference establishes the task of the feminine self as the realisation of her irreducible difference. In this enterprise she is offered strategic support in the guise of an image of a 'women's divine'. A patriarchal culture offers an image of the difference of the feminine specified negatively as a lack of masculine qualities. Irigaray's God seeks to project a transcendent image of her own concrete difference which refuses to accept the definitive status of a masculine subjectivity. The divine provides the horizon of irreducible feminine difference.

If women lack a God they cannot communicate or communicate among themselves. The infinite is needed, they need the infinite in order to share a little? Otherwise the division brings about fusion–confusion, division and tearing apart in them/her, between them. If I can't relate to some sort of horizon for the realisation of my genre, I cannot share while protecting my becoming.[24]

The pursuit of an ethics of alterity presents itself, then, as one major attempt to rethink the status of feminism in terms which might dissolve the problem of the grounding of normative criteria. An ethics of sexual difference seeks no general assent for the validity of its judgements on the rationality and legitimacy of given gender relations. With Lyotard, this interpretation of feminism thinks to judge 'without the least criterion'. An ethics of sexual difference offers itself up only as a strategic guidance to those individuals who find appeal in those free-floating images of autonomous femininity that it evokes. The image of an autonomous femininity evoked here seeks to present itself as the poetic truth of a particular subjectivity which invites sympathetic recognition but which does not seek to recommend itself as a quest for justice linked to the supposition of consensus.

This kind of reconstitution of feminism as an invitation to empathetically engage with the poetic truth of a particular embodied subjectivity underpins the authorial voice which directs Irigaray's text *Marine Lover of Frederich Nietzsche*:

Yes, I am coming back from far, far away. And my crime at present is my candor. I am no longer the lining to your coat, your—faithful—understudy. Voicing your sorrows, your fears and resentments. You had fashioned me into a mirror and I have dipped that mirror into the waters of oblivion—that you call life. And farther away than the place where you are beginning to be, I have turned back. I have washed off your masks and make up, scrubbed away your multicolored projections and designs.[25]

The dilemma of how to ground the normative judgements of feminism in terms which do not presuppose the 'truth' of a certain way of life is, seemingly, overcome by emptying feminism of all normative claims. Feminism, on this construction, enunciates only the poetic truth of particular selves who merely invite others to share in their experimentation.

This strategic interpretation of feminism as an aesthetics of existence buys into a quite particular construction of the character of postmodernism. It has, namely, adopted the suggestion that the problem of legitimation is dissolved by the recognition of the radical incommensurability of social language games characterising the postmodern world. Yet, clearly this portrait proposes its own definite vision and normative evaluation of the character of contemporary social relations. The prevailing meaning of the postmodern world appears, on this account, as a radicalisation of that polytheism which the theorists of modernity had long since diagnosed as characteristic of post-traditional societies. What, to Lyotard and others, distinguishes the attitude of the postmodernist from the modernist is not only an awareness of the accelerated heterogeneity of a fragmented modernity but the readiness also to jettison any hopes for reconciliation and consensus. Lyotard wants to 'wage war on totality'; to 'activate the differences and save the honor of the name'.[26] This construction of postmodernity as the dissolution of legitimacy and normativity as the false problem of modernism is, then, clearly committed to a certain interpretation of the character of contemporary social relations. It is, I suggest, an interpretation which merits close scrutiny from a postmodern feminism.

Living in a postmodern world

Lyotard attempts to capture the distinctiveness of the postmodern social environment via his conception of the logic of the 'differend'. The logic of the differend suggests that the differences among social language games are so extreme that their various claims to 'right' are simply incommensurable. Richard Wolin points out that, for Lyotard:

> . . . justice is attained by allowing the multiplicity of language games to subsist in their various states of difference, that is by our refusal to totalise them according to a repressive logic of consensus. In this way . . . the values of pluralism are best served.[27]

Two features of this characterisation of the logic of the 'differend' need to be looked at. First, as Seyla Benhabib has discovered, there is little of substance which distinguishes Lyotard's conception of the social as polytheism of social language games from neo-liberal interest group pluralism.[28] And, she goes on to point out, the trouble with traditional liberal conceptions of pluralism is the neglect of the structural sources of inequality, influence, resource and power among competing groups. The model of society suggested by the image of incommensurable social language claims seeks to eliminate any conception of a common criterion which might be called upon to provide a perspective on the relations of inequality and disadvantage which characterise contemporary social life. This perspective of a social life characterised by a diversity of 'worlds' committed only to sustaining the integrity of their difference is finally unable to satisfy one of the most crucial demands of a feminist politics whose call for social justice requires some capacity to reflect upon the ways in which difference in modern societies is constructed as disadvantage and inequality.

The perspective on social life embedded in the image of incommensurable social language games does not, I suggest, offer an interpretation of social life capable of reflecting upon and clarifying what is at stake in contemporary feminist struggles. The call for the exercise of 'judgement without criterion' suggests a totally heterogeneous social experience in which individuals and groups do not experience themselves as differently placed in relation to a set of potentials and goods posited as universal. As I argue at a later point, a model of social interpretation adequate to contemporary feminism must above all be able to offer some account of that experience of radical dissatisfaction and sense of frustrated potential with the life choices available to women which has prodded the modern women's movement into existence. The neo-liberalism, which Benhabib sees at the core of the social vision harboured by the theory of the differend, is precisely without any means for reflecting on and clarifying the sources of the experience of dissatisfaction with given social arrangements which continues to vitalise feminism as a modern social movement.

Just as the idea of incommensurable social language games attempts to overcome the problem of normativity, so, too, the conception of an 'aesthetics of existence' developed by Foucault in his later years attempts to transcend the necessity of characterising those criteria used to justify one's judgements on a preferred way of life.[29] The theme of an 'aesthetics of existence' elaborated by the later Foucault seeks to disassociate an ideal of autonomy from any modern ideal of universal justice. The later Foucault endeavours to evoke an ideal of autonomy, conceived in terms of an image borrowed from antiquity, which departs radically from the Enlightenment commitment to the idea of self-legislating subjectivity. The 'aesthetics of existence' construes the ideal of autonomy as a process of invention of the self; not, therefore, in the light of the struggles of the self to achieve authentic expression against an inhibiting world of convention and prejudice but, rather, as the playful, ironic engagement of concrete individuals with the governing codes and conventions of various cultural and institutional systems. On this point of view, the modern individual has the capacity to act voluntarily and intentionally within those cultural and institutional systems which organise his or her way of doing things and to make creative use of whatever space for self-formation that these systems permit or provide.[30] Foucault's conception of an 'aesthetics of existence' appears as an attempt to uphold an ideal of individual autonomy without, however, colluding with any of those repressive philosophies of history which look to a sovereign reason to effect the release of the modern self from the shackles of convention.

Foucault's conception of the aesthetic, playful relationship of the self to all those multifarious 'effects' opened up by the matrix of modern cultural and institutional systems proposes an image of the relationship between the self and the world of social conventions and routines which, in an earlier chapter, I characterised as typical of Romanticism. Denying the claims of a normalising, conventional social existence on the supremacy of the creative self, the Romantic seeks to transform his or her own acts into a work of art. This Romantic theme of the aestheticisation of life is very strong in Foucault's later writings. It is, for him, the positive meaning of that modern idea of the individual as a self-creating personality:

> That art is something which is specialised or which is done by experts who are artists. But couldn't everyone's life become a work of art? why should the lamp or the house be an art object, but not our life? . . . From the idea that the self is not given to us, I think that there is only one practical consequence; *we have to create ouselves as a work of art.*[31]

Foucault, as the above clearly shows, considered that the aestheticisation of life is an attitude in principle open to all. It does not presuppose the normativity of any particular kind of social subjectivity but encourages only an attitude of playful experimentation towards all those culturally produced effects which represent both the limit and the potential of the modern self. Yet, as we saw in the earlier discussion of the attitude of the Romantic ironist, this attitude of playful appropriation does indeed, contrary to its own self-representations, presuppose a particular kind of social subjectivity and its characteristic relations with others. The task of self-invention described by the concept of an aesthetics of existence calls upon special capacities in the heroic personality. The recognition that 'we have to create ourselves as a work of art' does not offer itself as a reflection of creative processes supposedly immanent to the production and reproduction of modern subjectivities. It does not offer itself to us as an account of the way in which the uniqueness of each personality might produce itself through the critical appropriation of the contingencies of a life context. The 'aesthetics of existence' is not a quest for authenticity—for making something of what we, by force of contingent circumstance, have become. It reflects, rather, a particular attitude of heroic resistance to those processes of carceral subjugation which are supposed by Foucault to characterise the production of modern subjectivity. The 'self-creating individual' construes the problem of self-invention not in the mode of a struggling, critical appropriation of a world of convention and cultural ritual but, rather, in the mode of the playful ironic engagement of concrete individuals with the governing codes and conventions of various cultural and institutional systems.

Richard Wolin has pointed to the undemocratic dimensions of Foucault's conception of an aesthetics of existence.[32] He maintains that this conception of the self presupposes a particular kind of subjectivity endowed with the capacity and the will to insist on its irreducible difference from the conventions and rituals of the modern historio-cultural life context. Paradoxically, Foucault's conception of an aesthetics of existence is also invaded by a normative construction of a particular kind of privileged subjectivity.

> Can the complex problems of modern self-individuation really be remedied, let alone solved by way of a simple assertion of will, by the 'choice of a beautiful life', as Foucault seems to suggest? And if the techniques of carceral subjugation are in fact as all-pervasive and inescapable as Foucault has described them, wherein lie the resources of selfhood upon which we might draw to combat them? Or is the model of aesthetic self-assertion to be reserved solely for the heroic few, who thereby acquire perogative over the aesthetically displeasing hoi polloi?[33]

The conception of an aesthetics of existence promises a way of formulating a commitment to the idea of autonomous subjectivity in terms which do not presuppose the normativity of any particular kind of social subjectivity and its characteristic way of life. As Wolin suggests, however, the project of universalising an aesthetics of existence does presuppose a particular, privileged kind of social subjectivity and its typical relations with others. One might be even stronger and suggest that it presupposes an instrumentalising relation with others in which the self is seen to measure the significance of the worlds inhabited by others in terms only of his or her own insatiable needs to imaginatively extend the scope of their own possibilities. And, because the aesthetics of existence confers an implicit normativity on an instrumentalising construction of intersubjective relations, it provides, I suggest, a very inadequate way of interpreting the goals and main concerns of a social movement committed to the idea of a democratic intercourse between differently placed social subjects.

The attempt to forge new identity descriptions, to experiment with new ways of understanding the potentials of images of femininity, is clearly an important and revitalising aspect of the concerns of feminism today. The point is not, then, that contemporary feminism should only concern itself with explicit questions of social justice. My argument is, rather, that the standpoint of an 'aesthetics of existence' obscures from us the fact that we do, constantly, make, at least implicit, judgements on the character of a desirable and worthwhile life and that we need to be as aware as possible of the character and the implications of the criteria we use in making such judgements. Feminism's dissatisfied consciousness judges the present from the standpoint of frustrated hopes and needs; it appeals, namely, to criteria in terms of which the current context is seen as a radical failure and disappointment. We need, then, a theory of the character of modernity which will help us to understand and to reflect upon those universalising value commitments which form the grounds for our restless dissatisfaction with, and sense of injustice at, the character of the life chances allocated to women in contemporary society.

The question framed by Fraser and Nicholson retains its pertinancy. How, they ask, can we combine a postmodern incredulity towards metanarrative with the social–critical power of feminism?[34] The experience of dissatisfaction at the frustration of hopes and expectations which, I suggest, continues to be a major reference point and motivation for feminism today suggests that feminism continues to be inspirited by a commitment to a description of social goods which it infuses with a normative status. Despite the postmodern incredulity towards metanarrative—a scepticism fuelled by contemporary feminism itself—the women's movement continues to appeal to value commitments upon which it confers a normative status.

It is, perhaps, possible to construe an alternative to both an attempted retreat from postmodern incredulity towards metanarrative and the rhetorical option of a retreat from the social, critical powers of contemporary feminism. In the following part of the discussion I turn to a brief review of the relevance to feminism of an interpretation of the postmodern condition understood, not as the abolition of the 'masternarratives' which have accumulated and proliferated in modernity, but as a new consciousness of the historically contingent character of these masternarratives which continue, however, to have a normative, universalistic significance for us.

Dissatisfaction in the conditions of postmodernity

Heller and Feher offer a diagnosis of postmodernity which attempts to grasp the implications of the breakdown of the grand narratives for the political landscape of a postmodern condition. To them, postmodernity describes a definite experience of inhabiting a world which has seen the collapse of those grand narratives whereby the moderns had attempted to supply a teleological interpretation of human history.

> . . . those dwelling in the postmodern political condition feel themselves to be after the entire story with its sacred and mythological origin, strict causality, secret teleology, omniscient and transcendent narrator and its promise of a happy ending in a cosmic or historic sense.[35]

Postmodernity is distinguished by its perspective on the world as a plurality of heterogeneous spaces and temporalities. It is a posture incompatible with any redemptive politics aimed at the messianic realisation of 'humanity's cause'. The anti-messianic posture of a postmodern political condition makes it vulnerable, however, to the dismissal of any kind of utopianism and hence to an undermining of the possibility of any critical engagement with the present from the standpoint of its own immanent potentials. The postmodern political condition is vulnerable to 'easy compromises with the present as well as susceptible to "doomsday myths" and collective fears stemming from the loss of future'.[36]

For Heller and Feher, the characteristic mark of the postmodern is the attitude that one is living after 'the grand narrative'. Yet this positioning does not mean that the postmodern eschews all commitment to the universalising values which had been supported by these grand narratives. Certainly, for the postmodern, there can be no criteria we can use to fix the meaning and implications of these universalising values. However, Heller and Feher insist that the universality of such modern values as freedom and life can and must be upheld by those who understand themselves as postmoderns. The value ideas of freedom and life are the, not always compatible, universals of modernity.[37] The grounds upon which the universality of these value ideas is established for us does not refer back to any construction of an essential 'species truth' or anthropological given. They are the immanent product of a long historical odyssey. The values of freedom and life are posited as 'empirical universals'; they are values which we postmoderns grasp as historically produced, therefore as contingent and vulnerable, and yet their impact and presence can be now seen 'everywhere on our globe'.[38]

In a monograph which appeared in 1986 called *Doomsday or Deterrence? On the Anti-Nuclear Issue*, Feher and Heller make the point that the anti-nuclear movement has, more than any other, given focus to the exclusive universality of the modern values; freedom and life.[39] By necessity, the anti-nuclear movement assumes an interest in global, not merely regional survival. Its success depends, they argue, in asserting both the universality of these values and their equal priority. The anti-nuclear movement gives a practical articulation to that historical process of universalisation which has been 'taking place from the early eighteenth century onward, and covering the whole period of the Enlightenment'.[40] The anti-nuclear movement speaks on behalf of the fate of all humanity in terms which do not presuppose the normativity of any particular way of life. It is a voice raised on behalf of the future of life itself and on behalf of the freedom of all to determine for themselves those goods without which life would not be worth living.

For those dwelling in postmodernity it has become possible to affirm the values of freedom and life as universals without, at the same time, attempting to underpin these claims to universality by any recourse to traditional natural rights theory. In a more recent essay, Heller attempted to clarify what distinguishes her account of the 'empirical universality' of value ideas of freedom and life from the normative construction of 'universalism' in traditional grand narratives.

> In traditional grand narratives 'universalism' was seen as one of the major manifestations of the—coming or just accomplished—'end of history'. Philosophers saw the whole human race gathering under the same canopy, and they understood the pasts of people and cultures from this vantage point as the lengthy preparation for this final outcome. All particularities were supposed to wither (for example, in Marx) or become sublated (for example, in Hegel). This was a strongly normative concept of universalism. My concept of universalism is empirical. It is not an idea or manifestation of superiority, rather a simple observation that the modern social arrangements have set foot everywhere on the globe, and that the niches of the premodern social arrangement are dwindling fast. Empirical universalism, thus simply stands for 'everywhere on our globe'.[41]

To Heller and Feher, the postmodern political condition does not mean that we seek to 'judge without criteria'. It means, rather, that, constituting ourselves as coming after the 'grand narrative', we understand the status of the criteria we use in a distinctive, highly self-reflexive mode. We postmoderns do continue to affirm universalising values; values through which we interpret and place requirements on the particular local contexts we find ourselves in. The meanings of the value ideas of freedom and life are not encountered by those dwelling in postmodernity as fixed by their correspondence to the universalising aspirations and local experiences of any particular social subjectivity. The universality of these value ideas does not mark 'an idea or manifestation of superiority' of any one parochial way of life. It is, rather, the fact that the influence of these value ideas are felt everywhere on our globe with its wealth of diverse cultural contexts, local traditions and priorities which, to Heller and Feher, establishes their universality.

> The universal values of freedom and life are universal and general precisely because they can inform all kinds of aspirations related to all types and forms of human interactions, institutions and forms of life which are defined as 'goods', as 'valuable'. Human relations based on equality and on the free and mutual recognition of persons are such goods; they are valuable, no matter whether they refer to relations between genders, friends, associates or citizens.[42]

Heller and Feher go on to point out that these universal value ideas of freedom and life are experienced by concrete modern individuals as a need for self-determination; a need which generates dissatisfaction, more or less clearly understood, with those aspects of one's inherited life-context encountered as a limit on one's own chosen projects. Dissatisfaction is, to Heller and Feher, central to a contemporary life experience: we live in a 'dissatisfied society'.

The Feher–Heller theory of a dissatisfied modernity is emphatically historical.[43] A dynamic modernity, which has left behind the closure, stability, fixity and contentment of traditional society and which breeds in us expectations and hopes which have set modern individuals on a restless chase after autonomy, self-development and celebrity. In precapitalist epochs, needs are strictly allocated and limited according to social hierarchies and their established norms of conduct. By contrast, the limitlessness of the modern structure of needs has placed an experience of dissatisfaction, which even the expanded provision of satisfiers will not quell, at the centre of a contemporary social experience.[44] Feher and Heller underline that modernity expands the structure of needs *as a whole*. The modern abstract values of freedom and life have played a pivotal role in universalising the need for self-determination and justice. These values feed omnipresent modern dissatisfaction just as much as commodities and scientific rationalism. A gnawing dissatisfaction at the inability to sate one's unlimited needs is, for Feher and Heller, central to the modern social experience.[45]

The idea that modernity has meant the universalisation of the values of freedom and life is construed by Heller and Feher from the evidence everywhere on our globe', of the dissatisfied need for self-determination and justice. Clearly, Feher and Heller are not among those who wish to deny the emancipatory achievements and potentials of the 'masternarratives' which have taken shape in modernity. On the one hand, the Feher–Heller diagnosis of the postmodern political condition grasps the barbarisms which have flowed from the pursuit of those modern 'masternarratives' according to which human history is 'progress' measured as a accumulation of freedoms. Yet, whatever the distortions generated by the restless dynamism of modernity, Feher and Heller reassert, against the push of some post-structuralist thinkers, that the emancipatory Enlightenment commitments of modernity to humanity, freedom and rationality and to the uniqueness of the individual personality cannot be reductively assimilated to a monolithic instrumental reason. As Grumley writes: 'For Feher and Heller this commitment underwrites both the unique regulative humanitarianism of modernity—its capacity to condemn its own barbarisms—and the modern individual's, bold desire to be judged not by local, provincial standards but to assert their unique individuality'.[46]

An insistence on the universalising status of Enlightenment commitments need not, however, be underpinned with the strong assertion that these aspirations are today recognised 'everywhere on our globe'. For my present purposes, all that needs to be said here is that *for those who recognise them*, these values are conferred with a unique universality. Those who dwell in postmodernity recognise the historio-cultural contingency of the value ideas born of Enlightenment hence also their fragile vulnerability. At the same time, however, for all those who recognise them, these values have come to acquire a universal status; the due of all 'everywhere on our globe' by virtue of their humanity. With this recognition that the normativity of the universalistic value commitments 'freedom' and 'life' cannot finally be evaded, comes also the responsibility to recognise only formal limits on the meaning with which these historically evolved value ideas can be construed.

According to Fraser and Nicholson, contemporary feminism's own credentials as a postmodernism are established by its vital participation in the critique of all attempts to ground modern 'masternarratives' in transcendental claims of various sorts; in traditional natural rights theory or in teleological constructions of the dynamic movement of human history towards some appointed goal. Yet, where Fraser and Nicholson discover that Lyotard's reflections on the meaning of postmodernism go too quickly from the premise that philosophy cannot ground social criticism to the conclusion that criticism itself must be local, *ad hoc* and non-theoretical, the Feher–Heller reading of the postmodern condition avoids the temptation to 'throw out the baby of large historical narrative with the bathwater of philosophical metanarrative'.[47] This latter interpretation, which insists on the continuing relevance to those dwelling in postmodernity of the 'large historical narratives' which have taken shape throughout modernity, has significant advantages for a feminism concerned to grapple within this climate of postmodernism.

The Feher–Heller account of postmodernity looks upon the defence of a reconstructed rationality as vital to the possibility of a democratic politics. 'Postmodernity' does not, to them, signal the defeat of rationalism as an ideal. It means, rather, a review of the nature of the grounds evoked in any claims about the rationality and justice of one's needs. For Feher and Heller, rationality needs to be understood as the capacity to 'give reasons' for why one's needs ought to be met even though they are not. 'A person whose needs are not met can be said to be rationally dissatisfied whenever his or her needs can be related to claims and thus justified by claims.'[48] The concept of rationality evoked here is very different from a philosophical conception of reason described in terms of the innate powers and capacities of a particular subject. 'Rationality' here describes a fragile, contingent historical institution: it refers to the character of relations between subjects in which unmet needs are raised as claims for which reasons are given.

The point here is that, if we wish to defend the ideal of cultural critique, we need to discover how our judgements might appeal to criteria which render the legitimacy of our claims communicable to others. If we seek to 'judge without criteria' we surrender that interest in defending the justice of our claims which is necessary to the practice of social criticism. The construction of rationality, seen as the capacity to give reasons for one's claims, does evoke the existence of a common currency of values through which need claims can be recognised and interpreted. This currency need not be metaphysical properties or innate anthropological traits but the immanent value reservoir of our own, contingent, halting and fragile historical self-creation. Such an account of the universality of value ideas in modernity in no way suggests a return to philosophical metanarrative. Moreover, as we have seen, to Heller and Feher, the universality of these values does not present itself through a perception of the 'shared meanings' of a common culture in any narrow, parochial sense. The universality of these value ideas is, on the contrary, deduced from the way in which the need for self-determination is seen to inform a huge range of diverse aspirations and is related to all forms of human interactions in modern society.

In what sense does the radical humanism proposed by Habermas and by Heller and Feher allow us to better understand the status of those universalising value claims constantly raised in feminist discourse itself? In both cases we see the concerted efforts of a 'post-metaphysical' humanism to preserve the ideals of humanism expressed in the ideas of a self-conscious life, authentic self-realisation and autonomy in terms which disassociate all such commitments from the will and aspirations of any particular social subject. In each case, these cultural ideals are seen to enjoin a commitment to the cause of radically non-coercive processes of communication and interaction between subjects. I am, however, not suggesting here that feminism should seek to understand the character of its own contribution to the meaning of contemporary humanism only in terms of any pre-existing formulations of humanist ideals. As we have seen, even those feminists who generally endorse the universalistic moral and political ambitions of Habermas' theory typically find in his own formulations unjustified assumptions about the character of politically qualified subjectivity. Through its own reflection upon these theoretical elaborations of the dilemmas of a 'post-metaphysical' humanism, contemporary feminism can, I suggest, achieve a sharper focus on the inevitable tension between the universalistic character of those value claims which, at least implicitly, inform its dissatisfactions at existing gender relations, and the always particularistic, culture-bound terms in which these universalistic ideals are encountered, communicated and contested.

Conclusion

Since the late 1970s, the idea of a homogeneous feminism united by the ideology of 'sisterhood' has come to be seen as an increasingly unrealisable and unattractive ideal. The motto of 'sisterhood', which had implied the desirability of a consensus over the main aims of the contemporary women's movement, has now been largely dropped by a movement which is today more alerted to the significance of the diverse experiences and aspirations of modern women. Within feminist theory, this new-found sensitivity to difference has been widely conceived as a challenge to the universalising spirit of humanism. Seen as the enemy to difference, humanism appears committed to a false homogenisation of the diverse experiences of modern women. Humanism has now been identified as an oppressive attempt to assimilate a monolithically conceived feminism into the wider category of 'humanity's cause'. Humanism is, then, widely regarded as an ideology antipathetic to the radicalism of a contemporary feminism concerned to gain public recognition for the significance of feminine difference. To the later Iris Young, the ideals of modern humanism appear politically passé:

> Humanist feminism, which predominated in the nineteenth century and in the contemporary women's movement until the late 1970s, finds in any assertion of difference between women and men only a legacy of female oppression and an ideology to legitimate continued exclusion of women from socially valued human activity.

> Humanist feminism is thus analogous to an ideal of assimilation in identifying sexual equality with gender blindness, with measuring women and men according to the same standards and treating them the same way. Indeed, for many feminists, androgyny names the ideal of sexual liberation—a society in which gender difference itself would be eliminated.[1]

I have attempted to show in this book that this sort of conception of the battle between feminism and modern humanism rests on a very one-sided construction of the nature of humanist ideals. Modern humanism does not merely raise the idea of the unity of the species; the idea that we might recognise in each other a common, shared humanity. Modern humanism clearly does assert that, beyond the constellation of contingencies which shape our particular affiliations and integrations, each individual has a primary status as a member of a common humanity. Yet modern humanism also, precisely by virtue of this recognition of the humanity of each individual, raises a principled commitment to the idea that each individual should be free to seek expression and development of their own sense of the uniqueness of their personality. As I argued in an earlier chapter, only in the presence of modern humanism's dynamic concept of person, described as that belief, ushered in by the Renaissance, 'in the unity of the human race and man's potential to perfect himself by his own efforts', is it possible to raise the value idea of a diversity of identities and to insist on the necessary recognition of a plurality of images of the good life.

The central claim raised in the book is that feminism is a humanism. The anti-humanist's attempt to establish that modern humanism is hostile to the principle of diversity and difference— that it insists on 'measuring women and men according to the same standards and treating them in the same way'—is an assessment which fails to recognise humanism's universalising claims as the underside of its own commitment to the idea of the unique difference of each personality. Each time a feminist theory raises, once called upon to account for its own motivations, a principled commitment to the idea of the autonomy, the unique and rightful diversity of feminine selves, it speaks in the language of humanist values.

Is it all, then, a case of mistaken identity? Do I ask only for a redescription of the character of the values evoked in anti-humanist feminisms? Does modern humanism now stand revealed as the 'good guy', waiting only for the persistent misconstructions of its benevolent attitude to end? Actually, no. This, I hope it is clear, is not my standpoint.

I have argued that a contemporary defence of humanism does not insist on the essential innocence of modern humanism. 'Radical humanism', as I have characterised it, recognises that modern humanism is pinned on a dilemma which invades its very core. It recognises that modern humanism is caught in a paradoxical relation between the universalistic character of its own aspirations and the always particularistic, culture-bound terms in which these universalising claims are raised. Radical humanism is, as we have seen, distinguished both by its determination to defend the ideals of modern humanism as contingent, historical values and by its efforts to grasp the consequences which this recognition of its historically contingent character might have for the 'cause' of modern humanism itself. For the radical humanism of, for example, Feher, Heller and Bernstein, allegiance to these universal value ideas neither prevents a deep questioning of the particularistic shape in which these historical forms appear nor does it prevent augmenting their meaning as new horizons are opened up by a range of contemporary social struggles.

Hence the argument has not been that feminism needs to simply 'come home' to any pre-existing formulations of the meaning of modern humanism. Mainstream formulations of humanist ideals can offer no home to a contemporary feminism struggling with questions of the difference and significance of being a woman in the modern world. Throughout the book, I have been particularly concerned to demonstrate the success of feminism's critique of the gendered, privileged character of those images of human subjectivity which underpin some of the major interpretations of the meaning of modern humanism. The affirmation of feminism's character as a particular dynamic interpretation of humanism means, however, that, despite the determination of its own challenge to the prejudiced character of those images of humanity and personhood that infiltrate modernity and its culture at every level, modern feminism should not lose sight of its own fundamental allegiances to the value ideas of modern humanism.

The self-recognition of feminism's own engagement with the ideals of modern humanism means, not only a challenge to existing formulations of these ideals but also serious implications for the ways in which we think about the character of contemporary feminism itself. Above all, the turn from an anti-humanist feminism would be inconceivable without a fundamental shift in the terms in which modernity and its achievements are assessed. The call for a recognition by contemporary feminism of its own dynamic engagement with the value commitments of modern humanism implies an appreciation of feminism's own character as a particular expression of the progressive potentials of modernity. If contemporary feminism sees in modern humanism only the cultural reflection of a modernity steeped in a phallocentric logic which insists on measuring men and women according to the same standards and treating them the same way, then feminist theory can only seek to underline its own radical alienation from the homogenising attitude articulated by modern humanism. The way in which feminist theory conceives its own character and role crucially turns, then, on whether it is prepared to grasp the nettle of its own status as an interpreter of modern humanism. If contemporary feminist theory persuades itself that it can have no dialogue with the formulations of humanist ideals which have rooted themselves (albeit in an incomplete, flawed and fragile form) in modern social life, then, it inevitably severs itself from a reflective, interpretative relationship with the sense of frustrated potentials and dissatisfied cultural needs which have, from the first, galvanised the modern women's movement.

How, then, does anti-humanist feminism seek to understand the nature and sources of the resistant consciousness to which it also gives expression? And what might be the consequences of this kind of self-interpretation? Chapter 3, which examined a certain trend to a Romantic self-interpretation in contemporary feminism, specifically attempted to address such questions. In this context, I looked at a particular image of feminism as an heroic refusal to enter into any communicative relation with the world of mundane, phallocentric conventions where women can only feel themselves 'wholly and permanently annihilated in a masculine order'. Here, and in a later chapter which investigated various conceptions of feminism and postmodernism, I argued that the temptation of an anti-humanist feminism to conceive itself as an advocate for the principle of feminine difference against the homogenising attitude of modern humanism actually means the production of a particular image of the nature of feminine difference. In this case, rebellious femininity is not understood as being preoccupied with how differently placed women might manage to transgress the boundaries of, and to confer new significance on, the diverse contexts they find themselves in. Subversion cannot, on this viewpoint, be seen as a matter of assessing the consequences of the particular ways in which I go about pursuing the questions: 'who am I?' and 'what difference does it make that I am a woman?'. Rather, 'subversion' is given the homogeneous meaning of heroic refusal to engage with the temptation to respond to any call to express who I am.

Against this image of a rebellious femininity, construed only as a refusal of the quest for self-realising subjectivity, Chapter 4, which looked at feminism's eventful relations with liberalism, identified an alternative attempt to construct the meaning of autonomous femininity. Here I sought to clarify further some of the dilemmas which beset anti-humanist feminism's search for a way of conceptualising feminine differences in terms which might evade homogenising humanist constructions of the image of autonomous subjectivity. In particular, I considered a major dilemma which confronts Pateman's critique of liberalism. Because Pateman is persuaded that all images of politically qualified subjectivity made available to the political culture of modern liberal democracies are predicated on the subordination of women, she is, finally, unable to find terms in which she can respond to her own question: what can autonomy mean for a citizen who is a woman? Again the perspective of anti-humanism (which discovers no progressive potentials locked within the husk of mainstream formulations of humanist ideals) blocks the possibility of an interpretative, dialogic relationship between feminist theory and the practical efforts constantly made by women themselves to confer new significance on these humanist value ideas. In the absence of this kind of communicative relationship with social practice, anti-humanist feminism is constantly tempted to supply its own, inevitably homogenising, constructions of the character of feminine difference.

Among the range of attempts to conceive an image of a subversive femininity, it seems that the motif of an ironic non-compliance with all descriptions of a feminine identity has gained ground against, for example, conceptions of a rebellious femininity modelled after the idea of a 'return of the feminine repressed'. The limits of this image of heroic irony have been commented on in the main body of the book. At this point, I simply want to draw attention to what is missing from this image of feminine resistance. The ironic gesture is an explicitly anti-utopian gesture which is, I suggest, based more on a problematic understanding of the character of the processes of modern socialisation than on a sober appreciation of the practical impossibility of achieving significant, transformative changes in our sociocultural contexts.

The image of a self in a relation of non-compliant, ironic alienation from the ascribed meaning of its sociocultural context signals a conviction that there can be no creative appropriation of the meaning of our contingent life circumstances. The quest for authenticity, for self-realisation, is seen to be hopelessly deluded: all attempts at communicating who we are are inevitably alienated in the normalising grid of a monolithic, phallocentric culture. Ascribed social roles are, it seems, viewed as more or less stable, prepackaged descriptions which confront each individual as his or her alienating limit. Yet this strategy of the ironic gesture itself presupposes a culture which recognises authenticity and creative self-realisation as a fundamental value. The ironic gesture is not meant for the player alone: it communicates by its overdrawn, playful unseriousness, the serious conviction that this actor holds his or her potentials as very inadequately captured by the norms and typologies described by any definitional constructions of the self. Implicit in the strategy of the ironic gesture we see, then, the evocation of the values of authenticity and self-realisation. Given this unacknowledged commitment, the strategy of the ironic gesture is, finally, a very weak, limited one. Basing itself on a conception of socialisation understood as the appropriation by individuals of fixed social descriptions whose images of the self are hermetically sealed traps for the unwary, the strategy of heroic irony refuses to engage in that task of participating in the process of protest at, and creative reinterpretation of, imposed images of femininity which has, from the beginning, driven the modern women's movement.

Carol Lee Bacchi seems to think that feminism should not be tempted into a preoccupation with the politics of personal identity. In her view, 'perceiving issues in terms of women's sameness to or difference from men diverts attention from the inadequacy of social institutions. Focusing upon this question is, therefore, politically unwise.'[2] The point I wish to make is somewhat different. It is, as I see it, 'politically unwise' to seek to introduce any kind of limitation into a consideration of the kinds of issues and concerns which can be appropriately raised by feminism today. In recent feminist discussions the questions: what is a woman? and, how is a woman different from a man? have provoked lively debate and wide interest. This new level of interest in the politics of gender identity is particularly evident in an increased preoccupation with the question of the cultural production and signification of feminine bodies. The politics of gender identity are, then, among the leading concerns for feminist theory today and, unlike Bacchi, I suggest that such concerns are very legitimate. To my mind, problems only surface if a feminism of difference contrives to see itself as the true advocate of the principle of feminine difference against a false, humanist attempt to construct the essential sameness of men and women. In this case, the question: what is a woman? can only be answered in terms of reifying, homogenising images of feminine difference.

I have throughout the book tried to highlight the perils of this kind of attempt to speak on behalf of a marginalised, repressed femininity conceived as a principled opposition to the false totalisations of a humanist ideology. The main point I want to highlight here is that, if the ideals of humanism are taken to be reducible to a mere advocacy of women's sameness with men, then 'women's difference' will tend to be construed in reified terms as a principled opposition to the homogenising, totalising logic of modern humanism. I suggest that questions such as 'how is a woman different from a man?' need to be grasped as a contemporary participation in the reconstitution of the ideals of modern humanism. Only if questions about the difference of feminine identities are conceived, explicitly, as articulations and interpretations of the value ideas of modern humanism (in terms namely, of the idea of the moral autonomy of each individual and the notion of authentic self-realisation) do they move firmly out of the terrain of reified cultural descriptions of an essential femininity. Seen as the articulation of the value ideas of modern humanism, the question of the particularity of feminine selves resolves into the question; what have women themselves sought to make of the contingency of their found social and cultural contexts?

At this juncture, I have referred to one major consequence which an unequivocal recognition of its own character as a dynamic interpretation of modern humanism might have for the self-understanding of feminist theory. A contemporary feminism which affirms its own character as an articulation and interpretation of historically acquired humanist values does not feel itself called upon to supply an image of feminine difference against an homogenising humanist culture. Women's difference appears, on this perspective, as a matter of the diverse attempts made by women themselves to respond to the question: 'who am I, being a woman in the modern world?'. And, in this case, feminist theory undertakes to reflect upon the consequences and to elaborate on the significance of a plurality of representative attempts to find ways of answering this still insistent question.

I have already attempted to establish that feminism *is* a humanism. It offers a distinctive set of interpretations of these historically evolved value ideas and stands as an index to their practical force. Historically, feminism has extended and added new meaning to the idea of the civil rights of all individuals, it has qualitatively expanded our understanding of the character of publicly significant human needs and enriched our sense of the many-sided uniqueness of each human personality. The openness of modern humanism to new historical contents generated by diverse social struggles has conferred humanism with the elasticity and vitality which has enabled it to hold out against the choking grip of that instrumentalising rationality and brutal indifference which has also characterised the modern world. I suggest, then, that only by explicitly and proudly affirming its own humanist commitments can contemporary feminism seek to secure those diverse institutionalised and cultural conditions which it, at least implicitly, recognises as necessary to its own reproduction and development as a modern social movement.

Notes

Introduction

1 Bernstein, R., *The New Constellation: The Ethical-political Horizons of Modernity/Postmodernity*, The MIT Press, Cambridge, Massachusetts and London, England, 1992, p. 2
2 Heller, A., *The Power of Shame: A Rational Perspective*, Routledge and Kegan Paul, London, 1985, p. 303
3 ibid., p. 303

Chapter 1

1 De Beauvoir, S., *The Second Sex*, Penguin Books, UK, 1972, p. 29
2 Harding, S., *The Science Question in Feminism,* Open University Press, UK, 1986, p 15
3 Soper, K., 'Feminism, Humanism and Postmodernism', *Radical Philosophy*, 55, Summer 1990, pp. 11–17
4 ibid., p. 11.
5 Heidegger, M., 'Letter on Humanism', *Martin Heidegger Basic Writings*, Krell, D. F. (ed.), Routledge and Kegan Paul, London and Henley, 1978
6 Vattimo, G., *The End of Modernity*, The Johns Hopkins University Press, Baltimore, 1991
7 See Lacoue-Labarthe, P., *Heidegger: Art and Politics,* Blackwell, Oxford, 1990
8 Bernstein, R., *The New Constellation: The Ethical/Political Horizons of Modernity/Postmodernity*, The MIT Press, Cambridge, Massachusetts and London, England, 1992, p. 104

141

9 Lacoue-Labarthe, P., *Heidegger: Art and Politics*, Blackwell, Oxford, 1990, p. 95

10 Hindess, B., 'Heidegger and the Nazis: Cautionary Tales of the Relations Between Theory and Practice', *Thesis Eleven*, 31, 1992, pp. 115–31

11 Ferry, L. and Renaut, A., *Heidegger and Modernity*, University of Chigago Press, Chicago, 1990, p. 1

12 ibid., p. 1

13 Heller, A. and Feher, F., *The Grandeur & Twilight of Radical Universalism*, Transaction Publishers, New Brunswick, New Jersey, 1991, p. 562

14 ibid. and also Bernstein, R., *The New Constellation: The Ethical-Political Horizons of Modernity/Postmodernity*, op. cit.; Habermas, J., *Postmetaphysical Thinking: Philosophical Essays*, The MIT Press, Cambridge, Massachusetts, London, England, 1992 and Benhabib, S., *Situating the Self: Gender, Community and Postmodernism in Contemporary Ethics*, Polity Press, Cambridge, 1992

15 See Habermas, J., *Postmetaphysical Thinking*, op. cit.

16 See Heller, A., *Renaissance Man*, Routledge and Kegan Paul, London, 1978, see especially 'Introduction: Is there a "Renaissance ideal of man"?'

17 Fromm, E., 'Introduction' to *Socialist Humanism: An International Symposium*, Fromm, E. (ed.), Doubleday and Company, USA, 1965, p. viii

18 Heller, A., *Renaissance Man*, op. cit. p. 1

19 ibid., p. 4

20 ibid., p. 9

21 ibid., p. 18

22 ibid., p. 53

23 See Heller, A., and Feher, F., *The Postmodern Political Condition*, Polity Press, Cambridge, 1988, Chapter 2; Heller, A., 'Modernity's Pendulum', *Thesis Eleven*, no. 31, 1992, pp. 1–13

24 Heller, A., 'Modernity's Pendulum', op. cit., p. 3

25 Feher, F., 'Between Relativism and Fundamentalism', in Heller, A. and Feher, F., *The Grandeur and Twilight of Radical Universalism*, Transaction Publishers, New Jersey, 1991, p. 562

26 Chapter 5 considers aspects of Habermas' response to the dilemma of contemporary humanism. Chapter 6 looks more closely at the views of Feher and Heller

27 See McCarthy, T., 'Introduction' to Habermas, J., *The Philosophical Discourse of Modernity*, The MIT Press, Cambridge, Massachusetts, 1987, p. viii

28 Fraser, N., 'Michel Foucault: A "Young Conservative"?,' *Unruly Practices: Power, Discourse and Gender in Contemporary Social Theory*, University of Minnesota Press, Minneapolis, 1989, p. 43

29 McCarthy, T., 'Introduction' to Habermas, J., *The Philosophical Discourse of Modernity*, op. cit., p. x.

30 ibid., p. x

31 See, for example, the critique developed by Lloyd, G., *The Man of Reason: 'Male' and 'Female' in Western Philosophy,* Methuen and Co., London, 1984

32 ibid., p. 101

33 ibid., p. 101

34 Grosz, E., 'Feminism and Anti-Humanism', *Discourse and Difference: Post-Structuralism, Feminism and the Moment of History,* in Milner, A. and Worth, C., *Centre For General and Comparative Literature,* Monash University, Melbourne, 1990, pp. 63–75; 71 and 72

35 ibid., p. 72

36 Grosz, E., 'Conclusion: A Note on Essentialism and Difference', *Feminist Knowledge: Critique and Construct,* Gunew S. (ed.), Routledge, London and New York, pp. 332–344, 340

37 Fuss, D.J., ' "Essentially Speaking": Luce Irigaray's Language of Essence', *Hypathia,* vol. 3., no. 3, winter 1989, pp. 62–80

38 ibid., p. 68

39 Haraway, D., 'Ecce Homo, Ain't (Ar'n't) I a Woman, and Inappropriate/d Others: The Human in a Post-Humanist Landscape', *Feminists Theorise The Political,* Butler, J., and Scott, J.W. (eds), Routledge, New York, London, 1992, p. 86

40 Cixous, H., 'The Laugh of the Medusa' *New French Feminisms: An Anthology,* Marks, E. and de Courtivron I. (eds), The Harvester Press, Sussex, 1981, pp. 245–64; p. 256

41 Scott, J., 'Deconstructing Equality Versus Difference: Or the Uses of Post-Structuralist Theory For Feminism', *Conflicts in Feminism,* Hirsch, M. and Keller, E. F. (eds), Routledge, New York and London, 1990, p. 134

42 See Weedon, C., *Feminist Practice and Post-Structuralist Theory,* Basil Blackwell, Oxford, 1987, p. 21

43 ibid., p. 21

44 Fox-Genovese, E., *Feminism Without Illusions: A Critique of Individualism,* University of North Carolina Press, Chapel Hill and London, 1991, p. 19

45 ibid., p. 19

46 Grosz, E., 'Conclusion: A Note on Essentialism and Difference', *Feminist Knowledge: Critique and Construct,* Gunew, S. (ed.), op. cit.

47 Barrett, M., *The Politics of Truth: From Marx to Foucault,* Polity Press, Cambridge, 1991, p. 89

48 See, for example, Fox-Genovese, E., *Feminism Without Illusions,* op. cit.; Soper, K., 'Feminism, Humanism and Postmodernism', op. cit.; Benhabib, S., *Situating the Self: Gender, Community and Postmodernism in Contemporary Ethics,* op. cit.

49 Benhabib, S., *Situating the Self,* op. cit. p. 2

50 ibid., p. 2

51 Cixous, H., 'The Laugh of the Medusa', op. cit., p. 256

52 See, for example, Butler, J., *Gender Trouble: Feminism and the Subversion of Identity,* Routledge, New York and London, 1992

53 See especially Chapter 3 on the feminist appropriation of Romanticism

Chapter 2

1 See, for example, Jardine, A., *Gynesis: Configurations of Women and Modernity,* Cornell University Press, New York, 1985; Hekman, S., *Gender and Knowledge,* Polity Press, Cambridge, 1990; Flax, J., 'Post-modernism and Gender Relations in Feminist Theory', in *Feminism/Postmodernism,* Nicholson L. (ed.), Routledge, London and New York, 1990, pp. 39–63

2 Harding, S., 'Feminism, Science and the Anti-Enlightenment Critiques', in *Feminism /Postmodernism,* Nicholson, L. (ed.), op. cit., pp. 83–106, p. 99

3 Lovibond, S., 'Feminism and Post-Modernism', *New Left Review,* vol. 178, November/December 1989, pp. 5–29

4 Kant, I., 'What is Enlightenment?', Beck, L.W. (trans), *Kant on History,* Beck. L.W. (ed.), Bobbs-Merril Educational Publishing, Indianapolis, 1963, p. 3

5 See Jacob, M.C., *The Radical Enlightenment: Pantheists, Freemasons and Republicans,* Allen and Unwin, London, 1981. Jacob offers a very illuminating account of the diversity of intellectual trends at play throughout the eighteenth century.

6 Jardine, A., *Gynesis: Configurations of Women and Modernity,* op. cit., p. 20

7 Hekman, S.J., *Gender and Knowledge: Elements of a Post-modern Feminism,* op. cit., p. 1

8 ibid., p. 5

9 ibid., p. 9

10 Flax, J., 'Post-Modernism and Gender Relations in Feminist Theory', in *Feminism/Post-modernism,* Nicholson, L. (ed.), op. cit. p. 42

11 ibid., p. 43

12 See, for example, Grosz, E., 'Feminism and Anti-Humanism', *Discourse and Difference,* Milner and Worth (eds), op. cit.

13 Harding S., 'Feminism, Science and Anti-Enlightenment Critiques', in *Feminism/Post-Modernism,* Nicholson L.(ed.), op. cit., p. 99

14 Gay, P., *The Enlightenment: An Interpretation: The Rise of Modern Paganism,* vol. 1., Alfred Knopf, New York, 1966, p. 174

15 Cassirer, E., T*he Philosophy of the Enlightenment,* Beacon Press, Boston, 1951, p. 13

16 See D'Alembert, J., *Introduction to Preliminary Discourse on the Encyclopaedia of Diderot,* Bobbs-Merrill Educational Publishing, Indianapolis, 1963, p. xxxv

17 Cassirer, E., *The Philospohy of the Enlightenment,* op. cit., p. 13

18 I borrow this interpretation from an analysis developed by Gyorgy Markus in his 'Society of Culture: The Constitution of Cultural Modernity', transcript of an unpublished paper presented to *Thesis Eleven* Conference, Melbourne, August 1991

19 ibid.

20 Bauman, Z., *Legislators and Interpreters: On Modernity, Postmodernity and Intellectuals,* Polity Press, Cambridge, 1987

21 Márkus, G., 'Society of Culture: The Constitution of Cultural Modernity', op. cit.

22 Jacob, M. C., *The Radical Enlightenment: Pantheists, Freemasons and Republicans,* op. cit., p. 104

23 Diderot, D., *The Encyclopaedia,* Grendzier (trans. and ed.) Harper Torchbooks, New York, p. 97

24 Rousseau, J., *Emile,* Everyman, 1969

25 Luhmann, N., *Love as Passion: The Codification of Intimacy,* Polity Press, Cambridge, 1986, p. 99

26 See Spenser, S. (ed.), *French Women and The Age of Enlightenment,* Indiana University Press, Indiana, 1984, p. 98

27 See Jacob, M., *The Radical Enlightenment: Panthesists, Freemasons and Republicans,* op. cit.

28 Fox-Genovese, E., 'Property and Patriarchy in Classical Bourgeois Political Theory', *Radical History Review,* vol. 4, nos 2–3, 1977

29 Astell, M., *A Serious Proposal to the Ladies,* 1696 reprint, Source Books Press, New York

30 Astell, M., quoted in Smith, H., *Reason's Disciples: Seventeeth Century Feminists,* University of Illinois Press, Illinois, 1982, p. 63

31 Astell, M., *Reflections Upon Marriage* (1700); No pagination. Quoted in Mitchell, J., 'Women and Equality', *Feminism and Equality,* Phillips, A. (ed.), Blackwell, Oxford 1987, p. 31

32 See, for example, Luhman, N., *Love As Passion,* op. cit., p. 94

33 See Perry, R., *The Celebrated Mary Astell: An Early English Feminist,* University of Chicago Press, Chicago, 1986, pp. 79–80

34 Wollstonecraft, M., *A Vindication of the Rights of Woman,* The Norton Library, New York, 1967, p. 58

35 ibid., pp. 82–3

36 ibid., p. 122

37 ibid., p.122

38 Vogel, U., 'Rationalism and Romanticism: Two Strategies For Women's Liberation', *Feminism and Political Theory,* Evans, J. et al. (eds), Sage 1986, pp. 31–2

39 Condorcet, 'On the Admission of Women to the Rights of Citizenship', *Condorcet: Selected Writings,* Baker, K.M. (ed.), Bobbs-Merril Educational Publishing, Indianapolis, 1976, pp. 97–8

40 Reiss, T., 'Revolution in Bounds: Wollstonecraft, Women and Reason', in *Gender and Theory: Dialogues on Feminist Criticism,* Kauffman, L. (ed.), Blackwell, Oxford, 1989, pp. 11–51, p. 21

41 See, for example, passages from *A Vindication of the Rights of Women,* pp. 43 and 110. Norton and Company edn, 1967.

42 ibid., p. 110

43 ibid., p. 92

44 ibid., p. 115

45 Hazard, P., *European Thought in the Eighteenth Century,* Hollis and Carter, London, 1954, preface p. xvviii

46 See Márkus, G., 'Concepts of Ideology in Marx', *Canadian Journal Of Political and Social Theory,* vol. 7, nos. 1–2, 1983, p. 86ff

47 ibid., p. 86

48 Rendall, J., *The Origins of Modern Feminism,* Macmillan, London, 1985

49 Habermas, J., 'Modernity versus Post-modernity', *New German Critique*, no. 22, winter 1981, pp. 3–15, p. 9

50 Bauman, Z., *Legislators and Interpreters: On Modernity, Postmodernity and Intellectuals*, Polity Press, Cambridge, 1987, p. 191

51 See Adorno, T. W. and Horkheimer, M., *Dialectic of Enlightenment*, Allen Lane, London, 1973

52 Habermas, J., 'The Entwinement of Myth and Enlightenment: Rereading Dialectic of Enlightenment', *New German Critique*, no. 26, summer/spring 1982, p. 18

53 See Grumley, J., *History and Totality; Radical Historicism from Hegel to Foucault*, Routledge, London and New York, 1989, p. 214

54 Foucault, M., 'What is Enlightenment?' *The Foucault Reader*, Rabinow P. (ed.), Random House, New York, 1984, pp. 32–51

55 ibid., p. 42

56 ibid., p. 50

57 Kant, I., 'What is Enlightenment?', op. cit., p. 10

58 ibid., p. 15

59 Márkus, G., 'Concepts of Ideology in Marx', op. cit., p. 86

60 ibid., p. 86

61 See Márkus, M., 'Women, Success and Civil Society: Submission to, or Subversion of, the Achievement Principle', *Feminism As Critique:Essays on the Politics of Gender in Late-Capitalist Societies*, Benhabib S. and Cornell, D., Polity Press, Cambridge, 1987, pp. 96–110

Chapter 3

1 Vogel, U., 'Rationalism and Romanticism: Two Strategies For Women's Liberation', *Feminism and Political Theory*, Evans, J. *et al.* (eds), Sage Publications, 1986 p. 109

2 Cassirer, E., *The Philosophy of the Enlightenment*, Beacon Press, Boston, 1951, pp. 197–8

3 Lovejoy, A. O., *The Great Chain of Being: A Study in the History of an Idea*, Harper Torchbook Edition, New York, 1960

4 Peckham, M., *The Triumph of Romanticism*, University of South Carolina Press, South Carolina, 1970, p. 8

5 ibid., p. 14

6 ibid., p. 39

7 ibid., p. 39

8 See Wilson, J. D., *The Romantic Heroic Ideal*, Louisiana State University Press, USA, 1982, p. 12

9 See Peckham, M., T*he Triumph of Romanticism*, op. cit., p. 31

10 Rousseau, J. J., *Confessions* (Paris 1897), cited in Wilson, J. D., *The Romantic Heroic Ideal*, op. cit. pp. 1–2

11 See Rosenblum, N., *Another Liberalism: Romanticism and the Reconstruction of Liberal Thought*, Harvard University Press, Cambridge, Mass. and London, 1987, p. 2

12 ibid., p. 40

13 Taylor, C., *Sources of the Self: The Making of the Modern Identity*, Harvard University Press, Cambridge, Mass. and London, England, 1989, p. 375

14 See Richardson, A., 'Romanticism and the Colonisation of the Feminine' and Ross, M. B., 'Troping Masculine Power in the Crisis of Poetic Identity', in *Romanticism and Feminism*, Mellor, A. K. (ed.), Indiana University Press, 1988; see also Jacobus, M., *Romanticism, Writing and Sexual Difference*, Claredon University Press, Oxford, 1980

15 Wordsworth, W., *The Prelude*, Oxford University Press, Oxford, 1933, p. 211–13

16 Wordsworth, W., *The Prelude*, cited in Richardson, A., 'Romanticism and the Colonisation of the Feminine', in *Romanticism and Feminism*, Mellor, A. (ed.), op. cit., p. 18

17 Ross, M., 'Troping Masculine Power in the Crisis of Poetic Identity', *Romanticism and Feminism*, Mellor, A. (ed.), op. cit.

18 I am adopting a different interpretation here from the reading suggested by Ursula Vogel in her 'Rationalism and Romanticism: Two Strategies For Women's Liberation', in *Feminism and Political Theory*, Evans, J. *et al.* (eds), op. cit.

19 Schlegel, F., *Lucinde*, University of Minnesota Press, Minneapolis, 1971

20 Schlegel, F., *Theorie der Weiblichkeit*, Insel Verlag FAM, 1982, p. 140 (my translation)

21 Firchow, P., 'Introduction' to Schlegel's *Lucinde*, op. cit.

22 Jacobus, M., *Romanticism, Writing and Sexual Difference*, op. cit.

23 ibid., p. 206. See also Rabine, L., 'Feminist Writers in French Romanticism', *Studies in Romanticism*, no. 4, Fall 1977, pp. 491–509. Rabine points out that for Julia Kristeva, the Romantics posit the feminine as the 'polymorphous, spasmic, desiring, and laughing body' essential to those efforts on the symbolic level to isolate the principle of a Law—one, sublimating, transcendent, guarantee of the ideal interest of the community.

24 Wordsworth, W., *The Prelude*, p. vii., cited in Jacobus, M., ibid., p. 213

25 ibid., p. 208

26 ibid., p. 209

27 ibid., p. 223

28 Cited in Peckham, M., *The Triumph of Romanticism*, op.cit. p. 21

29 I have borrowed this formulation from the unpublished transcript of György Márkus's paper 'A Society of Culture: The Constitution of Modernity' presented at the Melbourne *Thesis Eleven* conference, Sociology Department, University of Melbourne, August 1991

30 Schlegel, F., *Kritische Aufgabe*, vol. 2, p. 319, cited in Habermas, J., *The Philosophical Discourse of Modernity*, Polity Press, Cambridge, 1987, p. 90

31 Peckham, M., *The Triumph of Romanticism*, op. cit., p. 38

32 ibid., p. 38

33 Schmitt, C., *Political Romanticism*, Oakes, G. (trans.), The MIT Press, Cambridge, Massachusetts, 1986, p. xx
34 ibid., p. xviii
35 ibid.
36 Butler, J., *Gender Trouble: Feminism and the Subversion of Identity*, Routledge, New York and London, 1990
37 ibid., p. 33
38 Jardine, A., *Gynesis: Configurations of Women and Modernity*, Cornell University Press, New York, 1985
39 ibid., p. 25
40 ibid., p. 48
41 Butler, J., *Gender Trouble: Women and the Subversion of Identity*, op. cit., p. 18
42 Grosz, E., *Sexual Subversions: Three French Feminisms*, Allen and Unwin, Sydney, 1989, p. 118
43 Fuss, D., 'Essentially Speaking: Luce Irigaray's Language of Essence', *Hypatia*, vol. 3, winter 1989, p. 68
44 Irigaray, L., 'This Sex Which Is Not One', *New French Feminisms*, Marks, E., and de Courtivron, I. (eds), The Harvester Press, Sussex, 1981, p. 103
45 Cixous, H., 'The Laugh of the Medusa', *New French Feminisms*, op. cit., p. 257
46 Fuss, D., 'Essentially Speaking: Luce Irigaray and the Language of Essence', op. cit., p. 68
47 Irigaray, L., 'Women's Exile', *Ideology and Consciousness*, 1, 1977, p. 68
48 See Simmel, G., *The Sociology of Georg Simmel*, (ed.) Wolff. K. H. as cited in Izenberg, G. N., *Impossible Individuality: Romanticism, Revolution, and the Origins of Modern Selfhood 1787–1802*, Princeton University Press, Princeton, New Jersey, 1992, p. 4–5
49 ibid., p. 4
50 Simmel, G., *The Sociology of Georg Simmel*, cited in Izenberg, G., ibid., p. 4
51 ibid., p. 5
52 Habermas J, *Postmetaphysical Thinking*, op. cit., pp. 149–205
53 ibid., p. 164
54 ibid., p. 83
55 Forging a conception of the self along these kind of lines has become a main theme in the work of, for example, Jessica Benjamin in her *The Bonds of Love: Psychoanalysis, Feminism and the Problem of Domination*, Pantheon Books, New York, 1988; Seyla Benhabib in *Situating The Self*, op. cit. and Agnes Heller in her *The Postmodern Political Condition*, op. cit.

Chapter 4

1 Pateman, C., *The Sexual Contract*, Polity Press, Cambridge, 1988

2 Mouffe., C., 'American Liberalism and its Critics: Rawls, Taylor, Snadel and Walzer', *Praxis International*, vol. 8. no. 2, July 1988, pp. 193–206

3 Okin, S. M., *Women in Western Political Thought*, Virago, London, 1979

4 See Mill, J. S., 'The Subjection of Women', *John Stuart Mill and Harriet Taylor Mill Essays on Sex Equality*, Rossi, A. S. (ed.), University of Chicago Press, Chicago and London, 1970, p. 191

5 ibid., p. 190

6 ibid., p. 191

7 ibid., p. 166

8 ibid., p. 190

9 Okin, S. M., *Justice, Gender and the Family*, Basic Books Inc., New York, 1989, p. 61

10 Eisenstein, Z., *The Radical Future of Liberal Feminism*, Longman, New York and London, 1981, p. 4

11 Goldman, E., 'The Tragedy of Woman's Emancipation', *Anarchism and Other Essays*, Dover Publications, Inc., New York, 1969, pp. 213–25

12 ibid., p. 214

13 Jordan, J., 'Declaration of an Independence I Would Just As Soon Not Have', *Civil Wars*, Beacon Press, Boston, 1981, pp. 115–21, p.102 cited in Di Stefanano, C., 'Dilemmas of Difference: Feminism, Modernity, and Postmodernism', *Feminism/Postmodernism*, Nicholson, L. (ed.) Routledge, New York and London, 1990

14 Okin, S. M. 'Humanist Liberalism', *Liberalism and the Moral Life*, in Rosenblum, N. L. (ed.), Harvard University Press, Cambridge Massachusetts, 1989

15 ibid., p. 41

16 Pateman, C., *The Sexual Contract*, Polity Press, Cambridge, 1988, p. 10

17 ibid., p. 11

18 ibid., p. 91

19 Noddings, N., *Caring: A Feminine Approach to Ethics and Moral Education*, University of California Press, Berkley and London, 1984

20 Okin, S. M., *Justice, Gender and the Family*, op. cit., p. 15; O'Niell, O., 'Friends of Difference', *London Review of Books*, 14 September 1989, pp. 20–1

21 See McMillan, *Women, Reason and Nature: Some Philosophical Problems with Feminism*, Basil Blackwell, Oxford, 1982

22 O'Niell, O., 'Friends of Difference', *London Review of Books*, 14 September 1989, pp. 20–1

23 Pateman, C., *The Sexual Contract*, op. cit., p. 231

24 See Walzer, M., *Spheres of Justice: A Defence of Pluralism and Equality*, Basic Books Inc., New York, 1983

25 See Okin, S. M., *Justice, Gender and the Family*, op. cit.; Rosenblum, N., *Another Liberalism: Romanticism and the Reconstruction of Liberal Thought*, Harvard University Press, Cambridge, Mass. and London, England, 1987

26 Communitarianism has been described thus: 'It involves an attempt to recapture political control in local communities, to reconstruct the social basis to support stable family structures, i.e., to provide a totalising context for social existence and personal identity. It could be characterised as a "will to overcome" the overbearing reality of a normless isolation in mass society—a reality often attributed to rise of liberalism and secularism and the resulting supremacy of individual rights over the "common good" '. Anderson, K., Piccone, P., Siegel, F., Taves, M., 'Roundtable on Communitarianism', *Telos*, no. 76, summer 1988, p. 2

27 MacIntyre, A., *After Virtue: A Study in Moral Theory*, Duckworth, London, 1981

28 ibid.

29 Walzer, M., *Spheres of Justice*, op. cit., p. 19

30 Mouffe, C., 'American Liberalism and its Critics', *Praxis International*, vol. 8, no. 2, 1988, pp. 193–206

31 See Rosenblum, N., *Another Liberalism: Romanticism and the Reconstruction of Liberal Thought*, op. cit.

32 ibid., p. 178

33 Okin, S. M., *Justice, Gender and the Family*, op. cit., p. 112

34 See Mouffe, C., 'American Liberalism and its Critics: Rawls, Taylor, Sandel and Walzer', *Praxis International*, op. cit., p. 193

35 ibid.

36 Okin, S. M., *Justice, Gender and the Family*, op. cit., p. 115

37 Walzer, M., *Spheres of Justice: A Defence of Pluralism and Equality*, op. cit., p. xiii

38 Honneth, A., 'The Limits of Liberalism: On the Political–Ethical Discussion on Communitarianism', *Thesis Eleven*, no. 28, 1991

39 Pateman, C., *The Disorder of Women: Democracy, Feminism and Political Theory*, Polity Press, Cambridge, 1989, p. 14

40 ibid., p. 234

41 'The most profound and complex problem for political theory and practice is how the two bodies of humankind and feminine and masculine individuality can be fully incorporated into political life.' *The Disorder of Women; Feminism and Political Theory*, Polity Press, Cambridge, 1989

42 ibid., p.14

43 See Young, I., 'Impartiality and the Civic Public: Some Implications of Feminist Critiques of Moral and Political Theory' and Benhabib, S., 'The Generalised and the Concrete Other: The Kohlberg–Gilligan Controversy and Feminist Theory', in *Feminism as Critique*, Benhabib S. and Cornell, D. (eds), op. cit.

44 Benhabib, S., 'The Generalised and the Concrete Other', op. cit., p. 95

45 Young, I. M., 'Impartiality and the Civic Public: Some Implications of Feminist Critiques of Moral and Political Theory', in *Feminism As Critique*, Benhabib and Cornell (eds), op. cit., pp. 56–77

46 See Noddings, N., *Caring: A Feminine Approach to Ethics and Moral Education*, op. cit.

47 See McMillan, C., *Women, Reason and Nature: Some Philosophical Problems*, op. cit.

48 See Gilligan, C., *In A Different Voice: Psychological Theory and Women's Development*, op. cit.; Márkus M., 'Women, Success and Civil Society: Submission to, or Subversion of, the Achievement Principle' and Benhabib, S., 'The Generalised and the Concrete Other', in *Feminism As Critique*, Benhabib, S. and Cornell D. (eds), op. cit.

49 Márkus, M., 'Women, Success and Civil Society: Submission to, or Subversion of, the Achievement Principle', op. cit., p. 97

Chapter 5

1 See Eisenstein, Z., 'Developing A Theory of Capitalist Patriarchy', in *Capitalist Patriarchy and the Case For Socialist Feminism*, Eisenstein, Z. (ed.), Monthly Review Press, 1979 and Rowbotham, S., 'The Women's Movement and Organising For Socialism' in *Beyond The Fragments: Feminism and the Making of Socialism*, Rowbotham, S., *et al*, (eds), Merlin Press, London, 1979

2 See, for example, Hartmann, H., 'The Unhappy Marriage of Marxism and Feminism: Towards a More Progressive Union', *Women and Revolution*, Sargeant, L. (ed.), South End Press, UK, 1981; O'Brien M., *The Politics of Reproduction*, Routledge and Kegan Paul, Boston, London and Henley, 1981

3 See Benhabib, S., *Situating the Self: Gender, Community and Postmodernism in Contemporary Ethics*, Polity Press, Cambridge, 1992

4 Eisenstein, Z., 'Developing A Theory of Capitalist Patriarchy', in *Capitalist Patriarchy and the Case for Socialist Feminism*, Eisenstein, Z. (ed.), op. cit.; Rowbotham, S., 'The Women's Movement and Organising For Socialism', in *Beyond the Fragments: Feminism and the Making of Socialism*, Rowbotham, S. *et al*, (eds), op.cit.

5 Eisenstein, Z., ibid., p. 7

6 ibid., p. 9

7 It is not my objective in this discussion to contest the 'truth' of the Marx interpretations being recounted. The point is only to chart the fate of an early feminist appropriation of humanism. It is, perhaps, worth noting, however, the controversial character of this anthropologised reading of Marx. Eisenstein's formulation of the theory of alienation evokes a philosophical anthropology which Marx, himself, explicitly rejects from the time of the *German Ideology*. Marx's humanism categorically rejects the reduction of humanity to some purely 'natural' basis; he constantly reiterated the view that human essence and human activity are essentially historical: that 'man makes himself in history'. See Márkus, G., *Marxism and Anthropology*, Van Gorcum and Co., The Netherlands, 1978. Márkus elaborates an account of the historicising character of Marx's humanism.

8 ibid., p. 9

9 See Márkus, G., *Marxism and Anthropology*, Van Gorcum and Co., The Netherlands, 1978. Here Márkus offers an elaborated account of the historicising character of Marx's humanism.

10 Hartmann, H., 'The Unhappy Marriage of Marxism and Feminism', *Women and Revolution*, Sargeant, L. (ed.), op. cit., p. 52

11 Young, I. M., 'Beyond the Unhappy Marriage', *Women and Revolution*, Sargeant L., op. cit., p. 52

12 O'Brien, M., 'Reproducing Marxist Man', in Clark, L. and Lange, L. (eds), *The Sexism of Social and Political Theory*, University of Toronto Press, Toronto, 1979, p. 114, cited by Nicholson, L., 'Feminism and Marx', op. cit., p. 27
    This reading is challenged by others like Márkus for whom production is also a process of consumption of those products which embody definite culturally acquired skills and abilities. And to conceive production as a process of consumption embodying certain cultural acquisitions and skills means that their replenishment or reproduction appear as an essential theme within the paradigm of production. See Márkus, G., *Marxism and Anthropology*, op. cit.

13 See, for example, Benhabib, S., *Situating the Self: Gender, Community and Postmodernism in Contemporary Ethics*, Polity Press, Cambridge, 1992. (See especially the standpoint adopted in the Introduction, pp. 1–32.)

14 Benhabib, S. and Cornell, D., 'Introduction', *Feminism As Critique*, op. cit., p. 2

15 See Young, I. M., 'Impartiality and the Civic Public: Some Implications of Feminist Critiques of Moral and Political Theory', *Feminism As Critique*, Benhabib S. and Cornell, D. (eds), Polity Press, Cambridge and Oxford, 1987, pp. 31–56

16 As elaborated in, for example, Habermas, J., *Theory and Practice*, Heinemann, London, 1974

17 Habermas, J., *Theory and Practice*, Heinemann, London, 1974, p. 209

18 Habermas, J., *Towards A Rational Society*, Heinemann, London, 1971, p. 104

19 Benhabib, S., *Critique, Norm and Utopia*, Columbia University Press, New York, 1986, p. 58

20 ibid., p. 58

21 See Benhabib, S. and Cornell D., 'Introduction', *Feminism As Critique*, op. cit.

22 This critique of the character and limits of Marx's paradigm of production is, by no means, uncontroversial. See Markus, G., *Language and Production*, Reidel Publishing Co., Dordrecht, Holland, 1986

23 Habermas, J., *The Philosophical Discourse of Modernity*, Polity Press, Cambridge, p. 63

24 Habermas, J., *The Structural Transformation of the Public Sphere: An Inquiry into a Category of Bourgeois Society*, Burger, T. (trans.), The MIT Press, Cambridge, Massachusetts, 1989

25 Benhabib, S., 'Models of Public Space; Hannah Arendt, The Liberal Tradition and Jurgen Habermas', in *Habermas and the Public Sphere*, Calhoun, C. (ed.), op. cit., pp. 73–98

26 See Landes, J., 'Jurgen Habermas, The Structural Transformation of the Public Sphere: A Feminist Enquiry', *Praxis International*, vol. 12, no. 1, April 1992, pp. 106–27

27 *Habermas and the Public Sphere*, Calhoun, C. (ed.). See 'Introduction' by Calhoun, C., The MIT Press, Cambridge, Massachusetts and London, England, 1992, p. 3

28 Habermas, J., *The Structural Transformation of the Public Sphere*, op. cit., pp. 248–9.

29 ibid., p. 29

30 Habermas, J., *The Theory of Communicative Action*, Heinemann, London, pp. 342

31 Benhabib, S., *Critique, Norm and Utopia: A Study of the Foundations of Critical Theory*, Columbia University Press, New York, 1986, p. 285

32 ibid., pp. 94–95

33 See Márkus, G., *Language and Production*, op. cit., pp. 93–4

34 ibid.

35 Young, I. M., 'Impartiality and the Civic Public', in *Feminism As Critique*, op.cit., p. 68

36 See Habermas, J., *Communication and the Evolution of Society*, Beacon Press, Boston, pp. 93–4

37 Fraser, N., 'What's Critical About Critical Theory? The Case of Habermas and Gender', *Unruly Practices*, University of Minnesota Press, Minneapolis, 1989, pp. 113–44

38 Fraser, N., 'Rethinking The Public Sphere; A Contribution to the Critique of Actually Existing Democracy', in *Habermas and the Public Sphere*, Calhoun, G. (ed.), op. cit. and 'What's Critical About Critical Theory: The Case of Habermas and Gender', *Unruly Practices: Power, Discourse and Gender in Contemporary Social Theory*, University of Minnesota Press, Minneapolis, 1989

39 Fraser, N., 'Rethinking the Public Sphere', op. cit., p. 120

40 Landes, J., 'Jurgen Habermas. The Structural Transformation of the Public Sphere: A Feminist Enquiry', op. cit., p. 111

41 Calhoun, C., 'Introduction' to *Habermas and the Public Sphere*, Calhoun, C. (ed.), op. cit., p. 35

42 Benhabib, S., 'Afterward: Communicative Ethics and Current Controversies in Practical Philosophy', in *The Communicative Ethics Controversy*, Benhabib, S. and Dallmayr, F. (eds), The MIT Press, Cambridge, Massachusetts, 1990, p. 356

43 ibid., p. 357

44 Benhabib, S., 'The Generalised and the Concrete Other: The Kohlberg–Gilligan Controversy and Feminist Theory', *Feminism As Critique*, Benhabib, S., and Cornell, D. (eds) Polity Press, Cambridge, 1987, pp. 77–96

45 See Gilligan, C., *In A Different Voice: Psychological Theory and Women's Development*, op. cit.

46 Benhabib, S., *Critique, Norm and Utopia*, p. 341
47 ibid., p. 329
48 ibid., p. 336
49 ibid., p. 337
50 I borrow this phrase from Richard Rorty 'Habermas and Lyotard on Postmodernity', *Praxis International*, vol. 4, no. 1, April 1984, p. 31
51 Young., I. M., 'Impartiality and the Civic Public: Some Implications of Feminist Critiques of Moral and Political Theory', *Feminism As Critique*, Benhabib, S. and Cornell, D., op. cit.
52 ibid., p. 76
53 Márkus, G., 'A Society of Culture: The Constitution of Cultural Modernity', paper presented to Melbourne *Thesis Eleven* conference, Sociology Department, University of Melbourne, 1991, p. 15
54 ibid., p. 15
55 Taylor, C., 'What is Human Agency?', p. 27, cited in Wolin, R., *The Terms of Cultural Criticism: The Frankfurt School, Existentialism, Poststructuralism*, Columbia University Press, New York, 1992, p. 216

Chapter 6

1 Several feminists have commented on the difficulties associated with all attempts to constitute an external relationship between feminism and postmodernism. See Meaghan Morris *The Pirate's Fiancee: Feminism, Reading, Postmodernism*, Verso, London, 1988; Felski, R., 'Whose Postmodernism?', *Thesis Eleven*, no. 32, 1992, pp. 129–41
2 Fraser, N. and Nicholson, L. J., 'Social Criticism without Philosophy: An Encounter between Feminism and Postmodernism', *Feminism/Postmodernism*, Nicholson, L. J. (ed.), Routledge, New York and London, 1990, pp. 19–38
3 ibid., p. 21
4 Flax, J., 'The End of Innocence' and Butler J., 'Contingent Foundations: Feminism and the Question of "Postmodernism"', in *Feminists Theorise the Political*, Butler, J. and Scott. J. W. (eds), Routledge, New York, London, 1992
5 ibid. p. 451. 'Postmodernists believe philosophy occupies a constituting and legitimating position within the metanarratives of the Enlightenment that continues to structure Western culture. Hence, the deconstruction of philosophy is a political responsibility and (at least qua philosophers) their most salient and subversive contribution to contemporary Western culture.'
6 ibid., pp. 456–7
7 Lyotard, Jean-Francois, *The Postmodern Condition: A Report on Knowledge*, trans. G. Bennington and B. Massumi, University of Minneapolis Press, Minneapolis, 1984
8 Butler, Judith, 'Contingent Foundations', *Feminists Theorise the Political*, Butler, J. and Scott, J.W. (eds), Routledge, New York and London, 1992, pp. 3–21

9 ibid., p. 6

10 Hekman, Susan, J., *Gender and Knowledge: Elements of a Postmodern Feminism*, Polity Press, Cambridge, 1990

11 Diamond, I. and Quinby L., 'Introduction', in *Feminism and Foucault: Reflections on Resistance*, North Eastern University Press, Boston, 1988

12 Foucault, M., *Discipline and Punish*, Penguin, London, 1977, p. 194

13 Foucault, M., 'Two Lectures', *Michel Foucault: Power Knowledge: Selected Interviews and other Writings*, Colin Gordon (ed.), Harvester Press, Sussex, 1980, p. 98

14 Martin, B., 'Feminism, Criticism and Foucault' and Sawacki, J., 'Identity Politics and Sexual Freedom: Foucault and Feminism', in *Feminism and Foucault*, Diamond, I. and Quinby, L. (eds)

15 Martin, B., ibid., p. 13

16 ibid., p. 13

17 Foucault, M., 'Truth and Power'. An interview with Alessandro Fontana and Pasquale Pasquino, *Michel Foucault: Power Knowledge*, p. 117

18 Sawacki, J., 'Identity Politics and Sexual Freedom', op.cit., p. 190

19 Jay, M., 'The Morals of Geneaology: Or is there a Post-structuralist Ethics?', *The Cambridge Review*, June 1989, pp. 70–74

20 Lyotard, J.F. and Thebaud, J.L., *Just Gaming*, Godzich,W. (trans.), University of Minnesota Press, Minneapolis, 1985, p. 14

21 Jay, M., 'The Morals of Geneaology: Or is there a Post-structuralist Ethics?', op.cit., p. 70

22 ibid., p. 70

23 See Grosz, E., *Sexual Subversions: Three French Feminists*, Allen and Unwin, Sydney, 1989

24 Irigaray, L., *Divine Women*, Stephen Muecke (trans.), Local Consumption Occasional Papers, no. 8, p. 12

25 Irigaray, L., *Marine Lover of Frederich Nietzsche*, Columbia University Press, New York, 1991, p. 4

26 Lyotard, J.F., *The Post-Modern Condition*, op. cit., p. 82

27 Wolin, R., *The Terms of Cultural Criticism: The Frankfurt School, Existentialism, Poststructuralism*, Columbia University Press, New York, 1992, pp. 15–16

28 Benhabib, S., 'Epistemologies of Postmodernism: A Rejoinder to Jean-Francois Lyotard', *Feminism and Postmodernism*, Nicholson, L. (ed.), p. 123

29 This new posture is elaborated in several different contexts. See, for example, *The Use of Pleasure: The History of Sexuality. Volume Two*, Random House, New York, 1985 and *The Care of the Self: Volume Three of the History of Sexuality*, Random House, New York, 1986

30 See McCarthy, T., *Ideals and Illusions*, op.cit., especially Chapter 2, 'The Critique of Impure Reason: Foucault and the Frankfurt School' for a clear account of this episode in the development of Foucault's thinking on the contemporary legacy of Enlightenment

31 Foucault, M., 'On the Geneaology of Ethics', *The Foucault Reader*, Rabinow, P. (ed.), Penguin, 1984, pp. 348–351. I have adopted the

abbreviation of Foucault's statement constructed by Wolin, R., *The Terms of Cultural Criticism*, op.cit., p. 191

32 Wolin, R., *The Terms of Cultural Criticism*, op.cit., p. 192

33 ibid., p. 192

34 Fraser, N. and Nicholson, L., 'Social Criticism Without Philosophy', op. cit., p. 34

35 ibid. p. 2.

36 ibid. p. 4.

37 According to Feher and Heller, modern life is full of value conflicts between freedom and life. Priorities have constantly shifted. 'In the first half of the nineteeth century, life (in the form of the defense of the life of the worker against capitalist exploitation) had an almost absolute priority. Freedom, in states where the electorate, the number of practically free citizens had almost everywhere been reduced to the well-off, was the rich man's perogative and concern.' Feher, F. and Heller., A., *Doomsday or Deterrence? On the Anti-Nuclear Issue*, M. E. Sharpe Inc., New York, 1986, p. 13

38 Heller, A., 'Modernity's Pendulum', op. cit., p. 3

39 Feher, F. and Heller, A., *Doomsday or Deterrence? On the Anti-Nuclear Issue*, op. cit.

40 ibid., p. 8

41 Heller, A., 'Modernity's Pendulum', op. cit., p. 3

42 Heller, A. and Feher, F., 'On Being Satisfied in a Dissatisfied Society 1', *The Postmodern Political Condition*, op. cit., p. 23

43 See Grumley, J., 'Dissatisfied Modernity: Feher and Heller in Modernity', unpublished manuscript, Department of General Philosophy, University of Sydney, 1993

44 Feher, F. and Heller, A., *The Postmodern Political Condition*, op. cit., p. 27

45 ibid.

46 Grumley, J., 'Dissatisfied Society: Feher and Heller in Modernity', op. cit.

47 Fraser, N. and Nicholson, L., 'Social Criticism Without Philosophy', op. cit., p. 25

48 Feher, F. and Heller, A., 'On Being Satisfied in a Dissatisfied Society', *The Postmodern Political Condition*, op. cit., p. 23

Conclusion

1 Young, I. M., *Justice and the Politics of Difference*, Princeton University Press, Princeton, New Jersey, 1990, p. 161

2 Bacchi, C.L., *Same Difference: Feminism and Sexual Difference*, Allen and Unwin, Australia, 1990, p. ix

Bibliography

Anderson, K., Piccone, P., Siegel, F., Taves, M. (1988), Roundtable on Communitarianism', *Telos*, no. 76, Summer

Adorno, T.W. and Horkheimer, M. (1973), *Dialectic of Enlightenment*, Allen Lane, London

Astell, M. (1970), *A Serious Proposal To The Ladies*, 1696 Reprint, Source Books Press, New York

Bacchi, C.L. (1990), *Same Difference: Feminism And Sexual Difference*, Allen and Unwin, Sydney

Barrett, M. (1991), *The Politics of Truth: From Marx to Foucault*, Polity Press, Cambridge

Bauman, Z. (1987), *Legislators and Interpreters: On Modernity, Postmodernity and Intellectuals*, Polity Press, Cambridge

Benhabib, S. (1992), *Situating the Self: Gender, Community and Postmodernism in Contemporary Ethics*, Polity Press, Cambridge

——(1987), 'The Generalised And The Concrete Other: The Kohlberg–Gilligan Controversy and Feminist Theory', in *Feminism As Critique*, Benhabib, S. and Cornnell, D. (eds), Polity Press, Cambridge

——(1992), 'Models of Public Space; Hannah Arendt, The Liberal Tradition and Jurgen Habermas', in Calhoun, C. (ed.), *Habermas and The Public Sphere*, The MIT Press Cambridge, Massachusetts and London

——(1986), *Critique Norm and Utopia: A Study of The Foundations of Critical Theory*, Colombia University Press, New York

——(1990), 'Epistemologies of Postmodernism: A Rejoinder To Jean-Francois Lyotard', in *Feminism/Postmodernism*, Nicholson, L. (ed.), Routledge, London

Benhabib, S. and Dallmayr, F. (eds) (1990), *The Communicative Ethics Controversy*, The MIT Press, Cambridge, Massachusetts

Benjamin, S. (1988), *The Bonds of Love: Psychoanalysis, Feminism and The Problem of Domination*, Pantheon Books, New York

Bernstein, R. (1992), *The New Constellation: The Ethical–Political Horizons of Modernity/Postmodernity*, The MIT Press, Cambridge, Massachusetts

Butler, J. (1990), *Gender Trouble: Feminism and The Subversion of Identity*, Routledge, New York

Butler, J. (1992), 'Contingent Foundations', in *Feminists Theorise The Political* Butler, J. and Scott, J.W. (eds), Routledge, New York and London

Calhoun, C. (eds) (1992), *Habermas and The Public Sphere*, The MIT Press, Cambridge, Massachusetts and London England

Cassirer, E. (1951), *The Philosophy of The Enlightenment*, Beacon Press Boston

Cixous, H. (1981), 'The Laugh of The Medusa' in *New French Feminisms*, Marks, E. and de Courtivron, I. (eds), The Harvester Press, Sussex

Condorcet (1976), 'On the Admission of Women to the Rights of Citizenship', in *Condorcet: Selected Writings*, Baker, K.M. (ed.), Bobbs-Merril Educational Publishing, Indianapolis

De Beauvoir, S. (1972), *The Second Sex*, Penguin Books, UK

D'Alembert, J. (1963), *Introduction to Preliminary Discourse on the Encyclopaedia of Diderot*, Bobbs-Merill Educational Publishing, Indianapolis

Diderot, D. (1967), in *The Encyclopaedia*, Grendziers. (trans. and ed.) Harper Torchbooks, New York

Diamond, I. and Quinby, L. (eds) (1988), *Feminism and Foucault: Reflections on Resistance*, North Eastern University Press, Boston

Eisenstein, Z. (1981), *The Radical Future of Liberal Feminism*, Longman, New York and London

Eisenstein, Z. (1979), 'Developing A Theory of Capitalist Patriarchy', in *Capitalist Patriarchy and The Case For Socialist Feminism*, Eisenstein, Z. (ed.), Monthly Review Press, New York and London

Feher, F. (1991), 'Between Relativism and Fundamentalism', in Heller, A. and Feher, F., *The Grandeur and Twilight of Radical Universalism*, Transaction Publishers, New Jersey

Feher, F. and Heller, A. (1986), *Doomsday or Deterrence? On the Anti-Nuclear Issue*, ME Sharp Inc, New York

Felski, R. (1992), 'Whose Postmodernism?', *Thesis Eleven*, no. 32

Ferry, L. and Renault, A. (1990), *Heidegger and Modernity*, University of Chicago Press, Chicago

Flax, J. (1990), 'Post-Modernism and Gender Relations in Feminist Theory', in *Feminism/Postmodernism*, Nicholson, L. (ed.), Routledge, London

——(1992), 'The End of Innocence' *Feminists Theorise The Political*, Butler, J. and Scott J.W. (eds), Routledge, New York, London

Foucault, M. (1977), *Discipline And Punish*, Penguin, London

——(1980), 'Two Lectures' and 'Truth and Power', *Michel Foucault: Power, Knowledge: Selected Interviews and Other Writings*, Gordon, D. (ed.), Harvester Press, Sussex

——(1985), *The Uses of Pleasure: The History of Sexuality, Volume Two*, Random House, New York.

——(1986), *Care of The Self: Volume Three of History of Sexuality*, Random House, New York

——(1984), 'On the Genealogy of Ethics' and 'What is Enlightenment?', in *The Foucault Reader*, Rabinow, P. (ed.), Penguin, UK

Firchow, P. (1971), 'Introduction' in Schlegel, F., *Lucinde*, University of Minnesota Press, Minneapolis

Fox-Genovese, E. (1977), 'Property and Patriarchy in Classical Bourgeois Political Theory', *Radical History Review*, vol. 4, nos 2–3

Fox-Genovese, E. (1991), *Feminism Without Illusions: A Critique of Individualism*, University of North Carolina Press, Chapel Hill and London

Fraser, N. (1989), 'Michel Foucault: A "Young Conservative?", and 'What's Critical About Critical Theory: The Case of Habermas and Gender' *Unruly Practices: Power, Discourse and Gender in Contemporary Social Theory*, University of Minnesota Press, Minneapolis

——(1992), 'Rethinking The Public Sphere; A Contribution To The Critique of Actually Existing Democracy', in *Habermas and The Public Sphere*, Calhoun, G. (ed.), The MIT Press, Cambridge, Massachusetts and London, England

Fraser, N. and Nicholson, L.J., 'Social Criticism Without Philosophy: An Encounter between Feminism and Postmodernism', *Feminism/Postmodernism*, Nicholson, L.J. (ed.), Routledge, New York and London

Fromm, E. (ed.), *Socialist Humanism: An International Symposium*, Doubleday and Company, USA

Fuss, D.J. (1989), ' "Essentially Speaking": Luce Irigaray's Language of Essence" ', *Hypathia*, vol. 3. no. 3, winter

Gay, P. (1966), *The Enlightenment: An Interpretation The Rise of Modern Paganism*, vol. I, Alfred Knopf, New York

Gilligan, C. (1982), *In A Different Voice*, Harvard University Press, Cambridge Massachusetts and London, England

Grosz, E. (1990), 'Conclusion: A Note On Essentialism and Difference', *Feminist Knowledge: Critique and Construct*, Gunew, S., Routledge, London and New York

——(1990), 'Feminism and Anti-Humanism', *Discourse and Difference: Post-Structuralism, Feminism and The Moment of History*, Milner, A. and Worth, C., Centre For General and Comparative Literature, Monash University

——(1989) *Sexual Subversions: Three French Feminists*, Allen and Unwin, Sydney

Grumley, J.E. (1989), *History and Totality: Radical Historicism From Hegel To Foucault*, Routledge, London and New York

——(1993), 'Dissatisfied Society', *New German Critique*, no. 58, winter

Goldman, E. (1969), 'The Tragedy of Woman's Emancipation', *Anarchism and Other Essays*, Dover Publications, Inc., New York

Habermas, J. (1971), *Towards a Rational Society*, Heinemann, London

——(1974), *Theory and Practice*, Heinemann, London

——(1987), *The Philosophical Discourse of Modernity*, Polity Press, Cambridge, UK

——(1989), *The Structural Transformation of The Public Sphere: An Inquiry into a Category of Bourgeois Society*, The MIT Press, Cambridge, Massachusetts

——(1979), *Communication and The Evolution of Society*, Heinemann, Great Britain

——(1987), *The Theory of Communicative Action*, Polity Press, Cambridge, UK

——(1992), *Postmetaphysical Thinking*, The MIT Press, Cambridge, Massachusetts

——(1981), 'Modernity versus Post-modernity', *New German Critique*, no. 22, winter

——(1982), 'The Entwinement of Myth and Enlightenment: Rereading Dialectic of Enlightenment', *New German Critique*, No 26

Harding, S. (1986), *The Science Question in Feminism*, Open University Press, UK

——(1990), 'Feminism, Science and Anti-Enlightenment Critiques', in *Feminism/Postmodernism*, Nicholson, L. (ed.), Routledge, London and New York

Hartman, H. (1981), 'The Unhappy Marriage of Marxism and Feminism: Towards a More Progressive Union', in *Women and Revolution*, Sargeant, L. (ed.), South End Press, UK

Hazard, P. (1954), *European Thought in The Eighteenth Century*, Hollis and Carter, London

Haraway, D. (1992), 'Ecce Homo, Ain't (ar'n't) I a Woman, and Inappropriate/d Others: The Human in a Post-Humanist Landscape', in *Feminists Theorise The Political*, Butler, J. and J.W. Scott, (eds), Routledge, New York and London

Hekman, S.J. (1990), *Gender and Knowledge: Elements of A Postmodern Feminism*, Polity Press, Cambridge, UK

Heidegger, M. (1978), 'Letter on Humanism', in *Martin Heidegger: Basic Writings*, Krell, D.F. (ed.), Routledge and Kegan Paul, London and Henley

Heller, A. (1978), *Renaissance Man*, Routledge and Kegan Paul, London

——(1992), 'Modernity's Pendulum', *Thesis Eleven*, no. 31

——(1985), *The Power of Shame: A Rational Perspective*, Routledge and Kegan Paul, London

Heller, A. and Feher, F. (1991), *The Grandeur and The Twilight of Radical Universalism*, Transaction Publishers, New Brunswick New Jersey

——(1988), *The Postmodern Political Condition*, Polity Press, Cambridge, UK

Hindess, B. (1992), 'Heidegger and the Nazis: Cautionary Tales of the Relations Between Theory and Practice', *Thesis Eleven*, no. 31

Honneth, A. (1991), 'The Limits of Liberalism: On the Political–Ethical Discussion of Communitarianism', *Thesis Eleven*, no. 28

Irigaray, L. (1977), 'Women's Exile', *Ideology and Consciousness*, no. I

——(1981), 'This Sex Which Is Not One', *New French Feminisms*, in Marks, E. and de Courtivron, I. (eds), The Harvester Press, Sussex

——(1986), *Divine Women*, Muecke, S. (trans.), Local Consumption Occasional Papers, Sydney

——(1991), *Marine Lover of Frederich Nietzsche*, Colombia University Press, New York

Izenberg, G.N. (1992), *Impossible Individuality Romanticism, Revolution, and The Origins of Modern Selfhood, 1787–1802*, Princeton University Press, Princeton, New Jersey

Jacob, M.C. (1981), *The Radical Enlightenment: Pantheists, Freemasons and Republicans*, Allen and Unwin, London

Jacobus, M. (1980), *Romanticism, Writing and Sexual Difference*, Claredon University Press, Oxford

Jardine, A. (1985), *Gynesis: Configurations of Women and Modernity*, Cornell University Press, New York

Jay, M. (1989), 'The Morals of Genealogy: Or is There a Poststructuralist Ethic?', *The Cambridge Review*, June

Jordan, J. (1981), 'Declaration of An Independence I Would Just As Soon Not Have', in *Civil Wars*, Beacon Press, Boston, cited in Di Stephano, C., 'Dilemmas of Difference: Feminism, Modernity and Postmodernism', in *Feminism/Postmodernism*, Nicholson, L. (ed.) (1990), Routledge, New York and London

Kant, I. (1963), 'What is Enlightenment?', in *Kant on History*, Beck, L.W. (ed.), Bobbs-Merril Educational Publishing, Indianapolis

Lacoue-Labarthe, P. (1990), *Heidegger: Art and Politics*, Blackwell, Oxford

Landes, J. (1992), 'Jurgen Habermas, The Structural Transformation of The Public Sphere: A Feminist Enquiry', *Praxis International*, vol. 12, no. 1, April

Lloyd, G. (1984), *The Man of Reason: 'Male' and 'Female' in Western Philosophy*, Methuen and Co., London

Lovejoy, A.O. (1960), *The Great Chain of Being: A Study in The History of an Idea*, Harper Torchbook, New York

Lovibond, S. (1989), 'Feminism and Post-Modernism', *New Left Review*, no. 178, November–December

Luhmann, N. (1986), *Love As Passion: The Codification of Intimacy*, Polity Press, Cambridge, UK

Lyotard, J.F. (1984), *The Postmodern Condition: A Report on Knowledge*, University of Minneapolis Press, Minneapolis

Lyotard, J.F. and Thebaud, J.L. (1985), *Just Gaming*, University of Minnesota Press, Minneapolis

MacIntyre, A. (1981), *After Virtue: A Study in Moral Theory*, Duckworth, London

Márkus, G. (1978), *Marxism and Anthropology*, Van Gorwin and Co., The Netherlands

——(1986), *Language and Production*, Reidel Publishing Co., Dordrecht, Holland

——(1983), 'Concepts of Ideology in Marx', *Canadian Journal of Political and Social Theory*, vol. 7, nos 1–2

——(1991), 'A Society of Culture: The Constitution of Modernity', delivered at *Thesis Eleven* Conference, Sociology department, University of Melbourne, August. Forthcoming in Thesis Eleven.

Márkus, M. (1987), 'Women, Success and Civil Society: Submission to, or Subversion of, the Achievement Principle', in *Feminism As Critique*, Benhabib, S. and Cornell, D. (eds), Polity Press, Cambridge, UK

Martin, B. (1988), 'Feminism, Criticism and Foucault', in *Feminism and Foucault*, Diamond, I. and Quinby, L. (eds) North-eastern University Press, Boston

McCarthy, T. *Ideals and Illusions* (1991) Massachusetts Institute of Technology, Cambridge Mass

——(1987), 'Introduction', in Habermas, J., *The Philosophical Discourse of Modernity*, Massachusetts Institute of Technology, Cambridge, Mass.

McMillan, C. (1982), *Women, Reason and Nature: Some Philosophical Problems with Feminism*, Basil Blackwell, Oxford

Mellor, A.K. (ed.) (1988), *Romanticism and Feminism*, Indiana University Press, Bloomington and Indianapolis

Mill, J.S. (1970), 'The Subjection of Women', in *John Stuart Mill and Harriet Taylor Mill: Essays On Sex Equality*, Rossi, A.S. (ed.), University of Chicago Press, Chicago and London

Mitchell, J. (1987), 'Women and Equality', *Feminism and Equality*, Phillips, A. (ed.), Blackwell, Oxford

Mouffe, C. (1988), 'American Liberalism and its Critics: Rawls, Taylor, Sandel and Walzer', *Praxis International*, vol. 8, no. 2

Noddings, N. (1984), *Caring: A Feminine Approach to Ethics and Moral Education*, University of California Press, Berkley and London

Morris, M. (1988), *The Pirate's Fiancee: Feminism, Reading, Postmodernism*, Verso, London

O'Brien, M. (1981), *The Politics of Reproduction*, Routledge and Kegan Paul, Boston, London and Henley

Okin, S.M. (1979), *Women in Western Political Thought*, Virago, London

——(1989), 'Humanist Liberalism', in *Liberalism and The Moral Life*, Rosenblum, N.L. (ed.), Harvard University Press, Cambridge, Massachusetts and London, England

——(1989), *Justice, Gender and The Family*, Basic Books Inc., New York

O'Niell, O. (1989), 'Friends of Difference', *London Review of Books*, no. 14, September

Pateman, C. (1988), *The Sexual Contract*, Polity Press, Cambridge, UK

——(1989), *The Disorder of Women; Democracy, Feminism and Political Theory*, Polity Press, Cambridge, UK

Peckham, M. (1970), *The Triumph of Romanticism*, University of South Carolina Press, South Carolina

Perry, R. (1986), *The Celebrated Mary Astell: An Early English Feminist,* University of Chicago Press, Chicago

Rabine, L. (1977), 'Feminist Writers in French Romanticism', *Studies in Romanticism,* no. 4, Fall

Rendall, J. (1985), *The Origins of Modern Feminism,* Macmillan, London

Reiss, T. (1989), 'Revolution in Bounds: Wollstonecraft, Women and Reason', in *Gender and Theory: Dialogues on Feminist Criticism,* Kauffman, L. (ed.), Blackwell, Oxford

Richardson, A. (1988), 'Romanticism and The Colonisation of The Feminine', *Romanticism and Feminism,* Mellor, A.K. (ed.), Indiana University Press, Bloomington and Indianapolis

Rorty, R. (1984), 'Habermas and Lyotard on Postmodernity', *Praxis International,* vol. 4, no. 1, April

Rosenblum, N. (1987), *Another Liberalism: Romanticism and the Reconstruction of Liberal Thought,* Harvard University Press, Cambridge, Mass.

Ross, M. (1988), 'Troping Masculine Power in the Crisis of Poetic Identity', in *Romanticism and Feminism,* Mellor, A. (ed.), Indiana University Press, Bloomington and Indianapolis

Rousseau, J.J. (1969), *Emile,* Everyman, Dutton, New York

Rowbotham, S. (1979), 'The Women's Movement and Organising For Socialism', *Beyond The Fragments: Feminism and The Making of Socialism,* Merlin Press, London

Sawacki, J. (1988), 'Identity Politics and Sexual Freedom: Foucault and Feminism', in *Feminism and Foucault,* Diamond, I., and Quinby, L. (eds), North-eastern University Press, Boston

Schmitt, C. (1986), *Political Romanticism,* Oakes, G. (trans.), The MIT Press, Cambridge, Mass, and London, England

Schlegel, F. (1971), *Lucinde,* University of Minnesota Press, Minneapolis

Schlegel, F. (1982), *Theorie der Weiblichkeit,* Insel Verlag Frankfurt am Main

Scott, J. (1990), 'Deconstructing Equality Versus Difference: Or the Uses of Post-Structuralist Theory For Feminism', in *Conflicts in Feminism,* Hirsch, M. and Keller, E.F. (eds), Routledge, New York and London

Smith, H. (1982), *Reason's Disciples: Seventeenth Century Feminists,* University of Illinois Press, Illinois

Soper, K. (1990), 'Feminism, Humanism and Postmodernism', *Radical Philosophy,* no. 55, summer

Spenser, S. (1984), *French Women and The Age of Enlightenment,* Indiana University Press, Indianapolis

Taylor, C. (1989), *Sources of the Self: The Making of the Modern Identity,* Harvard University Press, Cambridge, Mass.

Vattimo, G. (1991), *The End of Modernity,* The John Hopkins University Press, Baltimore

Vogel, U. (1986), 'Rationalism and Romanticism: Two Strategies For Women's Liberation', in *Feminism and Political Theory,* Evans, J. *et al.,* Sage

Walzer, M. (1983), Spheres of Justice: A Defence of Pluralism and Equality, Basic Books Inc., New York.

Weedon, C. (1987), *Feminist Practice and Post-Structuralist Theory*, Basil Blackwell Oxford

Wolin, R. (1992), *The Terms of Cultural Criticism: The Frankfurt School, Existentialism, Poststructuralism*, Columbia University Press: New York

Wollstonecraft, M. (1967), *A Vindication of The Rights of Woman*, The Norton Library, New York

Wordsworth, W. (1933), *The Prelude*, Oxford University Press.

Wilson, J.D. (1982), *The Romantic Heroic Ideal*, Louisiana State University Press: USA

Young, I.M. (1981), 'Beyond the Unhappy Marriage' *Women and Revolution*, Sargeant, L. (ed.), South End Press, UK

——(1987), 'Impartiality and the Civil Public: Some Implications of Feminist Critiques of Moral and Political Theory' *Feminism As Critique*, Benhabib, S., and Cornell, D. (eds.), Polity Press Cambridge and Oxford

——(1990), *Justice and the Politics of Difference*, Princeton, New Jersey, Princeton University Press

Index